Hitler's New Command Structure and the Road to Defeat

Hitler's New Command Structure and the Road to Defeat

A Study through Field Marshals Kesselring, Rommel and Model

Andrew Sangster and Pier Paolo Battistelli

Pen & Sword
MILITARY

First published in Great Britain in 2024 by
Pen & Sword Military
An imprint of Pen & Sword Books Limited
Yorkshire – Philadelphia

Copyright © Andrew Sangster and Pier Paolo Battistelli 2024

ISBN 978 1 03610 694 2

The right of Andrew Sangster and Pier Paolo Battistelli to be identified as Authors of this Work has been asserted by them in accordance with the Copyright, Designs and Patents Act 1988.

A CIP catalogue record for this book is
available from the British Library

All rights reserved. No part of this book may be reproduced or transmitted in any form or by any means, electronic or mechanical including photocopying, recording or by any information storage and retrieval system, without permission from the Publisher in writing.

Typeset by Mac Style
Printed in the UK by CPI Group (UK) Ltd, Croydon, CR0 4YY.

Pen & Sword Books Limited incorporates the imprints of After the Battle, Atlas, Archaeology, Aviation, Discovery, Family History, Fiction, History, Maritime, Military, Military Classics, Politics, Select, Transport, True Crime, Air World, Frontline Publishing, Leo Cooper, Remember When, Seaforth Publishing, The Praetorian Press, Wharncliffe Local History, Wharncliffe Transport, Wharncliffe True Crime and White Owl.

For a complete list of Pen & Sword titles please contact

PEN & SWORD BOOKS LIMITED
47 Church Street, Barnsley, South Yorkshire, S70 2AS, England
E-mail: enquiries@pen-and-sword.co.uk
Website: www.pen-and-sword.co.uk
or
PEN AND SWORD BOOKS
1950 Lawrence Rd, Havertown, PA 19083, USA
E-mail: uspen-and-sword@casematepublishers.com
Website: www.penandswordbooks.com

Contents

Introduction ix

**Field Marshal Albert Kesselring:
Master of Defence and War Criminal**

Chapter 1	The Young Man	3
	Early Life	3
	The Great War 1914–18	6
	Chaos and Disorder 1918–1922	8
Chapter 2	The Interbellum Years	11
	Serving in the Reichswehr, 1922–1937	11
	Kesselring, the Nazis, and War Plans	14
	Kesselring, Luftwaffe Administration, 1933–37	16
Chapter 3	Luftwaffe Command	19
	Kesselring, Luftwaffe Command, 1937–1941	19
	Strategic/Tactical Bombing	20
	Kesselring in Battles of France and Britain	22
	Eastern Front	25
Chapter 4	North Africa	27
	Southern Command 1941–1945	27
	North Africa	29
	Operation Torch	33
	Contemporary views of Kesselring in Africa	35

vi Hitler's New Command Structure and the Road to Defeat

Chapter 5	**His Rise in Power**	38
	Sicily and Power Politics	38
	Kesselring and Italians	41
	Master of Defence, Contemporary and Historian Views	45
	Kesselring and the SS	47
	Military Intelligence	49
	The Policy of Plunder	50
Chapter 6	**Battles For Italy**	52
	Bari, Little Pearl Harbor	52
	Gustav Line and Monte Cassino	53
	Anzio	54
	Rome	56
Chapter 7	**North Italy and Partisans**	57
	Kesselring's Loyalty	57
	Retreat North	58
	The Partisan War	59
	Western Command	62
Chapter 8	**Prison and Trial**	66
	Prisoner	66
	The Trial	69
	Commutation of Death Sentence	74
	Life in Prison	75
	The Politics of Release	76
Chapter 9	**Once Free**	79
	Insensitivity to New World	79
	The Veterans	80
	Kesselring Mistakes	81
Chapter 10	**Final Thoughts**	84

Field Marshal Erwin Rommel: Reconsidering the Desert Fox

Chapter 1	The Younger Rommel	89
	Introduction	89
	The Young Officer	90
	Shaping a Commander	94
	Battle of Caporetto reveals Rommel's Potential	98
Chapter 2	Rommel Grows in Recognition	105
	Analysing Rommel	105
	The Path to Generalship	108
	Hitler on the Stage	110
Chapter 3	An Important Commander	114
	The Panzer Commander	114
	Summing up the 1940 Campaign	123
	To North Africa	127
	The Winter Battle	135
	Rise to the Top	145
	The Shadow of Defeat	158
Chapter 4	End Days	166
	Facing Decisions	166
	Rommel in the Contemporary Views	171
	The Historians and the Rommel Myth	176
	Final Thoughts	177

Field Marshal Walter Model: The Firefighter

Chapter 1	Early Life	183
	The reluctant soldier	183

Chapter 2	Interbellum Years	188
	Nature of his work	188
	From Staff Officer to Panzer Commander	192
Chapter 3	The Second World War	196
	Poland and War	196
	The Rise in Command	203
Chapter 4	Top Rank	214
	The New Field Marshal	214
	From East to Western Front	218
Chapter 5	End Days	225
	End of the Road	225
	Model as seen by Others	229
	Final Comments	231

Final Observations	234
Notes	236
Bibliography of Cited Works	247
Index	252

Introduction

The first book we wrote on German field marshals indicated how the power-hungry Hitler worked on the traditional German-Prussian army to encourage them to his policies of overturning the Versailles Treaty, and then expanding German power across the whole of Europe. He demanded obedience to his instructions as he eventually took over command of the military and its commanders. Because of his gains in Czechoslovakia, followed by Poland and the swift victory in the battle for France, he was adored by the German population and most of the military commanders. In the first book we demonstrated that the obedience of Field Marshals Keitel and Paulus was beyond question, but the third study of Field Marshal von Manstein indicated that not all commanders were prepared to accept his orders without question.

Following the defeat of the Germans and Italians in North Africa and the loss of the Sixth Army at Stalingrad, the war was clearly turning against Nazi Germany. It was inevitable with the massive manpower of the Soviets, the resources of the USA, the stubbornness of the British, and the activity of partisans across Europe. Many of the more intelligent military commanders recognised the dangers, but Hitler remained obdurate in his belief of eventual victory, and he was supported in this illusion by his sycophantic cabal, including some military commanders. Others rebelled against a man they saw as plunging their country into the abyss, and there were many attempts on his life, including the 20 July Plot.

Hitler was paranoid about having military leaders who were obedient, took and understood the value of his orders, and who would achieve victory. He was becoming more and more suspicious of his commanders, especially those who raised questions. He had made innovations to the structure of the German military, and pursued this further trying to identify field marshals who would achieve his aims, which were now focused on the many battlefields. Hitler did not need obedient bureaucrats like Keitel, failures like Paulus, or argumentative men like Manstein. He needed loyal men who could be trusted to win, even when their resources were poor and facing more powerful opponents. In this study three men emerged who gave a glimmer of hope to the German regime, mainly because they were fighting field marshals who could lead men in battle. All three were ostensibly obedient but managed to avoid some of Hitler's demands without raising suspicion of disloyalty, although Rommel finally fell at this hurdle.

Kesselring was a soldier and airman and in the Italian crisis of Mussolini's removal and the Allied invasion of Italy, he soon gained a wide reputation as an expert in defence, which by 1943 was becoming critical. Kesselring was intelligent, diplomatic, charming, and was constantly at the front examining the situation for himself. He was nearly shot down, his plane crashed, later he was seriously injured but fought to the very last days. Hitler even selected him above Rommel whose reputation postwar was almost worldwide. Rommel had fought with his own innovations in North Africa, was built up by Goebbels as a national hero and was even admired by the British enemy. Model lacked Rommel's popularity and Kesselring's charm, but as a career man, he had risen through the ranks because of his battlefield organisational skills, and by leading his officers and men in a highly professional way.

These three field marshals were amongst the best when it came to the battlefield, both in their strategies and battlefield tactics. They were all highly professional in military matters but lost because, to use a chessboard analogy, they were facing an opponent on the board who held all the pieces required by the game, whereas on their side they only had a diminishing group of pawns.

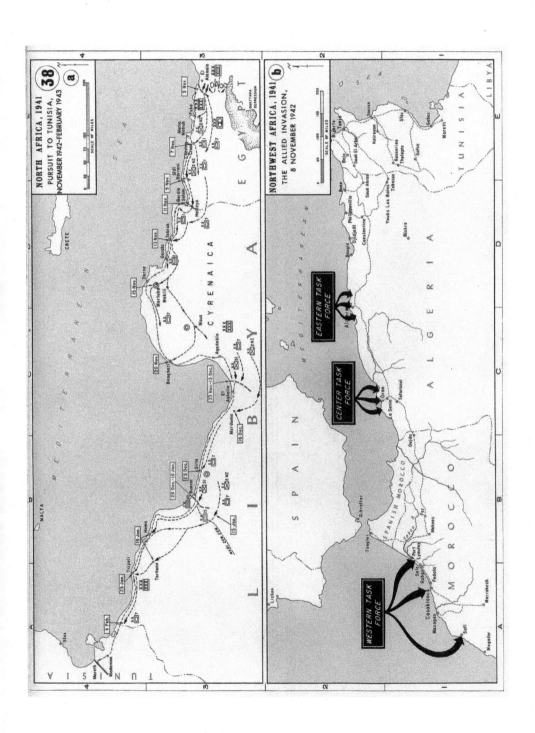

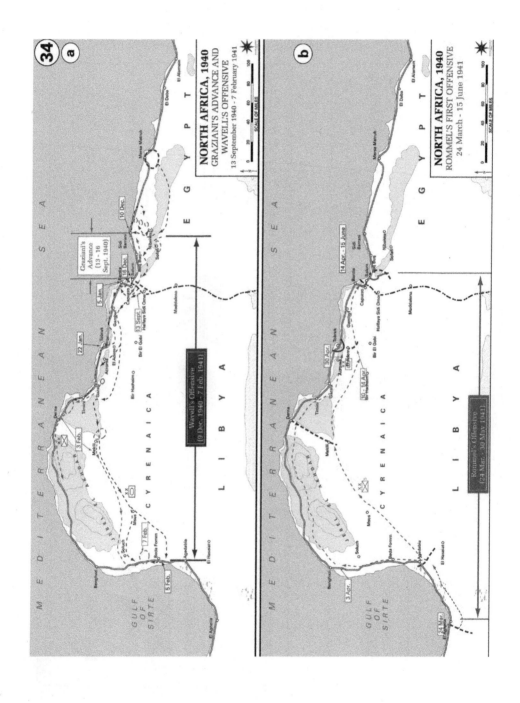

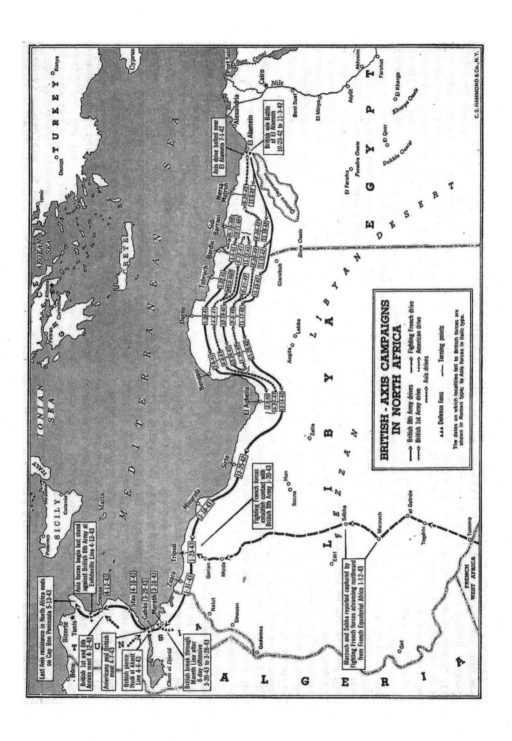

Field Marshal Albert Kesselring

Master of Defence and War Criminal

Chapter One

The Young Man

Early Life

Albert Konrad Kesselring was born on 30 November 1885, in Marktsteft, Bavaria, a small market town where the family worked the local brewery, and where he spent his childhood. He was the youngest child of six in the family, his father was Carl Adolf Kesselring, his mother, Rosina. His father was a teacher, later becoming the Schools Director in Bayreuth. Although middle-class, Kesselring regarded himself as having a past of 'knights, patricians, and priests'.[1]

At school he was of average ability, not following his brothers to university. The school record indicated he was 'good-tempered and upright, his behaviour as composed and decent', describing him 'as one who sought to battle his way to the top'.[2] He looked to the army which in Bavaria – as in Prussia – was regarded as being prestigious. It was a time of patriotism, changing to nationalism as elsewhere in Europe. In previous years, anyone born in the middle-class had little opportunity of officer rank, but times were changing. Dönitz, Kesselring, Keitel, Rommel, Paulus amongst many others were part of a development of 'officers of middle-class background succeeding in making substantial inroads…by 1913, they accounted for no less than 70 per cent of the total officer corps'.[3] Total obedience was the necessary demand for many senior officers, but Kesselring proved to be loyal though never obsessively obedient and could be critical. It was likely that military obedience was drilled into him by his background of the traditional German military values, but he was no robot.

Having no military connections, Kesselring entered as a *Fahnenjunker* (corporal-cadet), a person hoping to be an officer. It was often assumed that senior German officers carried the aristocratic *von*, an assumption made by Hitler about Kesselring, and by some historians. On 20 July 1904, he enlisted as a gunner in the 2nd Bavarian Foot-Artillery-Regiment, following the traditional route of becoming an *Unteroffizier* (NCO) on 25 October 1904, an officer cadet (*Fähnrich*) in February 1905, and was commissioned 2nd Lieutenant in March 1906. He served his first two years at the Munich *Kriegsakademie*, which was based on the Prussian model. Kesselring, like many others, was undoubtedly influenced by the Bavarian military anti-Semitic elements, 'because a general prejudice against Jews existed in the first place'.[4] This was widespread in Europe, pogroms in Russia, France with the Dreyfus affair, all having vast implications of inherent anti-Semitism, but curiously, 'Germany before the First World War was far from being Europe's heartland of anti-Semitism'.[5] Kesselring was undoubtedly anti-Semitic but although later found guilty of war crimes, he played no known part in the persecution of the Jews.

Kesselring joined his regiment at Metz, which had become a German city following the Franco-German 1870 war, a city which from the German point of view was pervaded with German success and victory. This war had given a self-perception of German military might, not lost on Kesselring's generation.

Kesselring was already noted for potential leadership, in the Munich War Archives there are reports on his progress:

> Among the young officers, Lieutenant Kesselring is by far the best; all indications are that he will distinguish himself above the average…in 1911 a qualification report noted his leadership qualities…he was allowed to attend the School of Artillery and Engineering in Munich from 1909 to 1910…he had a positive intellectual inclination…a superb sense of duty, a reliable and stable character…had authority over subordinates to whom his attitude was decisive, just and benevolent…his behaviour towards superiors was tactful and modest… Kesselring's good nature and polished social deportment were also mentioned.[6]

These reports reflected his early training, and later serving under the Crown Prince Rupprecht of Bavaria, Kesselring was described as infused with good manners with a charming approach to people, becoming one of his lifelong features, even during the years of imprisonment.*

From these early days, he developed an interest in weaponry, attending the artillery school in 1909. He was regarded as an 'expert with an understanding of the interplay between tactics and technology'.[7] He was interested in balloon-observation for directing artillery fire, later volunteering for the Balloon Companies at Metz, but the new aircraft soon made this tactic redundant. At this time artillery was regarded as the key weapon, and it was not until near the end of the Great War that aircraft and tanks were understood to be of growing importance.

His family background is scarce as he left no personal papers, but he married a wealthy lady on 29 March 1910 named Pauline Anna Keyssler, known as Liny. The arrangement brought money into the household, but on the proviso his mother-in-law lived with them.** Kesselring, once Lutheran, became Catholic for the marriage 'which prohibited divorce'.[8] They honeymooned in Italy which speculatively, may explain Kesselring's later knowledge of Italy's terrain and love of their culture. They had no children, but using their wider family, adopted a son called Rainer.

Kesselring became a dedicated officer under a nationalistic regime which had a world policy (*Weltpolitik*) always lurking in their home politics. The Wilhelmine period of German history was one where the military was given high status, with the belief that 'armed conflict was the natural state of affairs'.[9] Under Kaiser Wilhelm pacifism was 'regarded as a mixture of stupidity, cowardice, and treason'.[10] The German military was linked to the right-wing crown which held considerable power. This had a long-lasting influence on Germany, as noted by one historian: 'Wilhelmine Germany had a febrile, nationalistic, and superficial form of politics rather than a stable, democratic political culture…Wilhelmine politics were materialistic, populist, and irresponsible. And the search for

---

* Had there been war trials post-1918 Prince Rupprecht was on the list. See Hankey Rt Hon Lord, *Politics, Trials and Errors* (Oxford: Pen in Hand, 1950) p.5.

** In 1946 while Kesselring was in prison, Liny was still living in Telz with her 89-year-old mother.

antecedents of the Nazi seizure of power is justified and important'.[11] By 1914 Lieutenant Kesselring, aged 29, expecting promotion, was moulded into the nationalistic right-wing German tradition, from which he never departed.

The Great War 1914–18

The rise of nationalism and call for patriotism made the Great War inevitable, as it was a development taking place in many countries. There was almost 'a legend that Europe welcomed the conflict but is today heavily qualified, if not discredited...thoughtful people were appalled'.[12] In Berlin, '100,000 people demonstrated against war'.[13] It may have been different in military barracks, where young men hoped to prove their valour. Kesselring recalled the Commander-in-Chief of the Sixth Army as they moved into Belgium saying, 'now with the happy prospect of war', a sentiment shared by many in the military.[14] In the initial stages Kesselring stayed at Metz, but by September 1914 he was caught up in an early defeat under the Bavarian Crown Prince Rupprecht attempting to breach the lines at Marne. In his memoirs it was clear that Kesselring witnessed the devastation of trench warfare, appearing to accept that this was part of their soldierly profession, but he never spent time in the trenches, being involved with the artillery.

By 5 December 1914 Kesselring was appointed Regimental Adjutant to the 1st Bavarian Foot Artillery; in 1915 he was promoted to *Hauptmann*, spending time with the Sixth Army in Vosges involved in repulsing the French in their last assault on Vimy Ridge. This was his first command experience, where he observed the role played by planes and artillery. He was made Adjutant to the 2nd Bavarian Artillery fighting in the Arras area. Kesselring, who was on leave when the German front was collapsing, returned to repel 'a British bridgehead by means of a tactical dodge with operational consequences, subsequently closing the impending gaps in the line of defence and thus avoiding a retreat, a gambit he used in Italy thirty years later'.[15] He was noted by senior officers, and commended for 'his clear and carefully constructed orders despite being on duty for twenty hours'.[16] In the following January he was commended by Lieutenant-

General Kreppel for being an 'alert and persistent observer with very strong nerves'.[17] As a result of this action at Arras his Commanding Officer decided that Kesselring was ready for the General Staff.[18]

During the winter of 1917 Kesselring attended the meeting of Germans and Russians at Düna as a General Staff Officer of the 2nd Bavarian *Landwehr* Division.* It was the first time he had met communists, leaving a bad taste for the rest of his life. He was aware that the leading figures, including Leo Kamenev who was Trotsky's brother-in-law, were Jewish. There was a common opinion that the Bolsheviks were Jews, a belief of which Kesselring was aware. This experience of communists 'hardened his political views' against the left-wing and confirmed his own right-wing position.[19] Kesselring was not there long, but he had sufficient time to develop his right-wing bigotry and anti-Semitism. The historian Wette suggested that Ludendorff and Bauer may have started the *Dolchstosslegende*, because they believed that the 'Jews had created a secret international organization to promote revolutionary movements in several countries, first Russia in 1917 and then Germany in 1918'.[20] It was utter nonsense and used as a political excuse for failure.

Now on the General Staff, Kesselring was not required to attend the normal staff training at Sedan based on his experience and the opinions of senior officers. One of these was undoubtedly Prince Rupprecht, who was a major influence on Kesselring, especially in his style of leadership and social manners.** On 4 January 1918, Kesselring was appointed as a Staff Officer in the Quartermasters Branch to the II Bavarian Army Corps with the Sixth Army. Then on 15 April, he was appointed as GSO to Headquarters, III Army Corps. During this final period of the war, Kesselring participated in the preparations for what was to be the largest artillery attack produced by the Germans. Kesselring had learned much about defence against superior numbers. He was now entrenched in his anti-communist stance, bolstering his right-wing nationalistic views.

---

* *Landwehr*, or *Landeswehr*, meaning defence of the country.
** Prince Rupprecht went into exile in 1938 in Florence, as guest of the Italian king during the Second World War managing to avoid arrest, although his wife and children were interned in separate concentration camps until the war ended. He died in 1955.

8 Hitler's New Command Structure and the Road to Defeat

Chaos and Disorder 1918–1922

Following the defeat of the Great War, Germany was in chaos, with starvation, divided political opinions, and humiliated by the Treaty of Versailles. There were street fights between the two political extremes of the communists and right-wing extremists. The well-known *Freikorps* found Kesselring at odds with his commander, which later taught him to keep his political views private. The Weimar Republic, a sound democracy by all accounts, could not cope with the disorder. The Versailles Treaty was a failure in restoring stability as it left Germany, a potentially powerful nation, in total turmoil. Many Germans, especially the military, viewed the reparations with anger, because they were based 'on a manifestly false premise, the assertion written into the Versailles Treaty (Article 231), that Germany alone had been responsible for the war'.[21] This situation re-stimulated nationalism, and 'apart from the ostracism and humiliation of Germany, which in spite of the servitudes imposed by the treaty settlements, remained the most powerful nation in Europe'.[22]

Kesselring, as with many senior officers, would have been dismayed as parts of German territory were either returned to France or other areas annexed, leading to later demands of irredentist nationalism (return of territory). The reparations were crippling, and the military reduced on the grounds of stopping Germany starting another war. There is no doubt that the Versailles Treaty which had hoped for stability had caused further conflict. It has been noted that 'a harsh dictated peace must inevitably arouse a determination in the defeated side to reverse it'.[23] Later, in 1939, John Colville, a civil servant at 10 Downing Street, anticipating an early British victory, wrote in his diary there should be no 'guilt clause' in the next peace treaty.[24]

Kesselring found himself embroiled in a virtual civil war in his home of Bavaria. A place with 'exceptionally fertile soil for the development of right-wing extremism…the political pressures brought to bear by military and paramilitary groups in Munich were greater than anywhere else in Germany'.[25] For a moment, Kesselring considered leaving the army, but was persuaded otherwise by senior officers. He landed up in the Freikorps involved in ruthless street fights against various versions of the left-wing. This civil disorder was curious, because Germany now had a 'socialist led government which had authorised right-wing troops to stop workers struggling for a more democratic and socialist Germany'.[26] The danger, with the benefit of hindsight, was that anarchy was preparing the way for a dictatorship as it appeared to offer a firm hand.

At the personal level it was a bleak time for Kesselring, which he described as the most 'humiliating moment of my life', and 'my cup of bitterness was full, when I saw my devoted work rewarded by a warrant for my arrest, for an alleged *putsch* against the socialist influenced command of my III Bavarian Army Corps'.[27] The Munich War Archives revealed more about this event. Kesselring had an argument with the leader of the Freikorps, refusing to carry out orders which 'he claimed made no sense', probably because the officer had sympathies for the left-wing.[28] It was a matter of questioning his commanding officer, whom he believed was influenced by Socialist opinions. His commanding officer claimed he had failed to 'display the requisite discretion', with the Brigade Commander, Major-General von Zoellner deciding Kesselring had been away too long from the troops. He deployed him as a battery commander, allowing him to re-join the General Staff once he had proved himself.[29] It was clear from the earliest of times that Kesselring's natural inclination was anti-left wing, especially the communists and socialists.

After this issue had been resolved Kesselring was made battery commander in the 24th Artillery in the same area. Little is known about him during these years, but he had been awarded four medals and held in some regard.* He continued to be employed in the German army's downsizing to a peace force known as the *Führertruppe*. Because of the demand of the victors, the army was reduced which was uncomfortable for officers serving in the *Reichswehr*.** On 1 October 1922, Kesselring was seconded to the *Reichswehr* Ministry in Berlin. He was back on the promotional ladder where he became active in what he perceived

---

* Including the Prussian Iron Cross 1st and 2nd class.
** The *Reichswehr* (German for National Defence) formed the military organisation of Germany from 1919 until 1935, when it was renamed the *Wehrmacht* (Defence Force).

as Germany's reconstruction. These years indicated that Kesselring was a right-wing supporter. His clash at the political level caused him embarrassment, probably confirming his policy to keep out of politics, or at least conceal his opinions, which some critics would see as leading to the dangers of blind obedience.

Chapter Two

The Interbellum Years

Serving in the Reichswehr, 1922–1937

As Kesselring turned 37 in 1922, he gave up smoking, deciding he had a sound military career ahead of him.[1] Herde, the German historian made an interesting observation about Kesselring:

> Great industry and self-discipline united with a certain warm-heartedness and exceptional deportment, perhaps here and there mixed with an exaggerated self-confidence, he was marked as an achiever…the genial behaviour of a well brought up Bavarian…with a zealot's pursuit of career advancement…but his political horizon was circumscribed…later in 1947 he would testify at his trial that the *Führer* had been placed in power legitimately…but he was more honest than most of his comrades who metamorphosed in the de-Nazification process to a group of serious resisters.[2]

Herde's view of Kesselring noted him as kindly and genial, with Overy referring to him as 'jovial', but he stayed firmly if not ruthlessly right-wing.[3] He had been encouraged by Prince Rupprecht, but in the early interbellum years was inspired by General von Seeckt, who typified German militarism, and encouraged men like Kesselring to pretend they were above politics.

On 1 October 1922, Kesselring was given a key appointment as GSO1 to the Chief of Staff Army Direction in the Berlin Reichswehr Office. This meant he was involved in training, technical developments, economics, personnel, administration, all of which was the German military secretly re-establishing itself. As Churchill later wrote, it was 'natural that a proud people vanquished in war should strive to rearm themselves as soon as possible'.[4] Churchill was writing with the benefit of hindsight, but the 1919 *Daily Herald* cartoonist Will Dyson had sketched a picture of the Versailles gathering, with a baby crying in the corner with the label '1940 Class [conscript]'.[5] It was a highly perceptive political cartoon which underlined that the more astute could foresee what might happen as a result of the Versailles Treaty.

The allies had established a Control Commission to keep an eye on Germany's restrictions, but lacking funds it was withdrawn in January 1927. The Germans had started to covertly rebuild their military, and Kesselring as *Sparkommissar des-Reichsheeres,* (Commissioner for Army Retrenchment) participated in the military expansion. When head of the Seventh Regional Command in Munich, he developed an interest in the embryo Luftwaffe based on his experiences in the Great War. By 1926 the Paris Air Agreement gave total freedom in civil aviation, giving the Germans the opportunity to develop their commercial aviation, generating the growth of flying clubs. As well as this benefit, Germany and Russia signed the Treaty of Rappallo (1922), which normalised relationships between the two countries, linked only by their pariah status, with Germany intending to circumnavigate Versailles restrictions. Kesselring between 1923 and 1924 made several visits to the Soviet Union, as he 'worked in the T-4 (Training) Department, where he was involved in the secret instruction of airmen in the Soviet Union'.[6] Given Kesselring's scepticism of communism, this demonstrated his resolve to see the German military grow. Seeckt always held the view 'that Germany needed to recapture the prestige, powers, and territories of which it had been stripped', even if it meant cooperating with communists.[7]

Seeckt was a dominant military figure during these years and influenced many up-and-coming officers with his attitudes. One historian wrote that Seeckt's attitude towards Weimar 'ranged from an angry denial of its legitimacy at worst to lukewarm support at best...contributed in no small way to the downfall of the republic and the rise of Adolf Hitler. Such is the political indictment; as for Kesselring's military abilities there have been very few complaints'.[8] Liddell-Hart suggested that although

Seeckt died three years before the next war, and had been retired for nearly ten years, he remained the single German general who had the greatest influence on the Second World War.[9]

Kesselring worked at the recruiting and training of pilots, finding training space in Russia and Italy. By the mid-1920s firms like Krupps, Stolzenberg, Junkers, were producing ammunition, aeroplanes and even poison gases.[10] Kesselring knew the airmen of the day, including Walther Wever, working with them on new concepts such as the Ural Bomber.* The new air force was strengthened in 1926 when the airline Lufthansa came into being. This innovation provided an opportunity for training pilots in long-range flying and navigational skills. One of the directors was Erhard Milch.**

Kesselring, promoted to major on 1 February 1925, was appointed First General Staff Officer of the Army Directorate to Seeckt. From 1 October 1926 until 1 April 1929, he was in the Defence Office (*Wehramt*), where he developed his administrative ability. Kesselring had no idea what the future held, but this work was useful, for 'when Hitler came to power in 1933, he found all the technical preparations for rearmament ready, thanks to the Reichswehr'.[11] Seeckt with men like Kesselring were busy re-establishing German military power, mainly for the defence of their homeland, not knowing that a fascist dictator would utilise their work, which soon turned Seeckt away from favouring Hitler.

The historian Carlo D'Este wrote that Kesselring was 'one of the originators of the blitzkrieg'.[12] This may be something of an exaggeration, but it contains a degree of validity. The core of Seeckt and Kesselring's strategy 'was founded on the harnessing of modern technology to armed warfare, and the utilisation of motorised armoured vehicles supported by self-propelled guns, aircraft and infantry'.[13] *Blitzkrieg* as a means of warfare remained effective until the Allies started to understand its nature:

---

* Wever, as a Luftwaffe commander, was an early proponent of strategic bombing, a supporter of Douhet (famous Italian air-theorist). Wever died in an air crash in 1936.

** Milch had been employed by a small air-transport company having worked at Junkers. By 1933 Milch was deputy to Göring, finding himself in charge of the Luftwaffe. This was to lead to a power-struggle after the death of Wever, when Milch became a general then shortly afterwards a field marshal.

14   Hitler's New Command Structure and the Road to Defeat

'it was a tactical innovation rather than a revolutionary form of warfare'.[14] However, *Blitzkrieg* 'proved Seeckt to be quite right…nobody could have foreseen that a clever combination of modern weapons untried in war would achieve such speedy results'.[15]

Kesselring, the Nazis, and War Plans

Postwar Kesselring would later explain he had no idea war was being planned, but it is hard to believe this claim once Hitler appeared. He may not have been privy to Hitler's inner circle, but the preparations were not merely defensive. 'German map production was deliberately stopped in 1931' so ensuring there would be no up-to-date maps of Germany when war started, but this could be seen as a defensive measure.[16] From the mid-1920s and throughout the 1930s Kesselring and other senior German military had prepared a war machine, with General von Senger later writing that 'the isolation of the Reichswehr is said to have undermined the democratic basis of the Weimar state. The Army had not become integrated with the state'.[17] The German military, under its own steam, had built up a powerful force which appeared to be more aggressive than defensive, and men like Seeckt and Kesselring could be viewed as playing a part in the crime against peace, but not until Hitler came to power. In 1930 Kesselring was promoted to the rank of Lieutenant Colonel, leaving Berlin for Dresden as a full Colonel and Divisional Commander with the 4th Artillery Regiment.

At the age of 48, Kesselring arranged to be discharged from the army on 1 October 1933, joining the Luftwaffe with the rank of Commodore (which was the time Hitler came to power) responsible for administration. This was the time when the military and politicians realised the importance of airpower. Kesselring continued in his postwar assertions that he had no idea about a war, claiming he was surprised when the demilitarised zone was occupied (7 March 1936). When the Germans entered Austria (11 March 1938) he purported he was just as surprised. His ignorance is difficult to believe, as it typified the postwar defence of many senior Germans. In March Hitler had 'delegated the diplomatic coercion of

Austria to Göring, who promptly put the Luftwaffe on a war footing', of which Kesselring would have been aware.[18] It was the same defence of ignorance that people later claimed about the escalating ill-treatment of Jews. In his memoirs he employed the lame excuse that 'I paid very little attention to the junketings in Berlin', and 'kept myself from gossip'.[19] It is inconceivable that he was unaware: his 'ignorance is bliss' belief was simply unsustainable. If anything, he was drawn to the NSDAP because of their stress on loyalty and duty, commenting that it was a 'brilliant and smooth-running organisation', thereby appealing to a military anticipating high standards of presentation.[20] The historian Burleigh presented the observation that 'the Nazi use of drum and trumpet, light and luridly coloured symbols resulted in what the satirist Karl Kraus called cerebral concussion', which Kesselring and many of his contemporaries failed to see as they succumbed to its effects.[21] After the early failed Putsch, Kesselring and others had regarded Hitler as keeping to the rules of the constitution, achieving power through participation in Germany's democratic process, and at the invitation of the lawful authorities. Kesselring believed Hitler was the legitimate head of Germany who therefore had to be obeyed.* Hitler had used the democratic process, but with the benefit of hindsight, democracy had been manipulated by wicked people as can still happen. There is no question that Kesselring knew war was being prepared. He mentioned his meetings with Hitler and Brauchitsch in the June of 1937, claiming military matters were not discussed. However, in the same year he was preparing airbases near the Czechoslovakian border. It was clear Kesselring and other commanders knew of Hitler's intentions. From mid-1937 Kesselring had overseen Air-Region III operating from Dresden, and from October he became Chief-of-Staff of *Luftflotte-I* operating from Berlin. He left the paperwork to his Chief-of-Staff, while he flew his own Ju52 with his personal flying instructor Zellmann visiting critical areas in the event of war.

---

* In 1932 the NSDAP received 37.3 per cent of the polls, the highest they were to receive in a free election, 'they now became Germany's largest party and had 230 delegates sitting in the Reichstag', see Weitz, *Weimar*, p.356. The constitution was manipulated but not broken.

Kesselring, Luftwaffe Administration, 1933–37

Kesselring was one of four colonels transferred to the Luftwaffe, with rapid promotion. On 1 October 1934, he was made a major-general and promoted again eighteen months later (1 April 1936) as Chief of Staff. Many were critical of army officers transferring, claiming that it was all too amateur, but men like Kesselring and Walther Wever learned to fly, following the military tradition that officers should not ask their men to do what they could not do themselves. Kesselring, Wever, and others as part of the traditional officer corps proved adaptable to the new life, and in many ways led the way.[22]

During 1933, with the growing relationship between the Nazis and Mussolini, German pilots had trained with the Italian Air Force, the *Regia Aeronautica*, at that time considered one of the best air forces in Europe.[23] The developing Luftwaffe was not just defensive, and there were discussions on dropping gas.* It was planned but never used, with the Germans advising Mussolini not to use this weapon. Also under scrutiny was the use of long-range bombers as proposed in Giulio Douhet's thesis on air power.[24] The Italian theorist Douhet had proposed the use of bombers to destroy factories, and even the homes of workers mainly as a way for avoiding of the attrition of World War trench warfare. An air force 'could project power in this way, so by default the bomber became the supreme instrument for waging what was now already being defined at the time as total war.'[25] The Germans had many leaders in their own study-groups evaluating airpower, but only four examined bombing, with most regarding the Luftwaffe's main task as supporting ground attacks. It was noteworthy that the 1936 Luftwaffe manual excluded using aircraft for terror raids.

Wever wanted a four-engine long-range bomber (known as the Ural), it was put aside because Kesselring considered it too costly.** Others protested, but Göring, wishing to ingratiate himself with Hitler who demanded large numbers of aircraft whether bombers or not, followed Erhard Milch and Ernst Udet's advice.[26] Historians immersed in Luftwaffe

---

* Only the Italians used gas, 103 times in 1935/6 Ethiopia, See Overy, Bombing, p.33.
** Each machine would require six tons of fuel per operation.

history have assigned the responsibility for the Ural Bomber's cancellation on different heads for various reasons. Richard Overy implied that because Kesselring was an ex-soldier, he was more interested in 'greater army-air cooperation'.[27] James Corum held that 'Kesselring strongly supported the programme to produce a long-range heavy bomber', and most tended to agree that there seems little question that both Udet and Milch did not, if only to please Göring.[28] There is no question that Kesselring as a soldier, always thought that victory was gained by 'boots on the ground' not planes, but smaller planes could serve the ground forces well, such as Stuka bombers and fighter planes.

However, Kesselring appeared to vacillate, as he published in a technical periodical an article where he stated that:

> I regard the purpose of the Luftwaffe in a total war by its very nature to have been achieved when lands are attacked, power centres annihilated, and the capacity of the people to resist smashed, so that occupation can follow more or less without a fight, or at least when the mere threat of occupation is enough to crash down the last vestiges of a people's will to resist.[29]

This ruthless argument tends to indicate that Kesselring leaned more towards Douhet than he later claimed in postwar times, though this same policy by the Italian theorist was proposed by Lord Cherwell to Churchill.

Kesselring and his fellow commanders had secretly rebuilt the Luftwaffe. When made public in 1935 it had 1,888 aircraft and 20,000 officers and men. At this size it could be argued that it was evidently not just a defensive force. According to one air-power historian, 'Kesselring played a major role in the construction of the Luftwaffe ground establishment and in creation of the parachute corps, during his tenure as Chief of the General Staff'.[30] He had worked hard ensuring personal contact with the aircraft industry, owners, and designers. In 1933 he arranged with Ernst Heinkel to build one of the largest aircraft factories, claiming the sales-orders would not stop.*

---

* Heinkel planes such as the Heinkel He59, He115 and He11 are well-known, Ernst Heinkel's interest in fast flight and rocket propulsion was regarded as important.

The petty politics of the new Luftwaffe were unsettled, with leaderships and policies in constant debate. When Wever was replaced by Kesselring as the Luftwaffe's Chief-of-Staff, he was described by a Luftwaffe historian as a good choice, with a dynamic personality, 'yet behind his friendly Bavarian demeanour he was as demanding as the toughest Prussian aristocrat'.[31] The growth of the Luftwaffe was hindered by Göring's tendency to interfere.

Despite the varying contentions Kesselring remained a major figure, working with Hans-Jürgen Stumpf on a major peacetime air and joint air/ground exercises, which would make the German war-machine efficient.[32] In June 1936 he organised night-fighter exercises to be held, and as a result the Luftwaffe's first manual on night-fighting was published in April 1937.[33] Kesselring also instigated the paratrooper (*Fallschirmager*) training programme, which by July 1938 was commanded by General Student. This unit was a powerful innovation designed for aggressive attack.

Göring signed a policy on 2 June 1937, which Kesselring had produced, proposing the Luftwaffe should be organised into groups of Air Fleets, after which Kesselring resigned from his administration tasks, seeking a field post. His son Rainer explained this change of direction was to avoid 'the frictional strife' which had constantly vexed members of the high command.[34] It has also been proposed that Kesselring did this to ensure that his plans worked. Another possible explanation was that it was because Kesselring had failed to work with Milch, with 'the back-biting between the two which led to Kesselring's replacement by Hans-Jürgen Stumpf within a year'.[35] A postwar study by the British Air Ministry suggests that Kesselring was replaced because 'Kesselring was a forceful character and potentially troublesome to Göring'.[36] Despite these politics concealed any accurate explanations, the various Air Fleets were suggestive that Kesselring knew an aggressive war was being planned.

Chapter Three

Luftwaffe Command

Kesselring, Luftwaffe Command, 1937–1941

The term *blitzkrieg* was used after the Polish invasion, by others, not by the Germans, to describe this form of 'mobile warfare'. It was Kesselring who had long been associated with this new method of rapid advance. 'The German armed forces blended the tactical lessons of the First World War with the new technologies of armoured vehicles, combat aircraft and radio communications to create a devastating new form of combined-arms warfare'…although in Poland they 'had still not perfected its novel tactics, and German casualties were relatively heavy for such a short campaign'.[1] Under Seeckt, Kesselring had made a careful examination of mobile war, and the historian Carlo D'Este was correct in his estimation of Kesselring's major input. Even the politician Leslie Hore-Belisha in a 1942 parliamentary debate, linked Kesselring's name with the military development of land and air working together.[2] It was Kesselring who always pointed out that only troops on the ground could provide victory, but more quickly achieve this by using the Luftwaffe. This working together of forces was the central theme of the so-called *blitzkrieg*.

After the war in 1947 the RAF wrote an objective account of the Luftwaffe. They realised the Germans had been able to test their men in the Spanish Civil War, and by coupling the air power with ground forces it had worked all too efficiently. It was decided that 'it was ideal for the type of continental warfare which the German High Command had planned'.[3] They also noted that 'Kesselring had written that beyond all other military arms, the Luftwaffe, by virtue of its mobility in space accomplished tasks which in former wars had been inconceivable…in this campaign the Luftwaffe learned many lessons and prepared itself for a second, more strenuous and decisive clash of arms'.[4]

20 Hitler's New Command Structure and the Road to Defeat

In May 1938, Kesselring was warned of the possible invasion of Czechoslovakia. Knowing their defences were minimal, he proposed to drop airborne troops behind the frontline, moving his operational headquarters to Senftenberg in the Lansitz to be closer to his units. However, it was seemingly resolved by the four-power conference in Munich, with Kesselring asserting postwar he was relieved at the solution. When the annexation of the rest of Czechoslovakia was ordered, Kesselring stated he had no time 'to speculate on the justification or need for intervention', he simply had to respond to orders.[5] He had learned from Seeckt that a soldier obeyed his orders, whether right or wrong. Kesselring, postwar, was vague about knowing about the preparations of the Polish campaign, despite being summoned to the Berghof to hear Hitler's plans.

Strategic/Tactical Bombing

The Polish campaign raised the issue of strategic and tactical bombing. Tactical bombing was intended to hit military or their resource targets, whereas strategic bombing was hitting a town or city, what is often called carpet or terror bombing. Such were the limited technical devices for bomb-aimers, tactical bombing was difficult to carry out successfully. It has proved over the years a highly contentious issue. It was hardly mentioned at the Nuremberg Trial because of the banned *tu quoque* argument (you did the same), because the British and Americans used strategic bombing much more than the Germans were able, and the British were the first to utilise this with their attack on Berlin.

Kesselring had been a major contributor of the regulations governing the *Luftwaffe-Manual/16*, which stipulated that it should only bomb military targets. As noted, the technology for accurate aerial bombing did not exist, although Kesselring had initiated scientific investigation, acknowledging it would be in the far future.* It has been claimed:

---

* Luftwaffe scientists experimented with radio direction, the *Knickebein* system, often known as the battle of the Beams.

> The Luftwaffe did not have a policy of terror bombing civilians as part of its doctrine prior to World War II…Rotterdam was bombed for tactical military reasons in support of military operations… the Luftwaffe leadership specifically rejected the concept of terror bombing in the interwar period, and one must look well into World War II, starting with the night bombing of selected British towns in 1942, to see a Luftwaffe policy of terror bombing in which civilian casualties are the primary desired result.[6]

It was further added that there was a 'prevalent myth that the Luftwaffe had a doctrine of terror bombing…in order to break the morale of an enemy nation', the evidence regarding Kesselring indicated that this was not part of original Luftwaffe development, and terror bombing only came into use later in the war, under the direction of Göring and Hitler, but it was taken to its zenith by the Allies because of their logistical superiority.[7] In general practice 'German air strategy was linked closely to the ground campaign', and did not prepare for terror bombing. This argument is probably correct, but even to this day would be disbelieved by many who still blame the Germans for initiating strategic bombing of cities.[8]

At the concluding moments of the Polish campaign Warsaw still resisted. The artillery and Luftwaffe were ordered to finish the war, which it did on 27 September. The bombing of military sites may have been Kesselring's policy, however, because of the nature of war it soon became unselective. Hitler wanted Warsaw erased, and the result was that '15 per cent of Warsaw was ruined brickwork; 60,000 homes were destroyed'.[9] The historian Hastings claimed that although Polish resistance was finished, Warsaw was left unoccupied 'only because the Germans wished to destroy it before claiming the ruins'.[10] However, other historians agree that some resistance continued, with the bombing during September, sometimes known as the Black Monday air-attack, when Wolfram von Richthofen was allowed to use 1,150 airplanes. Warsaw was all but destroyed, yet Kesselring stated that the war 'was conducted with chivalry and humanity as far as is possible', but aerial or artillery bombardment in civilian areas can never be chivalrous or humane, as both sides knew during the rest of the war.[11] It was the same issue in Rotterdam where Student called for support by bombing areas of resistance. Rotterdam was the key to Dutch defence, and Kesselring alleged that the aerial attack on the city's defences was 'not against the Geneva Convention', and that he had serious contentions with Göring who wanted the city destroyed; the veracity of this debate was later endorsed by Göring's biographers.[12] Kesselring later asserted it was justified as a tactical operation to aid ground troops. Precise figures are impossible to know, but it has been generally estimated that some '980 people were killed and some 78,000 were left homeless'.[13] Many have divided opinions as to whether it was tactical or terror bombing, but Kesselring's argument that it was aimed at military targets has had much support. There was also clear evidence that smoke signals indicating surrender amongst the turmoil of dust and confusion could not be seen by the pilots.

One thing is clear that Kesselring's missions and targets were mainly successful, and as Overy noted in his book on bombing, 'the German aggression against Poland which began on 1 September 1939 was a model of the modern exercise of air power', and more to the point Kesselring's work on mobile war with co-operation between land and air forces worked.[14] It was a successful campaign because of the previous build-up of military and careful planning, with men like Kesselring giving Hitler the tools he needed. Astonishingly, as Kesselring settled his *Luftflotte-I* in eastern Europe, he later claimed ignorance of Hitler's intentions in Western Europe.

Kesselring in Battles of France and Britain

Kesselring was not in the east long because he was ordered to take over *Luftflotte-II* in the West. This occurred because a Luftwaffe officer carrying the German plans had crash-landed in Belgium, infuriating Hitler, who sacked General Felmy, ordering Kesselring West to replace him for another conflict.* The battle for France was over so quickly the Germans

---

* See Manvell, *Herman*, p.177 (Reinberger was flown by fellow officer Hoenmanns): Felmy was also in Hitler's bad books, because of his 'frank appraisal on the capabilities of the Luftwaffe vis-à-vis the RAF', see Mitcham, *Eagles*, p.81.

were surprised, but the English Channel and the underestimated RAF closed the doors on Britain. During the final days of the battle for France, Kesselring once again had problems with Göring who had told Hitler that *his* Luftwaffe would destroy the British on the Dunkirk beaches.* The Luftwaffe had been seriously hit, and repairs were essential, and there was pilot fatigue with Kesselring's *Luftflotte II* reduced by nearly 50 per cent.[15] The Luftwaffe had been weakened but remained a serious threat. In his memoirs Kesselring was aware of the strafing of fleeing civilians on the French roads, noting that 'it is a matter of rueful reflection that in these high-and-low-level attacks civilians intermingled with the troops were hit'.[16] It was a popular image often portrayed in postwar films, but a war crime committed by all sides which did not justify such actions.

When the French Armistice was signed (22 June) Kesselring believed the English would ask for peace. Kesselring knew the battle had been costly in material, and the Germans had lost an estimated 1,279 aircraft between 10 May and 20 June. Since the start of the fighting in Norway the Luftwaffe had lost 36 per cent of its force.[17] Nevertheless, it was an instant promotion for Kesselring when on 19 July 1940, in the Berlin Kroll Opera House, Hitler offered Britain peace and promoted Kesselring to field marshal along with eleven others.

By mid-July 1940, Kesselring was ordered to attack Britain, and his pre-war planning enabled the rapid transfer of Luftwaffe units to Western Europe. There is much evidence that Kesselring was an able organiser and administrator capable of looking ahead to likely problems. Armed reconnaissance missions were directed against British shipping, some important ports, armament factories such as the Vickers Armstrong Aircraft works at Reading. Bombers were easy targets for British fighters, and experienced pilots were essential for both sides. Kesselring understood this as he observed aircraft from his underground HQ at Cape Gris Nez.**

---

* Halder was told by Brauchitsch following a conversation with Kesselring and Milch, that Göring wanted to deflect some of the army glory to himself, Shirer, *Rise*, p.733.
** Cape Gris Nez, advanced HQ; main HQ in Brussels. At Cap Gris Nez he was pinning a Knight's Cross on the famous German ace Galland when it was all interrupted by Spitfires, Galland Adolf, *The First and the Last* (London: Methuen, 1995) p.52–3.

German pilots parachuting over England were lost, but often the RAF pilot could return to duty the next day. One German pilot, Steinhilper, in his biography, explained many of them felt on the back foot, despite the myth that the Luftwaffe was all powerful.[18] Pilots who ditched in the English Channel were often rescued by both sides, but it was an easier task for the British.

Kesselring and others had underestimated British resistance and the RAF. In early August Göring instructed Kesselring 'to stun the island defences by sharp hammer blows and launch the attack with the Luftwaffe'.* Kesselring decided on two phases, first from 8 August to 6 September to prepare by diminishing the RAF and shipping, and postwar he insisted that terror raids were forbidden, only military targets and their resources were selected.

The attack known as *Adler Tag* on 12 August inflicted damage to some airfields. The German pilots were hampered by weather conditions, and Kesselring failed to understand the efficiency of British radar with the ground-to-air-communications. The attack could have been fatal, but there were many airfields, with weak German intelligence not pinpointing all the major sites, as many remained well scattered and hidden. The head of Luftwaffe Intelligence was Colonel Joseph 'Beppo' Schmid, whom Adolf Galland in post-war interrogations, described as 'a complete wash-out as an intelligence officer, the most important job of all'.[19] Kesselring later claimed the raids on London were to draw the RAF fighters up, but on 25 August 1940, the RAF had made five bombing raids on Berlin, probably because it was the only offensive action which could be taken at this time. They had done little damage but infuriated Hitler who on 4 September announced: 'when they declare that they will attack our cities in great strength, then we will erase theirs'. The command for city bombing came from above Kesselring's paygrade.[20] The poor Intelligence led Kesselring to believe the RAF was short of planes. He would have been astonished to know that although the British economy was smaller,

---

* Hitler's Directive No 17 issued 3 days earlier read 'The German Air Force must with all means in their power and as quickly as possible destroy the English Air Force...' Kesselring, *Memoirs*, p.68.

it out-produced Germany, and 'was ahead in aircraft from 1940 and in tanks in 1941–2'.[21]

The well-known attack on Coventry was organised by Kesselring, and postwar he correctly argued that Coventry was a place known for armament and military resource factories. The raid 'levelled twelve armament factories, gutted the medieval cathedral, and killed 380 people... Coventry was to become a symbol', and regarded by most as an unnecessary terror raid which it was not.[22] The raid was carefully observed by Kesselring who flew over the operation, which was 'entirely characteristic of a man who believed in leading from the front'.[23] The Coventry raid was a tactical operation, but indicative that accurate bombing was too difficult to achieve by either side, and that area-bombing was the consequence. Kesselring with good reason later argued that the first indiscriminate raids on cities were done by the RAF.

Eastern Front

When Hitler informed his military that Russia was the next target, Kesselring moved to Posen in occupied Poland, flying to Warsaw for a conference with von Kluge the commander-in-chief. The Luftwaffe was preparing the important and initial phases of preparation. In October instructions were issued to start 'long-range reconnaissance formations capable of photographic reconnaissance of Western Russian territory from a great height'.[24] This utilised advanced camera technology which the Americans followed a few decades later with the U-2 planes over Russia. Kesselring himself flew his FW-189 over the intended battle territories to study the terrain.

Despite the danger of a two-front war, in his memoirs Kesselring tended to agree with the decision to invade Russia. He accepted Hitler's claim about the ideological differences between the two countries, which was hardly a justifiable cause for war. He may have been one of the few who believed Hitler's claim that it was a preventative war to stop the Russians invading Germany. Kesselring had a deep distrust of the Soviet system following his experience at the end of the First World War with the communist delegation. He had developed a strong antipathy for their political philosophy, and he ignored the fact that Germany and Russia had assisted one another in the interbellum years, and they had signed a mutual pact in August 1939.

Like many others then and since, Kesselring wondered why Stalin had not seen the dangers, and believed following the disastrous Soviet attack on Finland that the German attack should not face many problems, seeing Russia as militarily weak. Given Stalin's views that Hitler would not attack, it was no surprise that the Luftwaffe had the surprise element, and quickly destroyed some 2,500 aircraft, mainly lined up on the ground making them easy targets.* The Soviet fighters were virtually wiped out during an attack sometimes described as the 'Pearl Harbor of the air'.[25] The figures of destroyed Russian aircraft are impossible to ascertain, but it has been proposed that more than 5,000 were destroyed by 5 October.[26]

Kesselring kept up with the fast-moving assaults; it has been noted that 'the Luftwaffe carried the German army to the gates of Moscow. After that point it became over-extended…now essentially a fire-brigade'.[27] *Blitzkrieg* had worked in the West, but was going to experience a long-term failure in *Barbarossa*, because of the 'infantry's inability to keep up with the armoured spearheads over a long distance', with the immense tracts of territory involved.[28] As the German forces moved north towards Leningrad and south towards Kiev, Kesselring understood that *Luftflotte-II* was now too diversified to help Guderian at Smolensk. There were disagreements over Hitler's direction of his forces, but Kesselring was about to be moved from the Eastern Front.

---

* The minimal figure is in excess of 2,000 'a casualty rate without precedent', See Clark, *Barbarossa*, p.50.

Chapter Four

North Africa

Southern Command 1941–1945

Kesselring received fresh orders and a new major command from Göring, with the title of *Oberbefehlshaber-Süd* (Commander-in-Chief, South). He was to be responsible for military matters in Italy, but subject to the 'complex Italian command and the OKW and Hitler'.[1] Hitler wanted to impose his military authority through Kesselring, but the Italians thought otherwise, regarding this implant as a liaison officer, who would one day be addressed by the Allies under the code name of 'The Emperor'.[2]

In his memoirs he acknowledged that despite Hitler's intentions, diplomatic reasons made the task difficult. He was obliged to subjugate his role to Italian command under Mussolini. Hitler had long been concerned about Italian weakness, the Greeks had proved to be formidable foes, Italian equipment was insufficient, the officers often seemingly inadequate. This had meant that with the ventures against Greece and forces in North Africa the Italians needed German support. However, the British were still having some success in North Africa and the *Afrika Korps* had serious supply problems, and not helped by Rommel complaining about the Italian military. Hitler probably regarded Kesselring as a problem solver because of his buoyant personality. He was known to have some diplomatic skills because of his pleasant easy-going character, was considered loyal, was a linguist, and knew Italy, having honeymooned there.

Despite Kesselring's pleasant and easy-going manner, the Italian Chief of Staff, Ugo Cavallero objected to Kesselring taking command, only offering some of the air force for Kesselring's use. Kesselring knew tact was essential, and in his words 'ignored Hitler's orders' by accepting Italian demands, writing in his memoirs that he was 'only a subordinate to the King and the Duce'.[3] It has been stated that he moved into 'a political balancing act, the precarious diplomatic course which was to govern his every subsequent move'.[4] The relationship between Kesselring and his hosts remained cordial for a time, but the Italians held information back from him. As General Westphal noted, the title *Oberbefehlshaber-Süd* was incongruous, as 'it was not until the beginning of 1943 that he became chief of the German Army formations in Africa and Italy'.[5]

However, as Allied successes occurred and the Italian forces gave way, Kesselring's power grew exponentially. Later Kesselring would become the only General to control all three services in a joint command, except for the *Afrika Corps*. Much later, with the arrival of the SS, it was obvious that Kesselring was never truly *Oberbefehlshaber-Süd*, but his insistence that he was in charge caused him problems in his postwar trial.

Rommel was often critical of Italian military command, with Kesselring having his own views which were more diplomatic when expressed. He felt the Italians had no sense of urgency. He based this insight on the calm lifestyle in Italy, compared to Germany. A White Russian aristocrat Marie Vassiltchikov wrote of 'the sense of normality and the abundance in Rome compared to Germany'.[6] Kesselring was never happy with Mussolini's failure to inspire a 'warlike manner', but later the Italian partisans demonstrated determined fighting not evident during Mussolini's time.[7] Many at the time and since, have derogated the Italians as soldiers. The war-photographer Robert Capa, commenting about the invasion of Sicily, wrote, 'it turned out to be a twenty-one-day race and in the lead was the Italian Army. They were afraid not only of the Americans, but of the Germans too, and ran in every direction'.[8] However, the fact that many Italians were unwilling to fight undoubtedly arose from disagreeing with Mussolini and the need for war, and they had poor leadership with hopeless equipment. The more perceptive General von Senger wrote that 'the Italian is by nature more critical and therefore politically more mature than the Germans', and the Italian soldiers knew they were in a hopeless situation.[9] Senger was probably right with some

Italians, but many of them were unhappy with fighting a war they did not want or think necessary.

Kesselring, responsible for supplying Rommel in North Africa, discovered that 'German and Italian equipment was invariably different and rarely interchangeable'.[10] Kesselring frequently spoke of 'total war', feeling Germany and especially Italy were not prepared for such a task.*

In his memoirs Kesselring believed there were leaks in Italian Intelligence, and he was correct. A history of MI6 indicated the British Secret Intelligence Service (SIS) was active, and their co-operation with the Italian *Servizio Informazione Militaire* (SIM) may have started early in the war.[11] Kesselring never knew the Enigma code had been deciphered, which would hound him throughout his military life. In early 1943 a 'whole air-transport wing of Ju-52s and six-engine Giants' were caught by British fighters and destroyed, and again 'Ultra had revealed where they would be flying'.[12]

North Africa

Another issue he faced was his relationship with Rommel, who was the hero of success, much loved by Goebbels' propaganda, and even respected if not admired by the British. Kesselring had met Rommel at the Dresden Infantry School, meeting him again in the Polish campaign. Their fathers had both been schoolmasters, and whereas Kesselring was respected for his modesty, Rommel was believed to be overconfident. The one thing they both had in common was that the allied opponents admired their respective skills. The relationship between Kesselring and Rommel often faltered, usually when the *Afrika Corps* failed to receive critical supplies, and especially on one occasion when the Luftwaffe mistakenly attacked German troops. Kesselring later wrote that Rommel's independence was risky, because of what he called 'fatal insubordination' which could lead to disharmony.[13] However, when Hitler ordered them to stand and fight,

---

* 'Total War' is sometimes seen as peculiar to German thinking, but it was a phrase often employed by Churchill, 'modern war is total war,' see Winston Churchill, *Onwards to Victory* (London: Cassell, 1944) p.97.

it was acknowledged as an order and not just one of Hitler's whims. A retreat from El Alamein was the only sensible move, but 'Rommel was shaken and bewildered by the insanity of the command', but 'assured by Kesselring's support Rommel ordered a general retreat' which, as Westphal pointed out, avoided the entire loss of a German army.[14] This situation underlined the fact that Kesselring was not always totally obedient to Hitler's orders when it came to military matters, and seemed to escape Hitler's usual wrath.

Relations between Rommel and Kesselring were not always easy, especially later clashing over the command in Italy, but on Rommel's death Kesselring wrote to Frau Rommel 'there were times when I did not always agree with him, just as he did not always understand me… but I was glad when he was appointed to an important command in the West, because I knew his experience of fighting against the British and Americans would be of the greatest value'.[15] This was a letter of condolence, but it was clear that Kesselring disliked Rommel and had clashed with him on many occasions, not least in their work in Italy.

One of the main problems was Allied supplies through Malta, which was active as a naval and airbase. The OKW, namely Hitler, had forbidden the use of Tunis and Bizerta because of French sensitivity. Hitler had anticipated that Kesselring would stabilise the military situation, and annoyed at Kesselring's insistence that Malta should be occupied. Hitler could not understand its importance, having worried about the losses in taking Crete.

The year 1941 was a difficult time for German supplies to Africa; in August some '35 per cent of supplies and reinforcements were sunk and 63 per cent in October', causing concern and confusion.[16] Rommel's adjutant summarised the situation by pointing out that 'Malta probably has to be occupied first, as we cannot leave the English on our flank'.[17] Kesselring ordered intensive air attacks on Malta, but knew the island needed to be occupied. Later he complained in his postwar interrogation that Rommel kept changing his mind about Malta.[18] In the *Rommel Papers*, Rommel made it clear that he believed 'Malta should have been taken instead of Crete', which was commonsense.[19] He was undoubtedly correct, but Göring had probably selected Crete as the easier target, but which led to considerable losses in the eventual victory. Rommel later wrote that 'for some unaccountable reason our High Command abandoned this scheme [Malta]. My request to have this pleasant task entrusted to my own army had unfortunately been refused the previous spring'.[20]

The OKW had agreed in March that it would be the time for the Italians to invade Malta (Operation *Hercules*), but with Kesselring knowing Cavallero was reticent. Rommel was demanding that Malta should be occupied before he attacked Tobruk. On 29 April, at Obersalzberg, Hitler and Mussolini, with Kesselring and Cavallero present, had given permission for the attack. When Kesselring asked for a start date of 31 May, Mussolini and Cavallero wanted further delay, still clinging to August. It was a confusing situation for those involved and for historians to understand later.

Kesselring's plan had proposed that Student's airborne would seize the southern heights while the airfields were attacked by bombers. This would be followed by naval forces and landing parties attacking the harbour, during which there would be a diversionary attack at sea against the Bay of Marsa Scirocco, on the south-east of Malta. It has been proposed that these plans for Malta may well have been accomplished.* If it had succeeded the North African situation may have worked better for the Axis as supplies would have been more reliable. Later Kesselring stated the failure to occupy Malta was a blunder by the OKW, he also blamed the Italian leadership.[21] He criticised Keitel and Jodl for the failure which he said led 'to the loss of the Italian colonies and of the German and Italian armies'.[22] General Montgomery wrote later that 'the battle of El Alamein could not have taken place if Malta had fallen'.[23] Historically, the failure to take Malta is confusing with many postwar contradictions, but Kesselring's original plan looked likely to succeed.

At one stage Kesselring became personally involved in a ground battle when General Crüwell's pilot mistakenly landed amongst the British,

---

* 'Kesselring's feasibility study showed that an invasion was possible...' Nicolas von Below, *At Hitler's Side, Hitler's Luftwaffe Adjutant 1937–45* (London: Greenhill, 2004) p.124.

which for Crüwell was the end of his war: ironically, Kesselring had just sent him 'birthday greetings'.[24] Kesselring flew over his battle area to guide bombers, which critics would have thought too dangerous for a senior commander. Unlike many top commanders he often placed himself in danger, not just by his flying, but by constantly visiting the front lines. Later Kesselring landed at the Italian Headquarters and was fired upon, tearing a strip off the gunners for missing their target.

On 26 June Kesselring, Rommel, Cavallero and Ettore Bastico held a meeting when Kesselring pointed out the dangers of stretching supply lines, in which he had the backing of Halder in Berlin who thought Rommel had gone 'stark mad'…[and]…he was 'sharply critical of Rommel's pathological ambition'.[25] Kesselring, who referred to himself as a glorified quartermaster without total control, had a major if not impossible task on his hands. There were at least '91,000 German soldiers vis-à-vis about 146,000 Italian soldiers' using different equipment, making their supply lines complicated.[26] Kesselring was supposed to be the superior commander, but his cynical self-description as quartermaster was close to the truth. Hitler was demanding too much, Rommel was overstretched, and Kesselring had few supplies. While the RAF controlled the air space, the Luftwaffe lacked fuel, and it was estimated that less than 20 per cent of essential fuel and equipment was arriving. It was not helped by Rommel complaining to Kesselring that the 'air reconnaissance has been completely inadequate', which it probably was because of the lack of adequate supplies.[27]

The postwar British review was kinder to Kesselring, stating 'the British also knew that Kesselring had responded to Rommel's request for fuel with alacrity and sent five ships with fuel under foggy conditions therefore anticipating its safe arrival'.[28] Enigma had decoded the messages, and an old English acquaintance of Kesselring, Frederick Winterbotham, asked permission to sink these vessels without pretending to spot them with aircraft. Rommel, as it transpired, suspected an 'Enigma system' at this stage, but 'Winterbotham sent messages thanking Italian informants that he knew would be picked up by German interception.'[29] It was not surprising that Kesselring and other German commanders hardly trusted Italian security. This same postwar British review concluded that Kesselring was not guilty, stating the blame 'can hardly be laid at his door, but was rather the result of the short-sighted policy of Hitler and the Supreme Command' which was an incisive observation.[30]

Operation Torch

The British had managed to persuade the reluctant Americans to launch a landing in North Africa, and such was their naval and air activity Kesselring requested an army base in Sicily, speculating the invasion could be on the African coast. He requested that U-boats scour the area to watch for any movement. Westphal later wrote that the OKW thought an African landing was inconceivable, while Göring 'even went so far as forbidding Kesselring to let the Luftwaffe make any preparation for a North African landing'.[31] Only the day before the invasion Göring assured Kesselring the invasion would be Southern France, but the submarines indicated that possible invasion convoys were heading south-east. During this period, it was proved that Kesselring had a more realistic approach than those above his paygrade.

In a postwar newspaper article, it was purported that Kesselring suggested to Dönitz that Spain be invaded to take Gibraltar, thereby avoiding a North African landing.[32] Kesselring rightly considered the landings might be on the west African coast, and believed the Luftwaffe would have made Sicily, Sardinia, or Corsica impossible, and that the invasion force was too small for the south of France. As noted, he had more perception in war matters than his seniors who appeared to be in a state of panic. Hitler ordered the reinforcement 'of troops in Tunisia and occupied South France', which diverted numerous troops and Luftwaffe resources. 'Göring's formations had lost 40 per cent of their entire strength in the Mediterranean'.[33] The French situation was complex with not knowing where Vichy France stood. The collaborating Admiral Darlan who disliked the British was in North Africa for family reasons, and the Free French with de Gaulle in London; there was a developing uncertainty about French reactions.

Meanwhile, Kesselring ordered a bridgehead for Italian troops from Libya joining German troops, taking over an old French defensive position called the Mareth Line, defending the eastern border, and occupied Tunisia. The Mareth Line was an old system of forts built by the French in the 1930s and extended to protect Tunisia from the Italians. It had been demilitarised after the French armistice by a German-Italian commission. Kesselring stabilised the military situation, using Tunisia as the supply point for the Axis forces. By 16 November, the Axis had occupied most of Tunisia, but German paratroopers had failed to take the airfield at Souk-el-Arba, which had been countered by Allied paratroopers landing at the same time, due, once again, to the use of Ultra.

In addition to all these unexpected problems Rommel and General Bastico were in constant disagreement, and Hitler instructed Göring to Rome for a conference with Kesselring and Rommel. It was apparent that the complexity of working with allies was difficult, both in the Western alliance and proving somewhat strained between the Italians and Germans. There were also differences of opinion within the German ranks, with Kesselring describing the problems with subordinates General von Arnim and Rommel, describing them as 'pig-headed'.[34] These issues were known by the Allies. When Rommel was noted to have arrived in Berlin, the *London Times* speculated that Rommel could be suffering some tropical illness, or he was on bad terms with Kesselring, or because of his failures, which the journalist considered the least likely.[35] Kesselring took charge, and although Rommel and Arnim had their own plans, Kesselring rejected them for his own, over which military historians hold differing views.

The Axis forces evacuated Tripoli (22 January), while German troops formed themselves at the Mareth Line, but Kesselring could not stop the Allied advance because the shortage of supplies and fuel was weakening the Axis forces. As noted above the Mareth Line consisted of only loosely connected block houses on the coast beside a mountainous area, but Kesselring continuously demanded 'that the enemy be held up as long as possible in the area before Mareth, since otherwise reception of the Panzer-Army-Rommel would be exceptionally difficult'.[36]

Kesselring's defensive plans worked in places such as at the Kasserine Pass, where inexperienced Americans were humiliatingly defeated.* However, Kesselring was not only facing a logistically superior enemy, but his own forces were dangerously short of supplies. In addition to this, at German command level there were problems, as the historian Carlo D'Este wrote: 'Kesselring exercised command through two independent-minded subordinates, von Arnim and Rommel', with Kesselring being 'an outwardly amiable bear of a man whose sunny disposition masked an iron will'.[37] For a brief time it appeared that Kesselring would succeed even knowing the lack of supplies would mean defeat, and the soldiers were making 'bitter jokes about Tunisgrad'.[38] However, it was a defeat, and Rommel left, with Kesselring recommending him for the Knight's Cross with Diamonds, but he could not persuade the Italians to offer him an award. Westphal in his memoirs blamed the 'poor supply-lines and lack of air and sea power'.[39] Kesselring suffered a logistical disadvantage and although the Allies suffered '76,000 casualties they also captured 238,000 prisoners of war', more than those who surrendered at Stalingrad.**

Contemporary views of Kesselring in Africa

Kesselring had overseen a massive defeat, and it is important to understand how others regarded him. Kesselring always claimed it had been a clean war, but only because they were not surrounded by millions of civilians. After the war various memoirs and autobiographies appeared pointing out the relationships between Axis and British forces. One curious book by a Panzer commander called Hans von Luck recalled an offer of '600,000 cigarettes' in exchange for a captured family member of the 'Player

---

* Kesselring recognised the American troops were inexperienced, and Eisenhower admitted his troops were unprepared, later writing 'it was the only time, during the war, that I saw a divisional or higher headquarters so concerned over its own safety that it dug itself underground shelters'. It led to the humiliating spectacle of some 4,000 Allied PoWs being marched through Rome. See Dwight Eisenhower, *Crusade in Europe* (London: Heinemann, 1948) p.157 and Andrew Roberts, *The Storm of War* (London: Allen Lane, 2009) p.312.

** Figures supplied by Dear (ed) *The Oxford Companion to WWII* (Oxford: OUP, 1995) p.818, but Liddell-Hart questioned their veracity.

cigarettes' company.[40] Some refer to exchanges of 'Schnapps for English cigarettes' but this bonhomie was countered by Italian prisoners being killed because of home news of bombing.[41] When Kesselring was shown captured British orders that German prisoners were 'not allowed to eat, drink or sleep before their interrogation', he reciprocated the orders which was perhaps understandable.[42] Hans von Luck wrote of Kesselring that 'he was a charming man of medium height with warm and sympathetic eyes. We respected him as he was the only high commander to come to Africa'.[43] Some of his pilots were less enamoured, Franz Stigler claiming that when Kesselring had 'heard that Marseille [a top ace] was casting doubt on the G [model of Bf109] he ordered Marseille to fly the new plane anyway', from which he died because of a technical failure.[44]

Most people recognised Kesselring had an impossible task. General Westphal recalled the frequent times they had visited Mussolini to keep him steady and offer him encouragement. Kesselring had declined Mussolini's dangerous idea of using gas, and hospital ships to transport fuel, both of which Mussolini had done.[45] Kesselring tried to keep Mussolini on side, and he did his best by ensuring that the Germans worked with their Italian counterparts.

After the defeat the blame fell on different people, but most especially on Kesselring. In Trent House England, where captured German generals were secretly monitored, they tended to blame the Italians, while others believed Tunisia had not been worth the effort.[46] Some criticised Arnim or Rommel, but Kesselring was mainly blamed, with Göring insulting him about running away. The defeat led to a heated postwar debate in which Kesselring felt he needed to justify himself, and according to the official German history, 'he did this in a dignified manner: he shouldered the responsibility'.[47] Kesselring had been the senior commander when the defeat occurred, and the issue of the supply lines was the main problem, but Kesselring cannot avoid all the responsibility. As *Oberbefehlshaber-Süd*, he failed to persuade higher authority for the immediate invasion of Malta, critical because of the island's sea and air dominance, but on the other hand, Hitler who controlled the OKW rarely changed his mind and had his thoughts on *Barbarossa*.

It has been suggested that Kesselring's success was the fighting defence persistently produced by his soldiers, but that he failed to evacuate the huge number of fighting troops to Italy. Again, with British naval dominance this would not have been an easy task. Rommel's papers indicated that he understood that the logistics meant the Axis forces were going to be captured, and he knew evacuation was essential; he approached Kesselring who told him 'That the Führer was unable to agree with my judgement'.[48] The obedience to Hitler's concept of mass suicidal missions by ordering his soldiers to fight to the last man was unreasonable, and Kesselring was obedient, although as Kesselring knew, an evacuation was highly dangerous in terms of lives.

Kesselring claimed that it had been a clean war, but Jews in Tunisia became forced labour, 'the rape of Tunisian Jewish women by German soldiers was far from uncommon. Walter Rauff the Gestapo Chief in Tunis, transferred from the killing fields of Eastern Europe, quickly instituted a reign of terror against the Jews of Tunis'.[49] Kesselring had 'responded favourably to the suggestion of Ambassador Rahn, that instead of deporting the Tunisian Jews' they were to be used as essential labour.[50] Whether Kesselring was aware that deportation meant extermination, or he needed labour for his defences will never be ascertained.

Chapter Five

His Rise in Power

Sicily and Power Politics

Kesselring, like other *Wehrmacht* commanders was often at odds with Hitler's views on military policy. Even as Operation *Husky*, the plan to occupy Sicily was being planned, the Axis leadership had no idea where the invasion would take place. Kesselring and Mussolini believed Sicily was the objective, but Hitler disagreed, and others were confident it would be Sardinia, but Kesselring rightly remained convinced it was Sicily.[1] He was certain that Sicily was the intended 'door to Fortress Europe'.[2] Hitler was convinced that Churchill's well-known obsession was the target, namely the Balkans. The Allied deception codenamed *Mincemeat* had convinced the German High Command that it would not be Sicily, motivating Hitler to send reinforcements to the Balkans.[3] Kesselring had based his reasoning on the fact that airpower would be the critical factor for the Allied plans, making Sicily the place, and he was proved right.

This exploration of Kesselring will not give the details of the various operations and battles in Sicily but examine Kesselring's role. He observed and was concerned by the effectiveness of the beach-landings in Sicily, and the rapid transfer of planes to occupied airstrips. Kesselring was agitated on hearing that the Italian Augusta Fortress had surrendered to the British almost immediately. He flew to Sicily to assist, 'and to check on the story that Italian formations were surrendering without a shot being fired'.[4] A Brigade Commander, Schmatz had sent Kesselring a telegram about the surrender of Augusta Fortress, affirming that 'the English had never been in there. Notwithstanding this the Italian garrison has blown up its guns and ammunition and set fire to a large fuel dump'.[5] The Italian surrender in large numbers was a shock to the Germans as well as to the

Allies. Sicily was an attack on the Italian homeland, and Galeazzo Ciano, Mussolini's Foreign Minister, and his son-in-law, told Admiral Maugeri that 'our people have no faith in the war, or in our leaders…they have lost their will to win'.[6] The Italians were not cowards and most of them never wanted the war in the first place.

As always, petty power-politics often dominated the scene. Kesselring was supposed to be the top German authority in Italy, but he was constantly tied by Hitler's intrusions and authority. During the highly successful evacuation of troops across the Messina Straits, often known as the 'mini-Dunkirk', Hitler even sent demands as to which troops should be the first to go. This habit of interference was continuous throughout the battles for Italy and beyond. Despite Hitler regarding Kesselring to be the leading man in charge, Kesselring only had command of German troops. He was nearly always regarded with suspicion by the Italians. After the successful occupation of Sicily by Allied forces, Hitler correctly suspected the Italians of trying to make peace overtures to the Allies. Ciano had already suggested peace with Russia, and Hitler accused Kesselring of being too sycophantic towards the *Commando Supremo* [Italian High Command]. Kesselring was known for his charm and diplomacy, and he had gained the confidence of some Italians. Even postwar his British interrogator in London, Lieutenant Colonel Scotland became a friend for life, and the American Historical Division Commander admitted he liked him. It was the Chief of the *Commando Supremo* Cavallero (until February 1943) with whom he gained some friendly co-operation, but Ambrosio who later took over remained hostile towards the German Field Marshal. Italy was now deeply divided with many plotting and planning the overthrow of Mussolini, with Hitler, being a politician, appearing more aware of these plots than Kesselring. The deviousness of Italian politics seemed beyond the grasp of Kesselring who was consumed by military matters.

Kesselring would have felt his authority was being challenged when Hitler appointed Rommel as his personal adviser (Rastenberg, 24 May) in the Mediterranean theatre, without informing Kesselring. There had always been a latent conflict between Rommel and Kesselring, and Hitler appeared to be stoking the fires. Both Rommel and Jodl had told Hitler that there should be one competent leader, implying Rommel. Kesselring would probably have felt he had been side-lined. However, it appears that Hitler was never certain about Rommel because he knew how many Italians disliked him, but Rommel was famous in German eyes, mainly because of his initial successes and Goebbels' propaganda.

When Sicily was occupied, Hitler created a 10th Army under General von Vietinghoff, with the implication that when Kesselring had finished, Vietinghoff would report to Rommel. It was possible that Rommel was scheming against Kesselring. At a critical meeting with General Roatta, (15 August) Kesselring was not invited by Rommel, and promptly resigned, but it was refused by Hitler, who remained undecided between the two commanders.

It must have been evident the Allies intended to advance up the leg of Italy. Rommel proposed to Hitler that the Germans concentrated on blocking any advance from the north, to stop any incursion into mainland Europe, known as Plan *Alarich*. Kesselring argued that it was better to fight from the furthest south as a major delaying tactic. Rommel 'believed that he would shortly take over from Kesselring as Commander in Chief South, especially since the latter had no control over what he was doing'.[7] Rommel 'interpreted the two opposing strategies in personal terms: this was a battle between himself and Kesselring for Hitler's Trust', and Kesselring must have felt this personally, although in later years he always denied this possibility.[8] Hitler stated that 'Kesselring doesn't have the name', meaning the necessary charisma.[9] Hitler also knew that although Rommel could be enthusiastic, he was an 'absolute pessimist when the slightest difficulties arise', while Kesselring was always the optimist.[10] Rommel had suggested a New Army Group B to hold northern Italy, but Kesselring won the debate for defending from the south.* This was a blow to Rommel, but Hitler, who once considered 'Kesselring as a replacement for Keitel or Jodl' tended to favour Kesselring because of his apparent sense of obedience.[11] What probably had a marked effect on

---

* The code breaker Ultra, revealed that the North Defence was the preference, 'but despite its many break throughs it could not predict Hitler's changes of mind'. See Max Hastings, *All Hell Let Loose* (London: Harper, 2011) p.443.

Hitler's mind was that the Salerno landing nearly failed, with Kesselring's delaying defence working well. Hitler ordered Rommel and Kesselring to meet him, but Rommel was depressed and unwell, whereas Kesselring was the eternal optimistic diplomat. Kesselring was finally in charge of Italy on 21 November. During the invasion of Sicily, Kesselring had little authority, and used his diplomatic skills to carry any weight. Many Italians continued to be deeply suspicious of him. Ciano had written that with Kesselring 'Mussolini has swallowed a toad', suggesting he had swallowed poison or something that would consume him in turn.[12]

Later, Kesselring's British interrogator, described Kesselring as 'the correct, proud, too proud field marshal', and this appraisal was probably close to the truth.[13] Kesselring insisted on being *Oberbefehlshaber-Süd* in total control, but he never was. He started as an officer on Mussolini's staff, and was the highest-ranking German in Italy, but he was 'far from supreme in executive powers'.[14] It had been an error by the Allies to refer to Kesselring as *Emperor*, but it was a delusion shared by Kesselring, and cost him at his trial.

Kesselring and Italians

Kesselring had struggled with the Italian military command, but he had done a better job than Rommel, who was known to praise the work of some Italian soldiers, but who often made it known how little he thought of Italian senior officers. Kesselring's diplomatic and buoyant nature were tested from the invasion of Sicily onwards.

The Italians had told Kesselring that Sicily's defences were sound, but after flying there he held a different view. He looked at gun-emplacements which he described as mere 'eyewash' and the defences as 'gingerbread'.[15] The Todt organisation used re-enforced concrete, but many of the Italian gun-emplacements were made from brick covered with thin cement.* Even with the tactical policies, he clashed with the Italians,

---

* The author saw such defences while studying German defence lines in Italy in 2012: many were red brick and thin concrete looking like 'gingerbread' and such examples tended to reflect those built by the Italians.

who were placing their defences out of sight of naval guns, but while Kesselring wanted them concealed he thought they should be closer to the beaches. 'The resulting controversy was still raging when the invasion commenced'.[16] Kesselring was surprised at the accuracy of the naval guns which made a lasting impression upon him, it was probably his first experience of naval gunnery.[17] In terms of the Italian mind-set Kesselring had his shortcomings. He never realised the Italians were deeply divided about fascism, that many were unsure concerning Mussolini's leadership, most were opposed to German interference, then the fear of German occupation, and they felt little antagonism for the British and Americans. Some fought under orders, others did not want to fight, and 'every soldier and every officer had to make that decision and it was very apparent when allied troops finally invaded Sicily on 10 July 1943, that the majority of Italian forces had decided not to do so'.[18] Kesselring had no idea that for many Italians, their heart was not in the war, with many regarding Fascism as either a mistake, or a failing system. He was a sound professional military leader, but he failed to have his finger on the pulse of the Italian population and their growing sense of scepticism.

If Kesselring failed to understand the man on the street and the foot soldier, he was often equally ignorant of the motivations of senior Italian officers. When Hitler offered help of three divisions to Ambrosio, Kesselring felt he accepted reluctantly. Hitler had offered Ambrosio five divisions but was refused. The Italians did not want too many Germans in their country with the persistent fear of a major occupation. In a conference with Dönitz, Kesselring claimed that the refusal was simply that the 'Italians wanted to remain masters in their own house', and he was close to the truth, but had not recognised the growing hostility.[19] Later Kesselring started to wonder whether Ambrosio had wanted to help an Allied takeover, or place German divisions where they could fall prey to the Allies.[20] Kesselring had anticipated that the Italians would hold firm with the Germans, feeling it confirmed when on 28 July, Badoglio sent Hitler a telegram explaining 'we shall carry on the war in the spirit of our alliance', but Hitler, always suspicious, was not fooled.[21] Kesselring was described by Hitler as trusting the Italians too much, and Goebbels wrote that 'Generals are usually too unpolitical to understand the background of such a scene'.[22] However, Kesselring followed OKW instructions, which were basically Hitler's demands, and who ordered him to prepare for a possible Italian collapse, but his understanding of the Italian military was disastrous. He was perplexed by the fall of Mussolini, but postwar Kesselring claimed that it was Mussolini who was out of touch, but that was with the benefit of hindsight. Kesselring had held a meeting with Mussolini, who explained that Dino Grandi, a leading political figure, was loyal, but who along with Mussolini's son-in-law Ciano, was at that time preparing to topple the dictator. Mussolini explained he had just spoken with Grandi saying, 'we had a heart-to-heart talk; our views are identical. He is loyally devoted to me'.[23] Postwar, Kesselring told the American Historical Division, 'Nothing could have surpassed Mussolini's blind confidence', and his overthrow could have been avoided with the support of the Germans and loyal Italians.[24] That Kesselring should have known about the proposed revolt would be asking too much, as many in the fascist party had no idea. The SS interpreter General Dollmann later wrote that 'whatever their former rank, unit and colour of uniform, any Germans who claim to have had advance knowledge of 8 September are simply lying'.[25]

When Kesselring's HQ was later targeted by Allied bombers, a map, retrieved from a downed bomber, pinpointed his headquarters. This map clearly indicated that some Italians had betrayed him. It later transpired that a disgruntled politician 'had obligingly ringed the field marshal's Headquarters in red on an aerial map which the Allies had provided him with in Lisbon'.[26] It was from this event that Kesselring changed his attitude towards the Italians who had now become the enemy. None of this was helped when the Italian Navy Minister, Count de Courten had explained to Kesselring that their navy had sailed to engage the British. According to Kesselring's Chief of Staff Westphal, 'Courten shed tears and...his invocation of the German blood that flowed in his veins from his mother's side, did not fail to make a deep impression'.[27] It never occurred to Kesselring that it was a ruse to lull German suspicions, because the Italian Navy had turned south to surrender as the Allies had demanded.

Kesselring's change of attitude towards the Italians took on a hard-line approach, and later developed into a ruthless brutality, which he explained as a military necessity. The first crucial moment was having to take over the Italian forces. Some willingly surrendered and like others asked to speak under a flag of truce. Kesselring instructed Westphal to carry out the demobilisation of Italian soldiers, adding that they could then return to their homes, which was at least a civilised policy. However, Kesselring now on his guard told the negotiators, if they did not agree to surrender, then he would bomb Rome.[28] Kesselring was prepared to be ruthless in his military control, and published the following public notice:

> Rome is under my command and is war territory, subject to martial law. Those organizing strikes or sabotage as well as snipers will be shot immediately, private correspondence is suspended. Telephone conversation should be brief as possible. They will be strictly monitored.[29]

Rommel, stationed up north, criticised Kesselring for not sending all Italian soldiers to Germany, which irritated Kesselring, because Rommel appeared to be acting as his superior. As it transpired, in North Italy many Italian soldiers deserted with their weapons, and later the partisan war had both men and arms because of Rommel's tougher stance and therefore failure to collect in the weapons.[30] According to an Italian historian, 'Kesselring's decision to disarm Italian soldiers and allow them to go home meant that Italian resistance was mainly focused in north-west Italy, in the area under Rommel's control'.[31] It should be noted that under Kesselring there were no massacres as in the Balkans and Greek islands.* Westphal later wrote of Kesselring's actions that 'the surrender of their war material was carried out without friction. Nor was the fear that they would at once join the partisan movement justified by events. Everyone was pleased that this loathsome business was over at last'.[32]

---

* On Cephalonia the Acqui Division fought the Germans; after the battle an estimated 5,000 prisoners were massacred.

Master of Defence, Contemporary and Historian Views

Kesselring's prestige grew in Italy among Allied leaders, praising him for his professional defence. Alexander, who suffered anxious moments at Salerno, Anzio, and Monte Cassino, wrote that Kesselring 'showed very great skill'.[33] The American General Bradley referred to him as 'the able field marshal'.[34] Even the London *Times* stated that Kesselring 'is manifestly too short of reserves: yet the German defence remains stubborn and dangerous'.[35]

Historians have continued in the same vein. With the exception of Richard Lamb, who fought in Italy, referring to Kesselring as 'a brute', most praise Kesselring as a master of defence.[36] His defence has been described as 'superb' (Hoyt); having the instincts of 'the true gambler' (Hapgood); 'bearing the stamp of genius' (D'Este); with 'few equals in the army' (Atkinson), and the 'master of delaying tactics' (Hickey).[37] Two respected historians refer to him 'as good a general as emerged from the German Army in the Second World War and certainly the best on either side in the Italian theatre'.[38] He has been described as 'superior even to Rommel' (Roberts); the 'canny commander' (Macintyre); 'in the front rank of commanders' (Hastings); 'talented and experienced' (Harper); and Beevor noted that the 'Wehrmacht in Italy under Kesselring proved far more durable than even Hitler expected'.[39] Many of these assessments paint the picture portraying the Kesselring image as a 'master of defence' to gloss over a flawed Allied opposition. It has been pointed out many times that defence in Italy, because of the terrain, was easier than attack. When Douglas Porch described Kesselring as a 'tough no-nonsense German General' he was closest to the truth.[40] Kesselring was a solid professional commander, experienced and brought up in a militaristic tradition, but he was no genius.

Kesselring's ability was assisted by poor Allied planning. As Bradley wrote, 'astonishing as it seems in retrospect, there was no master plan for the conquest of Sicily'.[41] According to Bradley some Allied intelligence believed Italians would flee, others believed 'that on home soil the Italians would resist fiercely'.[42] Few could have guessed how individual Italians would react; and Kesselring also failed to understand what was happening in Italian minds.

From the allied invasion of Sicily, it was clear that Allied planning, strategy, and often tactics were marred in many ways. After the war, referring to Sicily and Italy, Montgomery 'admitted to the New Zealand commander Major General Sir Howard Kippenberger, that we went in without a plan'.[43] In Sicily, there was no plan to attack Messina even though the Allies were aware of the evacuation. Senger, Kesselring's best strategic general who controlled Monte Cassino, later wrote that 'when I look at the Allied plans…I cannot refrain from criticism'.[44]

Salerno and its hinterland were tough, the London *Times* newspaper grudgingly admitted that in Italy 'the German resistance has been skilful, stubborn, and fierce…most of his [Kesselring] divisions are of high quality…some are exceptionally good…and his engineers have shown their customary skill'.[45] Mussolini having been reinstated by Hitler, became a puppet, and the Italians were descending into a vicious civil war. After Salerno, Kesselring's status as a defence commander continued to grow, but it was often Allied ineptitude that built his reputation.

Kesselring had recognised the value of escaping Sicily across the Messina Straits, having appointed General Hube to organise what has been called a mini-Dunkirk. The Salerno beachheads were dangerous for the Allied troops as Vietinghoff's Tenth Army launched a serious counterattack on 13 September. It nearly worked; it came dangerously close to cutting the bridgehead in two, and General Clark considered re-embarking the US 5th Army. Whereas the Allied planning appeared ignorant of the Italian weather and terrain, Kesselring and his staff had a thorough knowledge of Italian geography and its details. Montgomery working his way up the east coastline, was often, and with some justification, criticised for taking his time given the circumstances at Salerno. However, he was seriously hampered by skilful German hindrances and booby traps, which had made use of the narrow mountainous roads. The German defence under Kesselring had not forgotten Montgomery's whereabouts.

The terrain of mountain and valley, the slow progress of the Allies, permitted Kesselring to build defence lines across the breadth of Italy's peninsula, the first ran through Monte Mignano called the Berhardt/Reinhard, the Garigliano River to the Cassino line, the well-known Gustav line, and more were later established. Italy is long, narrow, mountainous, with narrow roads and cold winters, making it easier to defend than to attack. Ernie Pyle the war correspondent wrote:

> The war in Italy was tough. The land and the weather were both against us. It rained and it rained. Vehicles bogged down and temporary bridges washed out. The country was shockingly beautiful, and just as shockingly hard to capture from the enemy. The hills rose to high ridges of almost solid rock. We couldn't go round them through the flat peaceful valleys, because the Germans were up there looking down upon us, and they would have let us have it. So we had to go up and over. A mere platoon of Germans, well dug in on high, rock-spined hill, could hold out for a long time against tremendous onslaughts.[46]

The battleground of Italy had focal points which have since become well-known. After Salerno the Allies pressed north through heavily defended river crossings until they came upon the Gustav line with its pivotal point at Monte Cassino. The nature of the mountainous terrain demanded more amphibious landings, and although Kesselring believed the Allies would carry out another landing, Anzio still took him by surprise. Typical of his forward thinking, he had preparatory plans. Already organised was Operation *Richard* which entailed having reserve divisions ready to swing into action across the breadth of Italy. Even after Anzio he had remained convinced, because of Allied deception, that there would be another landing around Leghorn. Kesselring's strategy allowed reserves to be rushed from one to the other site when necessary.

Kesselring and the SS

Kesselring had held the rank of *Oberbefehlshaber-Süd* but was answerable to many chiefs in Italy as well as Hitler and the OKW, and it had been a mere designation more than a reality suggested by the grand title. However, as Italy's political structure disintegrated Kesselring's command-title became more meaningful and realistic. Nevertheless, following Italy's capitulation, Himmler's SS moved into Italy with their own command structure which again tended to limit his increasing authority. Although Kesselring claimed to be their technical superior it was a misleading claim, he never had total control, and even the Reich Foreign Labour Service, tasked to transport labourers, reported directly to Berlin. *SS-Obergruppenführer* Karl Wolff was responsible for security, and the war against partisans. Wolff proposed to Kesselring the idea that the SS did the policing within the army-controlled area. Kesselring nearly accepted the offer but was warned by Westphal, who was more disinclined to the SS than Kesselring.

There was command-confusion, and on 1 May 1944, Kesselring had demanded that Keitel send a signal defining his duties. Kesselring was made the highest authority, but the partisan war was given to *Obergruppenführer* Wolff and his guerrilla operations staff. They were subordinate to Kesselring only for the sake of military appearances. Where the army was involved, the SS and the Police shared combat-roles, but not within a 20-mile zone from the front.

Himmler wanted Rome evacuated, but Kesselring refused on the grounds of potential starvation and riot. Herbert Kappler (SS officer head of the Gestapo and Security Services in Rome) was ordered by Himmler to arrest 800 Jews, Kesselring had no authority to stop this, but he circumnavigated the order by not detailing troops to the task.[47] Kesselring was aware that the Italians were not generally anti-Semitic, so he avoided the issue where possible, and although anti-Semitic himself, Kesselring did not appear a rampant Nazi in this matter, as may be perceived from this reaction to Himmler's orders. Up until July 1943 frontier officials were known to permit Jewish refugees to find sanctuary in Italy.[48] Once Himmler's SS arrived the situation changed. Kesselring was a right-wing nationalist and undoubtedly anti-Semitic, but probably not to the Nazi level, and as noted he never played an active role in the Holocaust.

Rome had been declared an Open City, but the Pope, being concerned with a breakdown of law and order, had asked Kesselring to police the city. Some have argued that Kesselring's Open City was a mere pretence, but Kesselring had to use the city as a transport communication link because all the roads led towards the Gustav line and Anzio.[49] The population in Rome was anticipating that the war would soon finish, but during April the city was reaching starvation level. There were bread riots with the SS reacting by shooting 'ten women on a Tiber bridge' as an example to others.[50] No association of this incident was ever made relating to Kesselring, underlining that the SS had their independence. Himmler, without consultation, had ordered that south of Anzio where the Pontine Marshes had been drained by Mussolini for farming, the area be checked by hydrographers and malariologists. They knew 'by flooding it would revert to a larval nursery for *Anopheles Labranchiae*, which made the place dangerous, and, in many ways, it was probably the first and only example of biological warfare'.[51] Kesselring had little or no control over the barbaric SS, but postwar, his insistence that he was in overall charge weakened his defence, and later during the partisan warfare some of his orders were regarded as barbaric as those of Himmler's men.

Military Intelligence

Kesselring carried more responsibility than any other commander, though limited, as seen by the power of the Nazi political command, and much was beyond the sphere of his control. He was hampered by having his intelligence continuously breached, not least by Ultra and many spies. He tried to keep his new military HQ in Soratte secret because he was all too aware of spies, although in April 1944 it was heavily bombed.[52] His various Headquarters were attacked several times because of information leaked to the Allied forces. Kesselring eventually discovered a spy in his staff, 'an Italian operative...an ardent royalist who served as a liaison with the Fascist command in Rome, who secretly provided the German order of battle and details about the *Fischfang* (Anzio) counterattack'.[53] Torture failed to break him, and he was executed. However, there was a man called

Tompkins who was an SOE spy in Rome, providing detailed information about units, whom it was believed 'was the mole in Kesselring's camp'.[54] Kesselring was fighting a war in Italy against an enemy who was more welcome in that country than the Germans. Kesselring became suspicious, doubting various Italian commanders. Occasionally Allied plans fell into Kesselring's hands, but he never knew that most of his orders were decoded in Bletchley, being dispatched to Allied command the same day. In British 'central government circles the few who knew of their existence referred to them as Boniface'.*

The Policy of Plunder

Kesselring was an educated man who appreciated Italy's culture, as did Göring who was plundering art wherever he could. Kesselring alleged postwar that he questioned Göring's thefts, but acquiesced when told it was for the Reich's Museum of European Art. This revealed a naïve attitude, or it may have reflected his need for safety against the powerful opposition of Göring.

When members of the Herman Göring Division approached Abbot Dom Gregorio Diamare at Monte Cassino monastery, suggesting they save the treasures and the library, he was naturally suspicious because of Göring's reputation, who was known as 'the most celebrated snapper-up of unconsidered trifles in the Second World War'.[55] It was Kesselring with his General von Senger who authorised the priceless works of art be transported to the safety of the Vatican.** After the war Kesselring implied he was the true saviour of the monastery's treasures; he may well have signed the order, but the initiative probably started with General von Senger. This general was deeply religious, a Lay-Benedictine who went to mass in the Abbey whenever he was there. Some Italian treasures

---

* John Colville, *The Churchillians* (London: Weidenfeld & Nicolson, 1981) p.59. Boniface was English and known as the Apostle to the Germans.

** It was not until the German Ambassador Dr Rahn's memoirs were published that Hitler's intention to have the Vatican 'fumigated' by German troops became known. See Westphal, *German*, p.168. It was considered that the Pope should be imprisoned, and the Vatican was to be robbed of its priceless treasures: Kurzman, *A Special Mission*.

were purloined and many lost forever, but Kesselring's strongest critics accept that this was not his doing.

Kesselring once remarked that the Italian campaign was like 'waging war in a museum', and although he could have some credit for not plundering art, he was ruthless with Italy's economic future.[56] On 20 September 1943, under superior orders, Kesselring issued a directive to troops that industrial machinery was to be transported north. He ordered the demolition of communication systems, power plants, docks, and water supplies. It was a merciless mission, and when Benelli, a motorcycle manufacturer tried to avoid this order, 'the Germans kidnapped and held a Benelli brother as hostage until their cache was revealed'.[57] Museums, churches, monasteries, and hospitals were mainly spared under Kesselring's orders. It has been suggested that he ordered that 'milk-cows should not be killed because their milk was important for Roman children', but this seems unlikely.[58] This type of plunder by a retreating army was close to a scorched earth policy, and dangerous for civilians. It is estimated 90 per cent of all sheep and cattle with 80 per cent plus of poultry in South-Italy was taken by the retreating army, and German explosive experts left delayed action-bombs and booby-traps, but 'some Allied soldiers behaved no better than their enemies, vandalising priceless artefacts'.[59]

Chapter Six

Battles For Italy

Bari, Little Pearl Harbor

As a result of complacency in the Allied camp, a Luftwaffe raid on Bari was so successful it was dubbed a mini-Pearl Harbor. The Allied air superiority was overwhelming, with the number of German planes diminishing every month. In November 1943, Kesselring held a conference at his Frascati HQ with Richthofen and other senior officers, on how to slow the Allied advance. The Foggia airfields were first explored as the prime target. However, Richthofen argued for the bombing of Bari. He based his sound argument on the number of supplies delivered through the port, and Kesselring agreed. On the other side of the divide, Air Marshal Sir Arthur Coningham (1st Allied Tactical Air Force) had announced the Luftwaffe was finished, stating that 'I would regard it as a personal affront and insult if the Luftwaffe would attempt any significant action in this area'.[1] Richthofen had been informed that the Allies were unloading at night with all the lights on in Bari. When the raid took place on 2 December, the over-confidence of the Allies was evident with the port lit up like a funfair.

The Luftwaffe managed to sink seventeen ships, and damage the others, as well as the dockyards. Amongst these vessels was a Liberty ship called the SS *John Harvey*. This vessel was carrying mustard gas bombs causing many fatalities amongst combatants and civilians. This vessel's manifesto remained a secret for many years because she was carrying 2,000 M47A1 mustard bombs from Oran. It was claimed that they were sent into a theatre of operation in case the Germans resorted to chemical warfare.* The German propaganda radio known as the Berlin Bitch, broadcast how the Allies had harmed themselves with their own gas.

---
* Each bomb held up to 100 lbs of mustard gas.

Gustav Line and Monte Cassino

There were many destructive battles before the major assault on the Gustav Line. Kesselring was surprised by the slow progress of the enemy, and the Allied casualty rate was greater than the Germans. Italy was a game of chess, a positional war, and the British Official History wrote of Kesselring as a formidable commander. He had highly professional subordinates, such as von Senger, his Chief-of-Staff Westphal, Vietinghoff commanding the Tenth Army, with Mackensen as commander of the new Fourteenth Army.* One smaller battle which went badly wrong for the Allies was when the British had widened the bridgehead at the Garigliano River, and the American 36th Division arrived to find the wide Rapido River in flood, meeting heavy German artillery. It was during this time Kesselring's plane was shot down by Allied aircraft, crashing into a pond with Kesselring turning up in Vietinghoff's HQ covered in mud, but surviving. German resistance was strong, with Alexander writing to Churchill that 'the Germans are fighting magnificently. Never imagine they are crashing. Their staff work is brilliantly flexible'.[2] The Rapido River was a disaster for the Americans. It was poor planning by General Mark Clark ignoring advice from his officers on the spot about the German defence lines. They tried to point out to him that it was virtually suicidal to cross the river at this point because it was dominated by German guns. Clark insisted and many men were killed and injured. 'The officers and men of the 36th Division were unequivocal as to who was responsible…it was entirely Mark Clark's fault'.[3] In the immediate postwar years it would lead to a Congressional Hearing. The Allies made it easier for the Germans, and admiration was given to Kesselring instead of questioning Allied command leadership.

The Gustav line was a series of battles, but the Allied victory at Monte Cassino was drawn out, costing many lives.** Kesselring acknowledged that the use of the 'natural features with concrete armoured positions

---

* Friedrich von Mackensen (1889–1969) son of the famous Field Marshal August von Mackensen.
** The hill was heavily defended. 'In November the Germans had put 100 steel shelters into the Cassino position, and they added more later, as well as 76 armoured casements and a number of armoured machine-gun nests'. Harper, *Battles*, p.7.

and enfilading fire', made defence easier than attack, making the high mountains and deep valleys ideal.[4] It was wrongly believed by the Allies that the German forces were using the Abbey at Monte Cassino as it dominated the area. The occasional spotter-plane and misunderstood or mistranslated radio-messages seemed to indicate the presence of Germans. However, Kesselring refused the use of the Abbey, having 'given his assurance to the Vatican on 11 December 1943'.[5] Westphal confirmed that Kesselring had the Abbey cordoned off by military police for its protection.[6] The Abbot said the Germans had not broken the agreement; the Abbot's secretary, Don Martino Matronola's diary recorded that the Germans never entered the premises.[7] General von Senger, a Lay-Benedictine who used to attend mass, said he was the only German present; and even Churchill later admitted that the evidence indicated there were no Germans.[8] However, the Germans were all around the Abbey, within its shadows, but not in it. The decision was taken to bomb the site which destroyed the ancient edifice and caused serious collateral damage. Bombing the area made defence easier, providing hiding places for guns, and rubble restricting the use of the roads. This action surprised Kesselring and caused the Allies damage to their reputation. The Abbey was eventually taken by the Poles but after a considerable loss of life.

Anzio

The plan behind the Anzio landing (Operation *Shingle*), was to break the deadlocks of the Gustav Line, especially Monte Cassino. As with Salerno it was another precarious landing with Allied troops virtually trapped on the beach, with Churchill famously referring to it as the 'stranded or beached whale' and not the 'wild cat' he had anticipated. Unlike the Salerno landings, Kesselring was caught by surprise. However, as a professional officer he had planned Operation *Richard*, in case of an unexpected landing. His reserves were ready for orders, and with considerable speed he drew in additional manpower. News of the landing reached Kesselring by 3 a.m., by 5 a.m. troops were heading to the beach, and by 7.10 a.m. orders were given for northern reserves to move south. Kesselring flew to the front in the early morning and returned late evening to avoid Allied aircraft. In postwar interviews Kesselring was critical of the American General Lucas, whom, he claimed, stayed on the beachhead because the way inland was undefended. Westphal later wrote that 'the road to Rome was open, and an audacious flying column could have penetrated to the city'.[9] Lucas was generally criticised all round, some claim unfairly, but he did not receive sound instructions from senior command until the situation came close to an ongoing disaster.

As the Anzio landings started, Hitler issued *Order Number 52*, instructing that the fight should have no mercy, even against officers or units failing in their duty, referring to that 'hazardous enterprise which will be drowned in the blood of Anglo-Saxon soldiers'.* Hitler sent a message to the troops demanding, 'it must be fought with bitter hatred against an enemy who wages a ruthless war of annihilation…and strives only for the destruction of Germany and European culture'.[10] Kesselring's first biographer claimed that Hitler's ruthless orders 'weighed on his conscience', but this seems problematical, being all too typical of postwar claims.[11] At a critical stage Hitler instructed that the Infantry Demonstration (*Lehr*) Regiment be sent for the assault. Kesselring noted this was a home-defence force with no battle exposure. Hitler's interference cost 3,000 men and thirty tanks: Kesselring wrote 'they were thrown back disgracefully'.[12] By 1 March 1944, Kesselring realised they had failed because of the size of the Allied reserves, and Hitler's inane interference, but Kesselring never challenged him on these issues. Kesselring was up against a foe who was logistically superior in manpower and resources. As such, although Kesselring's defence plans had held months longer than the Allies had expected, they were now creaking against the latest Allied operations.** Kesselring asked for help to be placed at the disposal of the Tenth Army, but Mackensen objected, and Kesselring replaced him. He used Mackensen again, but it sent a warning to subordinates not to hesitate over orders, Kesselring was a no-nonsense general.

---

* The last Directive was No 51, thereafter they were Orders, see Hugh Trevor-Roper, *Hitler's War Directives*, pp.232–3.
** Operation *Diadem*.

Rome

Allied codebreaking had picked up Kesselring's message to Hitler asking permission for both armies to retreat north, and for Rome to be evacuated without a fight. To avoid Rome breaking out in mayhem, as in Naples, Kesselring ordered that Lieutenant-General Mälzer attend a gala performance of Gigli to give the impression of normality. This order demonstrated Kesselring's eye for detail.[13]

Field Marshal Alexander had ordered General Mark Clark in Operation *Buffalo*, to close the Valmontone Gap, thereby entrapping the whole southern wing of the Tenth Army. For his own long debated reasons, Clark ignored the orders, by so doing 'he deliberately committed what must be ranked as one of the most misguided blunders made by an Allied commander during World War II'.[14] Had the Valmontone Gap been closed, the Germans may well have been trapped, but Kesselring could see what 'Clark obsessed with his private goals could not see, that it was the combination of the Allied thrusts…that posed the threat'.[15] Alexander later wrote that 'every time we attacked Kesselring in Italy we took him completely by surprise; but he showed very great skill in extricating himself from the desperate situation into which his faulty intelligence had led him'.[16] Once again a senior Allied commander used Kesselring's growing reputation for failure of his own orders.

Chapter Seven

North Italy and Partisans

Kesselring's Loyalty

At one stage there were wishful rumours amongst the Allies that Kesselring was clashing with Hitler. 'Kesselring, whom Allied propaganda broadcasts had frequently suggested was not a strong supporter of Hitler, and who indeed often disagreed with the Führer' did not have the same reputation with the Italian civilians.[1] Kesselring claimed that when Hitler delivered his 'fight to the last man' order, Kesselring gave a 'short and heated reply', but this was stated in the safety of postwar memoirs.[2] Hitler's adjutant wrote that the Italian theatre was in Kesselring's hands 'and Hitler hardly ever interfered there', which again is highly dubious.[3] However, Kesselring was one of the very few field marshals never sacked, remained loyal, and in the last bunker days was listed by Hitler's aides as one of the nine generals 'most loyal to Hitler'.[4]

After the Stauffenberg 20 July bomb-plot, Kesselring claimed ignorance, but mentioned that Dr Karl Goerdeler had tried to 'approach me in 1942, but unsuccessfully, as I could not then be reached'.[5] Dollmann confirmed this, referring to Goerdeler as 'a ringleader.'[6] After the war Kesselring conceded to his son that he was aware 'that something was afoot'.[7] Generals Westphal and Senger knew about the plot, and Senger had informed Kesselring's son that he owed his life to his father's intervention at that difficult time.[8] It is known that General von Senger's Chief of Staff was a friend of Stauffenberg.[9] It also appears he saved another staff officer, two in all, it may have been Westphal.[10] The plot was probably organised because 'with Hitler the war [would] certainly be lost', but Kesselring was obedient to the fruitless end.[11] The 20 July plot involved many executions, and Kesselring did not seem to come under suspicion because of his undoubted loyalty. He had proved a success in defence, never questioned Hitler and remained obedient to the regime. He was now faced with the moral dilemma of fighting partisans embedded in the civilian population, with the uphill task of facing the defeat of Germany.

Retreat North

During the retreat north, Kesselring 'was slightly wounded while in the front line', but carried on after a field dressing.[12] As early as November 1944 the *Guardian* newspaper referred to the Italian campaign as 'the toughest of all side-shows', referring to Kesselring as the 'ex-airman' who transpired to 'be one of the most stubborn and least advertised of German generals'.[13] However, Kesselring was acting out a long-term defence, because 'no matter how skilled their conduct of defensive battles, the weight of Allied military power was wearing away the Wehrmacht's tactical advantages'.[14]

In Italy, both Germans and the Allies worked on the policy they were tying down the other side. Alexander wrote that 'it was the Germans, not the Allies, who were contained in Italy'.[15] It could be that the Germans, with fewer troops, were holding larger Allied forces, with Alexander commenting to a journalist in 1950, that who was holding who down 'permitted no easy answer, then or now'.[16]

On Wednesday 25 October, Kesselring was on the road from Bologna to Forli when his car crashed into a long-barrelled gun turning into a side road. His skull was badly fractured, his face cut open and he was unconscious for twelve hours. General Vietinghoff replaced him, holding back the Allies until the end of the year. The Allies had decided to rest, and although Kesselring was in hospital, he was given credit for conducting a brilliant defence.

In the New Year of 1945, Kesselring, after three months away, returned to his staff HQ. The Italian campaign was static, and Italy was of secondary interest after the D-Day Normandy. This new pressure had obliged the OKW to extract ten divisions for other fronts.

The Partisan War

Kesselring was known for his speed of reaction with aggressive fighting-retreats, 'by a series of rear-guard actions which, inch by inch, opposed the Allied vanguard up to the definitive withdrawal on the Gothic line [leaving] a horrifying trail of massacres splitting the peninsula transversely'.[17] What made this so appalling was Kesselring's reaction to increasing partisan activity, within the Italian civil war. Much of this issue revolves around the nature of the partisan, for some a terrorist, for others a patriot. The partisans and resistance fighters had Western support. Churchill had demanded that Europe be set alight, and Alexander asked Italians to kill Germans at every opportunity. However, the policy of encouraging partisans was important because it occupied German troops, but Kesselring regarded it as a 'struggle against gangs with most severe measures' needed.[18] The nature of the partisan was a vexed question. In 1942 the Wehrmacht had prepared a study on guerrilla warfare declaring it as illegal. 'International law did not provide any unambiguous rules for dealing with guerrilla warfare. The 1907 Hague Convention was full of contradictions and open questions concerning the rights and responsibilities of an occupying force'.[19] The historian Claudio Pavone explained the 'armed resistance of 1943–1945 was, simultaneously, a national war, a civil war, and a class war'.[20] This war was complicated by a lack of national identity: it has been suggested there was no unified Italy.

The communists, as in France, were the most aggressive, believing the 'blood of the martyrs' built their foundation. They provoked the reaction of a 'ten-to-one reprisal' which was soon 'inflicted in Florence' after the murder of a fascist official.[21] Sometimes partisans would kill a German to provoke a violent reaction, done in the hope it would stimulate or activate civilians to join with them because of their outrage at German reprisals. Although active and numerous the partisans failed to stop Kesselring's 150-mile retreat towards the Gothic line. However, Kesselring had underestimated the Italians, and 'the German troops felt furious with their former allies for their betrayal and took their revenge on civilians at the slightest provocation'.[22] At first, Kesselring limited retaliation, as when some partisans bombed the Flora Hotel where he had been the same morning. Eight days later eight Germans were killed by a grenade attack, and again 'Kesselring refused to be goaded into retaliation'.[23] A few months before he had issued an order that 'every German soldier now... conducts himself in an especially exemplary manner...officers are again to be warned of the necessity for the sharpest supervision'.[24] This was a period of rapid change in partisan activity, affecting Kesselring's attitudes. When 'communist partisans in Milan had killed nine German soldiers as well as eight passers-by', Kesselring now decided to apply the ten to one rule.* However, he relented on an appeal by Cardinal Schuster, but despite this a fascist firing squad executed fifteen political prisoners the day after. The SS units followed their own rules, and in October 1944 a Reichsführer-SS Division moved into Bologna, where they committed a massacre at Marzabotto 'and perpetrated a massacre three times the size of Oradour and ten times the size of Lidice'.[25] There eventuated an endless list of massacres and murders in Italy, some not even recorded.

Kesselring may have disagreed with some of the SS reactions, but he gave the order that 'fighting against the guerrillas must therefore be conducted with the utmost rigour...I shall protect any commander who, in the choice and severity of method the old principle still holds good, that a wrong choice of method is used to achieve one's object is better than neglect and indolence'.[26] The Ultra decoding note in the archives on this particular message is marked with a red-pen for attention, the ruthlessness being evident. He recommended that Italian fascists were to select hostages, and where the partisans were in abundance, 'hostages will be taken from among the local population – relatives or able-bodied sympathisers...and villages will be burnt down'.[27] The SS were brutal, but Kesselring was now expecting the same from the Wehrmacht, stating that 'anti-guerrilla warfare must in large measure be carried out by the army'.[28] One German observer later acknowledged the 'terror and brutality left in the wake of the security police as they retreated', but noted that the Wehrmacht and Italian fascist groups all played a part.[29] Northern Italy

---

* Ten Italians killed for every German soldier.

was looking more like the bitter battles of the Eastern front, a conflict without mercy.

The war against partisans seemed to have brutalised Kesselring. It has been stated that Kesselring rarely followed up reports on ill-discipline, but *Panzertruppen* General Traugott Herr testified that Kesselring had soldiers shot who had raped or looted.[30] Kesselring tried to heighten the deterrent effect by using posters connecting the death of Germans to reprisals. Later, he constantly claimed to be innocent, but he was aware of his own orders. It was reported by the Chinese Chargé in Berne that Kesselring had recently 'commissioned a genealogist named Furics to obtain proof that Kesselring's ancestors originally came from Argovie (Aargau) in Switzerland', knowing that in Swiss law 'it is comparatively easy for all persons of Swiss ancestry to obtain citizenship by application'.[31] Given the nature of this unusual archival note found by accident in the archives, it is not unreasonable to feel that Kesselring was looking to the future for an escape route from his deeds.

Kesselring constantly blamed the Italian partisans, claiming, with some justification, that his soldiers were hanged, drowned, crucified, frozen to death, and suffered every kind of torture. It had, as Kesselring correctly noted, 'involved both sides in committing the most abominable crimes with mathematical predictability'.[32] How much Kesselring knew of all the activities of the SS and the Wehrmacht units can never be established. However, the Italian Minister of Pardon and Justice wrote in 1947, 'it is not likely that the Commander of the German Forces in Italy is ignorant of such a massacre [SS massacre at Sant'Anna di Stazzema] of which we still do not know the authors'.[33] It was a myth that Kesselring fought a chivalrous war as he contended, and a pretence that he was ignorant of the massacres. His own commands are clearly written and reflect those of the OKW on the Eastern Front.

Before his road accident, it was claimed he had secretly encouraged Wolff, one of the moderate SS generals to contact the Americans in Switzerland. This was probably not the case as it was Wolff and Dollmann who took the initiative with Dulles.[34] Given Kesselring's character and background such an idea is inconceivable. It was at this moment that in a top-secret telegram relating to the Italian chaos, Alexander used the code 'Emperor', signifying the importance attached to Kesselring.[35] Wolff had wildly predicted that in a postwar Germany Kesselring would be a possible president. On 9 March, Kesselring was summoned by Adolf Hitler, and the next day was made Commander-in-Chief of the Western theatre. In effect the bitter Italian campaign would grind to a halt only just before the final surrender in Germany.

Western Command

Hitler had been infuriated by the loss of the Remagen Bridge, sacking Rundstedt, whom he accused of retreating. Kesselring was caught by surprise when told he was to be ordered to the Western front. He suggested he was needed in Italy, but Keitel warned him it 'would hold no water with the Führer'.[36] Hitler stated at a Führer conference on 9 January 1945 that, 'as you saw with Kesselring, if someone does it right, it does work'.[37] Kesselring was an 'arch-loyalist, always exuding real or contrived optimism, however grim the military situation'.[38] Kesselring kept out of the political machinations, and was known to be loyal to Hitler.

On 1 April 1944, Kesselring sent a highly emotive message to all troops, reading:

> I greet you, soldiers, the stake is Germany, our people, our children, and their future. To throw in our hand now is to betray Germany. Those who have fallen with a triumphant faith in the future of Germany expect their sacrifices shall not have been in vain. I appeal to each and every one of you, be a sworn brotherhood of warriors, rating honour higher than life, knowing only one thing: Germany.[39]

Kesselring never hesitated to use the Führer's melodramatic language of 'heroic final battles'.[40] Following Seeckt, he had never joined a political party, but he shared Hitler's views on communism, held a belief in German superiority, supremacy in Europe and firmly held that a soldier should never surrender. Hitler was forever commanding his troops to fight 'in a spirit of holy hatred for an enemy who is conducting a pitiless war of extermination against the German people'.[41] By this stage of events, the German situation was hopeless, and a Wehrmacht military judge remarked on the inevitability of defeat, asking why the leaders fought on, writing, 'will it take for the very last German to realise this?'[42]

According to Kesselring, Hitler was full of confidence with talk of new-fangled weapons. Kesselring kept his feelings concealed then and later, but perhaps a degree of self-cynicism can be detected when he introduced himself to his staff with 'I'm the new wonder weapon!'[43] The sadness was that 'research on the last phase of the war shows many Germans still invested improbable hopes' in projected wonder-weapons, when they were mainly a propaganda fantasy.[44]

However, Hitler was able to convince many that victory remained a possibility. Kielmansegg, an officer on the German General Staff, witnessed the effect Hitler had on senior commanders, calling it 'the Wehrmacht high command bug'.[45] Westphal described Kesselring as arriving in a cheerful fashion, declaring he was Hitler's new V3 weapon.[46] It appeared that Kesselring had absorbed Hitler's phantom troops and miracle weapons, but at the front-line the realities re-engaged him.

Postwar Kesselring claimed he fought on to save those fighting in the east, arguing part of the army should not surrender whilst another fought.[47] A report to the British War Cabinet in July 1944 noted that 'fear of the Russians continues to dominate their thoughts, and there are indications of widespread anxiety that the threat from the East should be staved off at all costs'.[48]

As late as 1 April, Kesselring was sending orders to his troops to 'fight to the end'.[49] His orders were brutal, stopping PoW transports 'marching with white flags as protection against fighter-bombers'.[50] Kesselring fought on, later claiming that Germany would need rebuilding, possibly based on managing to get his hands on *Eclipse*, the Allied plan to divide Germany into zones.[51] Hitler issued his 'Destruction Order' on 19 March, 'the Nero Order, a scorched earth policy of Soviet style', with Kesselring later claiming to have collaborated with Speer to avoid senseless destruction, but there is no reliable evidence of such an arrangement.[52]

On 18 March 1945, Kesselring had reported that the population 'was playing a negative role' in so far that town deputations were begging German officers to circumnavigate them, and they were agreeing to these pleas.[53] It is impossible not to have some sympathy with such requests from German civilians. It was evident the war was lost and by fighting through the towns and villages innocent people, women and children included, would be unnecessarily killed. Hitler was not impressed, but when 'the Americans were advancing on all fronts, both Kesselring and Model decided against any more destruction'.[54] Westphal claimed that Kesselring ignored Keitel and Bormann's instruction that every town and village should be defended, by ordering positions be taken up outside the boundaries. If Westphal were correct, then it was a sign of common-sense humanity in Kesselring, and probably reflected for the first time that Kesselring had accepted the hopelessness of the situation, which was absurdly late. Kesselring wrote that:

> I felt like a concert pianist who is asked to play a Beethoven sonata before a large audience on an ancient, rickety, and out of tune instrument. In many respects I found conditions which contradicted all my principles, but events were moving too swiftly for me to have time to influence them much. My post was too important and my rank too high for me to shirk the responsibility.[55]

In late March Wolff had visited Kesselring to persuade him to allow Vietinghoff to surrender. Kesselring was aware of this operation which the Allies had code-named *Sunrise*.* Kesselring argued with Wolff, but supported the steps being taken, adding 'that an end only came into question for him if the Führer was no longer alive'.[56] Kesselring's hesitancy was curious. He dismissed Vietinghoff for surrendering because Hitler still lived, which given the circumstances of the day was, as the historian Kershaw wrote, a 'graphic case' of following 'insane orders'.[57] The obsession

---

* The Americans appeared to trust Wolff and when later 'Nuremberg prosecutors gathered three folders of evidence relevant to Wolf's administrative involvement in war crimes, including the extermination of European Jewry' he still found protection from Dulles. see Salter, *Nazi*, p.25.

with obeying Hitler was typical of the higher command, as von Hassell wrote in his 1943 diary, 'none of the field marshals is acting as if he knew any higher concept of duty'.[58]

After the Remagen Bridge fiasco, Hitler had ordered 'Flying Special Tribunals West', which were drumhead courts for those who saw no point in fighting on. Kesselring said they 'would weaken morale along the entire Western Front', but used them.[59] It was claimed that Kesselring 'complained to his general staff that nowhere on his journey through the army area had he seen a hanged deserter, a sure sign of ineffective military leadership'.[60] It has been recorded that some '9,732 death sentences were carried out up to Dec 1944 with 8,000 in the army alone, possibly 15,000 to 20,000 in the whole war;' by contrast, in the USA there were 146, France 102, Britain 40 but the Soviets shot an estimated 994,300.[61] The whole issue was immoral, if not illegal, and Kesselring appeared to be involved.

It was decided that the German forces be divided, the southern area would come under Kesselring with a small OKW staff under General Winter, with Dönitz controlling the north. Macmillan, in his war diaries, noted as late as 4 May that Kesselring, through Wolff, had 'sent Alex a message asking to be put in touch with Eisenhower – a very interesting development'.[62] Kesselring, like other political and military leaders was probably regarding himself as important even in the face of defeat, an unreal world.

There was confusion over who was surrendering, and Kesselring complained that he was kept in the dark. By 6 May Kesselring's HQ staff was the only official group which technically had not surrendered. Kesselring had transferred his reduced staff to Himmler's personal train at Saalfelden. He claims to have considered suicide like Model, but he decided against it on the grounds that it would simply place the burden on someone else.[63] The question remains as to why Kesselring was the last one to fight to the end. It has been suggested by his son Rainer, that there was always in his mind the hope of at least some sort of negotiated peace with the Western Allies.[64]

Chapter Eight

Prison and Trial

Prisoner

An American major of the 101st Airborne took Kesselring to Berchtesgaden permitting him to keep his weapons, medals, and baton. 'Charmingly, but firmly, smiling Albert [his nickname because he often appeared smiling] refused to deal with anybody from the 101st Airborne Division, for they were all junior in rank to him. That the power he had once held was gone seemed not to have been realised'.[1] Dönitz's request that Kesselring be flown to join other German leaders was refused. Kesselring was beginning to learn that he would be given little respect. After surrender, he claimed his concern was feeding the troops and population, sounding like a man trying to maintain his status. Kesselring suggested to General Devers that his technical troops should not be disbanded, but be used in repairing bridges and communications. He claimed to have 15,000 signals service men ready to repair the various systems, but he was totally ignored.

As with Göring, Kesselring was interviewed by Allied journalists, but his request to speak to Eisenhower was refused. There was an interlude of freedom, but as Nazi atrocities were revealed, Kesselring's imprisonment became more restrictive. On 15 May, he was taken to the camp at Mondorf, where he had to leave his treasured medals and baton, now a mere prisoner of war.

Kesselring experienced different prisons, some tougher than others, his guards having seen or heard of the results of Nazi atrocities. Knowledge of the Holocaust was growing as was the question of whether the military leaders knew what had happened. Westphal wrote:

Naturally one knew of the concentration camps. Nevertheless, it was no more possible for the Army to know the number and nature of these camps and their occupants or their condition…right up to the end of the war the majority had only heard of Dachau and Oranienburg. Names such as Auschwitz, Belsen, and Buchenwald only became known after the capitulation.[2]

Kesselring claimed he knew nothing, which is impossible to verify, possible in terms of the evil deeds, but highly unlikely that he had not heard of the camps. The same response as Kesselring's would be heard throughout the Nuremberg Trial. The British had imprisoned senior German military officers in Trent Park holding camp, and professional eavesdropping revealed that knowledge of atrocities varied. However, 'the prisoners at Trent Park had been captured exclusively in North Africa, France and finally in Germany, where the 'fewest infringements of international law were committed', but knowledge of massacres was still widespread.[3] Those fighting in Africa and Italy experienced less atrocity than those in Eastern Europe, and the myth grew that it was a clean war. It has been suggested this myth was encouraged by Kesselring's later defence counsel. Nevertheless, there were massacres in Northern Italy. For many, including Kesselring, 'the focus on the SS, which had resulted from the Nuremberg trials, bore all the marks of an *Alibi of a Nation*'.[4]

Kesselring must have had some knowledge of the brutal anti-Semitism, if only because he was aware that Himmler demanded the Roman Jewish population be transported. In Tunisia, Ambassador Rahn had suggested that instead of deporting Jewish people, they were given work. Kesselring ordered the mobilization of Jewish workers for defence constructions, possibly, it has been suggested, as an artifice to saving that Jewish community.[5] One middle-ranking German diarist noted five times in his short compilation that Jews were being 'gassed and then burned', and the NSDAP had intended the 'liquidation of Europe's Jews'.[6] Kesselring may not have been involved, but it is unbelievable he was ignorant of these events. At his trial when asked about Jewish soldiers, he simply said there was no such thing. It is inconceivable that a man in his position was unaware of the policy.

In Mondorf, dubbed the Ash Cage, Kesselring found the officer in charge, Colonel Andrus unpleasant, but the officers and NCOs more sympathetic. At Oberursel he was well treated, complaining that too many emigrant Germans had been utilised, as they were biased. This was probably based on the fact the Allies relied upon German speakers, many of whom, for political-racial motives, had fled Germany pre-war, and were considered biased.

He attended the main Nuremberg trial as a witness for Göring. He was puzzled to be questioned whether he was telling the truth while under oath, as he was accustomed to not being doubted. Kesselring's first biographer suggested that his presentation of the air-bombing charges regarding Warsaw and Rotterdam, had stopped bombing-raids becoming an issue. This was not likely, as the Allies had already agreed that areas 'concerning their own policies and actions the defence was to be prohibited from raising in court, such as *area bombing* and the Molotov-Ribbentrop *annexatio*'.* The *tu quoque* argument (you did this as well) did not work at any of the trials given the vast incomparable atrocities committed by the Nazi war machine. Kesselring was now regarded as a minor war criminal, and by the London Agreement his trial was to take place in the country where the alleged crimes had been committed.

After solitary confinement, Kesselring was sent to Dachau with five other commanders, being placed in a cell with others for ten days in pitch-darkness. It was regarded as an opportunity to reflect that 'their continued allegiance to the Führer before and during the war represented a lapse in moral and professional judgment that no circumstance could mitigate'.[7] Following this internment in Dachau, Kesselring returned to Nuremberg, then on to Langwasser where he met some old comrades, and shared a heavily barred prison-hut with Otto Skorzeny.

---

* Burleigh, *Moral*, p.545 under charge of waging an aggressive war Ribbentrop's counsel claimed Russia had to be charged under the same count, it was ignored.

In the autumn of 1946, he was transferred to the London Cage in Kensington, run by Colonel Scotland. It was a centre for interrogating suspected war criminals, and later had a mixed reputation, one recent writer claiming 'it is certainly a sordid piece of British history'.[8] Scotland, a tough interrogator, found, like others had, that Kesselring transpired to be charming, and assisted him in his defence. Scotland referred to Kesselring as Kessie, admitting he liked him, writing that he was the most 'blameless of all the German army leaders who ever set foot in wartime Italy'.[9] Nevertheless, having read the evidence, Scotland explained to Kesselring he was to be tried as a war criminal. Scotland blamed it on Kesselring's pride, as his insistence on being Commander-in-Chief made him guilty. Such was this friendship that Kesselring, with one British officer, was allowed to explore London; few, if any other prisoner, had ever been allowed such a privilege.

From London Kesselring returned to Allendorf, where over the Christmas and the New Year of 1946 he spent some time with his wife. On 17 January 1947, Kesselring was removed via Salzburg to Rimini for his trial in Venice.

The Trial

Kesselring's trial was based on the London Agreement and held in Italy, the scene of the crimes of which he was indicted. There were many critics about holding the trial in the first place, as well as the nature of its proceedings. For many, especially in Italy, the demand for retribution was powerful. The court was presided over by Major-General Sir Edmund Hakewill-Smith and four lieutenant colonels. Colonel Richard Halse was the prosecutor, as he had been at Mackensen's trial. Some questioned whether the court was senior enough to pass judgements on international law. Scotland, Kesselring's London interrogator, wrote a protest about the court's constitution. Colonel Preston Murphy, an American observer of the early proceedings, wrote a critique that the court consisted of a 'major-general, who had commanded a Division in combat, and four officers of the rank of lieutenant colonel…their services were on a relatively low level…I am of the opinion the officers could not envisage and properly evaluate the field marshal's problems, actions and orders'.[10] This point was taken up by the *Guardian* newspaper, as well as the criticism that it was 'the British Army' who conducted the trial.[11]

To add to this criticism of being a form of victor's justice, it was widely accepted that the SS General Wolff should have been the person in the dock. He was generally believed to be the major culprit for the German crimes in Italy. Research in the book *US Intelligence and Selective Prosecution at Nuremberg* indicated that Wolff was under the protection of Alan Dulles during Operation *Sunrise*, and 'declassified intelligence documentation provided direct evidence of Dulles's interventions within the Nuremberg process'.[12] Scotland was highly critical of the proceedings, and he pointed out in a letter after the trial that he found it difficult to see how the guilty verdict could stand without a 'closer scrutiny of the role played by the SS'.[13]

The prosecution called nine witnesses, producing 57 exhibits, with Kappler, Head of the Gestapo and Secret Service in Rome as their key component. The main witness for the defence was Kesselring himself supported by his staff officers Beelitz and Westphal. Kesselring's defence was led by Dr Hans Laternser, an expert in Anglo-Saxon law, and the 'the most right wing of the defence attorneys'.[14]

Kesselring faced two charges; the first was specific, relating to the killing of 335 Italians in the Ardeatine caves. In this incident thirty-three policemen of the Bozen Regiment (not SS as is frequently claimed) were blown up in the Via Rasella by communist partisans trying to provoke a German response. Kesselring was supposed to be visiting the Gustav Line on this date, and Hitler's demand that hostages should be shot at a ratio of fifty to one was reduced by Kesselring's subordinates to ten to one. This incident was not the greatest barbarity committed in Italy, but it was regarded as one of the most infamous. Kesselring's defence was that on the day of the incident, he was at Monte Cassino, with Beelitz claiming he told the OKW officer that Kesselring would never have tolerated a ratio of fifty-to-one.[15] Kesselring's defence team further argued that Hitler had ordered the SD to carry out the executions immediately, and this order came through after the ratios had been reduced in the form of a second order.

The Judge Advocate was obliged to state that 'I feel there is some doubt in the law, the benefit of that doubt must be given to the field marshal'.[16] It was plausible that the deed was carried out by the SD, and a Count Ingelheim confirmed a telephone call that the reprisal had been ordered over the head of the field marshal, but no written evidence of the precise order has ever been identified. The defence requested the Vatican to pass on a certificated copy of Kesselring's letter, in which he had explained the Ardeatine killings involved only those already on death sentences.

More damaging and with reliable evidence was the second charge related to Kesselring's Command Orders, inciting his forces to kill civilians as reprisals against partisan activity. The prosecution outlined that on '1 May 1944 Field Marshal Keitel, as Commander-in-Chief of all German forces, issued an order' which gave Kesselring total command in the war against partisans, and it was therefore his responsibility.[17] The prosecution further argued that on 17 June 1944, Kesselring issued a similar written order:

> The fight against the partisans must be carried on with all the means at our disposal and with the utmost severity. I will protect any commander who exceeds our usual restraint in the choice of severity of the methods he adopts against partisans.[18]

On 1 July, Kesselring sent another order, stating that where large numbers of partisans were operating, then in such areas male hostages were to be taken as a warning. The prosecution cited over twenty instances of indiscriminate killing by Germans, mainly based on submitted affidavit evidence, all of which together accounted for killings of approximately a thousand Italian civilians. The issue on the second charge, as pointed out by the Judge Advocate, was whether Kesselring's orders were 'a definite incitement to kill Italians or just badly worded orders which were rather carelessly drafted'.[19] The affidavits were not always verifiable. It was upon these documents that the second charge indicted him for the death of over a thousand people.

For his defence Kesselring claimed the orders of 17 June and 1 July were legal. He had simply instructed his soldiers to be severe, but not to break the law. Many massacres were carried out by Italian neo-fascist formations such as the *Brigata Nera*, and partisan elements some wearing German uniforms. It was a confusing case reflecting complex times.

Kesselring never invoked the Nuremberg defence of obeying superior orders, arguing his actions were legal. He may possibly have been aware that in 1921, a German court in Leipzig applied the German military code which stipulated that even with knowledge of superior orders, the subordinate 'ought to have known that the orders constituted crimes' and would therefore be guilty.[20]

Laternser argued that the hostage/reprisal issue was legal, albeit unpleasant, and because of its complexity needed more legal experience than a court martial. The Allies had apparently used the same threat. When 'the French occupied Stuttgart in April 1945, it was announced that hostages would be shot in the ratio of 25 to 1 for every French soldier murdered by the German civilian population. When the Americans entered the Harz district, execution was threatened in the ratio of 200 to 1', though this was more a threat, and no one was shot.[21]

The hostage/reprisal was widespread and complex. This was demonstrated when the American and British army regulations with their manuals appeared to give some legitimacy to the hostage-reprisal practice. Laternser also underlined the illegality of partisans by international agreement, namely their lack of uniforms, no insignia, and being criminal activity to the rear of the occupier. The OKH had agreed that no commander in an occupied area can be expected to tolerate the ambushing and/or surreptitious killing of his soldiers or the sabotage of his industrial or military facilities behind the lines by civilians. Laternser's defence had three components. First, that Kesselring's orders had been legal, secondly, that the partisans were internationally illegal, thirdly, Kesselring had always been a pro-Italian officer who had saved much of the Italian culture and many ancient places.

This third line of defence attracted considerable debate. It has been argued that Kesselring 'was, of course, perfectly aware of the need to protect buildings and works of art' and this has been supported in the book *The Rape of Europa*, a study on finding stolen treasures.[22] It claimed that 'Considering the precarious position of the German Armies north of Naples, it was an extraordinary use of military effort'.[23] Following the Allied destruction of Monte Cassino several reputable Italians came to offer Kesselring their support. Kesselring and the Allies were faced with the same problems when fighting in Italy's treasure trove, and Italy being a western country, as well as the centre of Roman Catholicism, came under intense international interest. According to Kesselring he arranged the evacuation of Pisa, and in July neutralised Parma, Reggio, Modena; Bologna was declared open when the local Mayor and Archbishop pleaded for its preservation. Vicenza and Padua were completely demilitarised at the request of the Bishop of Padua. Kesselring received a letter from the Archbishop of Chieti:

> For eight months we, the people of Chieti, were only seven kilometres from the line of operations held by the Germans. During all this time I received no offensive treatment from the German commanders, especially not from Field Marshal Kesselring or the generals under him. On the contrary, they, and particularly Field Marshal Kesselring, supported and helped me in every conceivable way as far as the military situation permitted when the question arose of saving the town of Chieti and anything that could possibly be saved.[24]

In a bitter world war, the preservation of Italy's heritage did not register highly in postwar priorities. It has been claimed that Kesselring 'devoted far greater attention to supervising measures (for saving places and treasures) than he did to, for example, supervising the manner in which his troops treated the Italian civilian population'.[25]

In 2000, an American historian and medical practitioner, Dr Richard Raiber was about to present a thesis, demonstrating that Kesselring had perpetrated a major perjury during his trial, but Raiber sadly died

(2002) before the thesis was completed. However, a friend published his findings.[26] Raiber suggested false alibis, that Kesselring had lied about his whereabouts during the days of the via Rasella bombing and the subsequent Ardeatine massacre. Raiber argued Kesselring had used a fabrication to be tried for the Ardeatine massacre, rather than be faced with the charge of confirming orders for some American/Italian commandos to be executed, from Operation *Strangle*, generally known as the Ginny incident.[27] General Dostler, Kesselring's subordinate had already been executed for following Hitler's *Führerbefehl* and killing the Americans. Kesselring realised the shooting of hostages was more in the grey area than killing PoWs, and he knew the Allied courts showed no leniency in matters of killing Allied prisoners of war. In his estimation it was safer to be tried for massacring 335 Italians than fifteen Allied soldiers. Raiber's evidence while not conclusive is persuasive.

The Court in 1947, oblivious to the possibility of Kesselring's perjury, paid little attention to his saving Italian culture, they were only interested in the two main charges. One American observer, a Colonel Murphy, believed the evidence had been insufficient. However, the British Court sentenced Kesselring to death by firing squad, as some 'Italians there booed and cried assassin'.[28] Laternser always believed Kesselring was blameless, and Kesselring maintained his innocence. However, as noted above, he had secretly asked a genealogist named Furics to obtain proof of Swiss ancestry, which only came to light in this research.[29]

Commutation of Death Sentence

Kesselring's death sentence produced mixed reactions. Generals Lemelsen and Herr petitioned that Kesselring 'was always guided by the purest intentions. He always promoted proper conduct and not evil'.[30] Field Marshal Alexander, then Governor General of Canada, asked for the commutation of the death sentence.[31] General Leese followed Alexander by writing that Kesselring was 'a gallant soldier who fought his battles fairly'.[32] Churchill wrote to Attlee, and as usual from the political point of view, that 'regarding Kesselring…in my judgement it is a question of political policy: condemning to death the leaders of a defeated enemy has today ceased to have the usefulness which it could have had in the past'.[33] Fortunately for Kesselring, time was provided by Italy's abolition of the death penalty, the Italians explaining that even in the past, the sentence could only be enforced for premeditated murder, which they did not think applied to Kesselring.[34] The *Daily Mail*, which operated a European and British newspaper, published an article entitled 'Will it Help to shoot Kesselring?'[35] In May 1947 the *Guardian* printed an article stating 'that Kesselring is guilty is certain: that Kesselring is more guilty than other Germans who have escaped punishment is not'.[36]

Churchill was active in changing the sentence, using men like Bishop George Bell of Chichester, Maurice Hankey, and many others to protest at the court decision. He even encouraged a debate in the House of Lords on 13 May 1947, led by Viscount William de L'Isle and Dudley.* Churchill's animosity to the Nazi regime was well-known, once announcing to parliament that the German General Staff were a 'group of tight-lipped men who think it noble to use war, and the fewer Keitels, Kesselrings, yes, and Rommels that are allowed to survive this war, the more secure'.[37] After the war Churchill and others were worried by the perceived Soviet threat, namely the emerging Cold War, and the need to keep Western Germany within the Allied fold thereby explaining this plea for mercy. There was also the growing popular myth that the SS was the evil component, and the Wehrmacht leaders like Kesselring fought a clean war; thus, Kesselring avoided execution.

Life in Prison

It was not until February 1950 that his case review occurred, commuting his sentence to 21 years, with effect from 6 May1947.[38] In October 1947 Kesselring was transferred to the prison at Werl, a British Military establishment in Westphalia. A *Guardian* newspaper article reported he had a standard cell, 'containing bed, table, and a couple of stools, he had

---

* Lord de L'Isle won a VC fighting against Kesselring, *Guardian*, 5 July 1947, p.7.

to rise at 5.30, breakfast, and go to work at seven.'[39] Prison life was dreary, and Kesselring's work was gumming paper-bags. He never mentioned his Christian faith in his memoirs but attended Mass regularly. At one time the prison chaplain, Father Victor Kleyer, acted as a courier for Laternser and Scotland, secreting in newspapers documents relating to Laternser's efforts to secure Kesselring's release.[40]

The Americans requested that Kesselring assist their Historical Division, which gave him access to other German officers, better food, and improved self-esteem. The Americans wanted German military opinion, and his work provided an insight of their military strategy. His observations on partisan warfare were restricted for many years, indicating his policies were of interest.[41] Curiously, Otto Lehmann-Russbüldt, a one-time Peace Movement Chairman during the Weimar Republic, then Secretary General to the German League of Human Rights, who had fled to England where he edited a Refugee newsletter, returning to Germany in 1951, suddenly spoke out on Kesselring. Although he was no friend of Kesselring, he thought he might be the right person to be the new Chancellor of the Federal Republic.[42] Even for some of his one-time enemies some still saw him as a natural leader, which may have been true from the military point of view, but not necessarily politically.

The Politics of Release

It has long been understood that the postwar western powers needed Germany rearmed against the Soviet threat. To encourage German public opinion, it became necessary to release high profile military leaders, of which Kesselring was a prime example. The German historian Lingen wrote that the debate surrounding Kesselring's release, 'illustrated the manner in which the treatment of the war criminals was distorted by the debates surrounding German rearmament and integration into the Western Alliance'.[43] As it transpired Kesselring became something of a figurehead in this debate, more so than Manstein, who had been known to award Iron Crosses to *Einsatzgruppen* men, acknowledging he knew of the genocide.[44]

It is important to note that part of Kesselring's so-called rehabilitation started through the process called *Entnazifizierung,* (de-Nazification), based on Eisenhower's demand that German administration be cleansed of NSDAP influence.[45] On 22 November 1951, the Munich Court in Kesselring's case argued major culpability, but withdrew because the affidavits exonerated Kesselring.

Kesselring was gathering support through his lawyer Laternser and various lobby groups emerged. Laternser made a name for himself in the postwar years, and his fees came from the *Stahlhelms* (formed after the First World War as a veteran's league, dissolved in 1935 by Hitler, but again active) who raised funds for imprisoned comrades.

Kesselring was a British prisoner, and therefore their support was necessary. The motives for freeing Kesselring were mixed, but he had support for humanitarian and political reasons. The result was a continuous discussion in the press with the *Manchester Guardian* often striking a positive note for the release of the war-criminals.[46] Hankey sought reconciliation, and amongst his associates was Kesselring's London interrogator, Scotland, who had remained in constant touch with Kesselring. Scotland's involvement with Kesselring had little to do with placating the Germans, it was a friendship which had developed during the London interrogations. Scotland later wrote that 'I count it a privilege to have played some part in gaining him his freedom'.[47] Another influential member of Hankey's pressure group was Basil Liddell Hart, ex-military, who had written a book on military strategy, and was an historian sympathetic towards German prisoners. Bishop George Bell was convinced that Christianity could bring the nations together, and that the 'fundamental menace to our civilisations was Nihilism – the attitude of destruction and negation which calls evil good and good evil'.[48] However, British attitudes were mixed towards Kesselring. As noted, those seeking his release did so for a variety of reasons, but not all wanted him freed. There was a fear that men like Kesselring may be reliable soldiers but aggressive.

The British views varied between those upholding the trials, and those wanting compassion, with some concerned about the Cold War. Kesselring became a focus for this debate. The German historian Lingen argued that the need for German re-armament in the Cold War was the major factor in sanitising people like Kesselring and the Wehrmacht. Finally, it appeared clemency was the one way to release Kesselring legitimately without too much discord. There was further debate in the Lords (14 May 1952) just after George VI's funeral, with more discussion on the yet unresolved issue of blind obedience to orders. Eden was opposed to clemency, but Churchill remained outspoken. On 16 July 1952, Kesselring was admitted to hospital for throat cancer, an operation was carried out by Kesselring's doctor, but the British expressed suspicion when the doctor said Kesselring was recovering, but 'unfit for prison'.[49] On 22 October 1952 Queen Elizabeth II, under government direction, pardoned Kesselring.

The French were somewhat underwhelmed, and there was a hostile reaction in Italy, but parliament was informed that 'no protest has been received by Her Majesty's Government from the Italian Government'.[50] The German public had not accepted that the military leaders were guilty, it 'had simply not penetrated public consciousness, and careful explanation and education were now seen to be pointless'.[51] Chancellor Adenauer and the Bonn government became significant during these postwar years, and Adenauer always praised PoWs whenever possible. On a trip to America, Adenauer later wrote that 'I then turned to the subject of war criminals and commented that it was largely a psychological problem. The American occupation authorities had released the sentenced men in their custody more slowly and hesitantly than the British and French'.[52]

Lingen's argument that the Cold War necessitated a cleansing of history to release Wehrmacht leaders like Kesselring was undoubtedly correct; this must have influenced many politicians who wanted Germany rearmed. How far the government's recommendation for the Queen's pardon of Kesselring rested on 'genuine humanitarian reasons' or Cold War pragmatism can only be speculation.[53]

Chapter Nine

Once Free

Insensitivity to New World

Prison is never easy, and according to his son Rainer, Kesselring was a shadow of the man he had been.[1] This was understandable given his health, his age, and seven years imprisonment. The first part was harsh, plus the psychological blow of falling from being a highly respected field marshal to common criminal making envelopes. The Americans, whom Kesselring had helped in their research, gave him an apartment in Bad Wiessee, a popular spa and scene of the infamous Night of the Long Knives. He was joined by his wife helping him with thousands of telegrams and congratulations, and requests for his appearance. He had become a celebrity at a time when his energies were low, and the world he knew had changed. Even the Prussian State, which had been a bearer of militarism, had *de facto* ceased to exist. Germany was in a state of change with the Cold War changing policies and attitudes. Many of the old military commanders were being reactivated, but not Kesselring. In 1955, Germany was invited into NATO – 'with its membership came the return to near full sovereignty'.[2] During his last decade Kesselring witnessed the sustained economic growth, and 'by 1951, West Germany had regained pre-war levels of output'.[3] His world had changed, by the 1950s 'the old military elite had disappeared'.[4] However, Germany was aware that the outside world remained somewhat distrustful, watching the political pulse of Germany for fear of the rise of a new right-wing. It was how the Germans dealt with their past which was of growing importance. Most commanders had turned against Hitler, blaming him for everything, but Kesselring never criticised him, his stubborn loyalty being based on his insistence that Hitler had been the legitimate government.

One of the reasons behind Kesselring's release had been an appeal to the Germans to encourage their rearmament of West Germany, merging it into a defence force. This was demonstrated by the *Guardian* newspaper in December 1952, the year of Kesselring's release. The article focused on the developing relationship between West Germany and the Western powers.

> The most acute and superficially most dangerous of these is the question of German war criminals…why should they [the Germans] be asked to take up arms when some of their own countrymen, condemned by courts which were based on no legal precedents, continue to sit in Allied administered gaols on German soil.[5]

However, Kesselring's only official appointment was to the Medals Commission, and even this was challenged. Denazification had outlawed the swastika, but Kesselring persisted in wanting the symbol on the medals. He argued that the swastika was a national not a political symbol which underlined that Kesselring had lost his way in the new world. He refused to let go of the past, frequently broadcasting that the term *Wehrmacht* was preferable to *Bundeswehr*. This tarnished any chance that might have existed for him to participate in the recovering Germany. His poor publicity was to be a feature of his remaining years, as he was quite insensitive to the circumstances of the day. When on 12 December 1952, Adenauer gave Kesselring a half-hour audience, Kesselring raised the subject of PoWs, and the question of 'soldier-hood and the issue of those convicted in connection with the war', when most wanted to forget.[6]

The Veterans

Kesselring's relationship with the veteran associations was prolific and complex. The Chairman of the *Verband deutscher Soldaten* (VdS) had made many public announcements on Kesselring's behalf when he was in prison, even approaching Adenauer and contacting Hankey.[7] Kesselring felt loyalty towards the veterans because they reflected his past, respected him, and had offered their help for his release. During 1952 he accepted various positions in different ex-military associations including honorary chairmanships. There is no record of Kesselring's personal views, but his sense of so-called soldierly loyalty was unquestionably his motivation. The older association, mentioned previously, the *Stahlhelms* would cause Kesselring adverse publicity. The *Stahlhelms* (Steel Helmets) were traditionally right-wing, and most Germans were trying to distance themselves from this past. The VdS was divided on many issues, and Generalleutnant Heinz Trettner who served in Italy under Kesselring, attempted to persuade him to act as a spokesman for all the veteran associations. Kesselring was obliged to refuse because he had accepted the presidency of the *Stahlhelms*, which precluded similar appointments. Because of the recent unpleasant past these social unions were not always welcome in the wider world.

Kesselring was regarded as a symbol of the old regime, confirming this at the *Stahlhelm* Nuremberg convention when he appeared in their uniform, complete with medals demanding social justice for all old soldiers. Kesselring was causing concern amongst the emerging political leaders of West Germany, which had started with the Medals Commission. Kesselring had no grasp of the changing political scene, and even the *Stahlhelms* detected this and were marginalising him. Many in modern Germany did not appreciate the *Stahlhelms* who belonged to the past, as did Kesselring who was making too many errors of judgment.

Kesselring Mistakes

On 20 March 1954, Kesselring and his wife went on holiday to Austria, visiting veteran associations and organisations looking after ex-servicemen. Kesselring had been asked to avoid such visits, to stay private. There was a high degree of political sensitivity, mainly because the communists had suggested that Germany remained a threat to Austrian Independence.*
Against advice, Kesselring persisted with meeting an organisation caring

---

* Arising from the Soviet Foreign Minister speaking at Berlin Conference, Jan 1954.

for relatives of PoWs still held in Soviet prisons. The Austrian government wanted him to leave, and the local police chief asked him on behalf of the government to exit the country.[8]

A further embarrassment occurred later that year, when during a BBC interview Kesselring expressed the opinion that the invasion of Britain failed, because the Germans had not planned it in advance, thereby hinting that it was not because of the willingness of the British to defend their country. He claimed 'that had the invasion succeeded, as I hoped, the war would have been over much sooner, which after all would have been a good thing for all of us'.[9] It was insensitive with the old German military arrogance. He was to repeat these claims in an American interview on 30 August 1955, adding that the failure to invade England had been one of the four major errors that lost Germany the war.[10] It was abundantly clear that Kesselring was completely out of touch with the new postwar era, and he was committing too many gaffs and accumulating personal blunders.

During the 1950s a series of *Kameradenschinder* trials started, indicting those who had brutalised their comrades while in Soviet PoW camps. Kesselring started taking an interest in another type of trial, namely those of returning officers who during the closing months of the war had committed crimes against their own population. His unpopularity increased because of his persistence in defending such soldiers, who were regarded as war criminals even by old comrades, because they had ordered the death of Germans. There were many cases, but some of the most infamous were Colonel Berthold Ohm, General Tolsdorff and Field Marshal Schörner, in which Kesselring became involved, losing him what little popularity he had managed to accrue. It was clear that Kesselring would have approved of their actions. Kesselring again became headlines when he acted as a witness in the case of Colonel Berthold Ohm. This man had executed seven citizens of the town of Penzberg because they wanted to save their town from further destruction, by letting the Americans enter. He was defending the actions of the Nazi regime, and even in 1950 he had been quoted in the *Guardian*, in a column entitled *Sayings of the Week*, that 'next time there is a war they won't be able to have soldiers in command. They will have to have lawyers'.[11] No one wanted to be reminded of May 1945 when Germans killed Germans. The press attacked Kesselring who had failed to understand the new world, adding to his failure by ignoring public opinion. In the same year (1957) his wife died, while Kesselring was still busy as an expert witness. He was supporting Field Marshal Schörner who had been released by the Soviets, and promptly arrested and charged with killing German soldiers. Schörner was not popular, and nor was Kesselring by being supportive; the West German press was indicating the new national feelings.

Kesselring had become an embarrassment. Modern Germany wanted no reminder of its past, and Kesselring, the so-called non-party member, remained to the end the right-wing nationalistic military man he had always been. He died on Wednesday 20 July 1960, in the sanatorium in Bad Nauheim. The *Stahlhelms* fired a volley over his grave, though he was not given a military funeral. General Kammhüber spoke about Kesselring's leadership, while distancing himself from Kesselring's postwar activities. Westphal spoke of Kesselring's strength of character and the care he had shown for men of all ranks. The funeral closed in a heavy rainstorm. The obituary in the *Guardian* mentioned that after prison 'Kesselring showed how irreconcilable and unteachable he was', which was perceptive and reflected the opinion of many Germans.[12]

Chapter Ten

Final Thoughts

A brief biography of a German field marshal is not about sanitising or vilifying, but setting him within a context, and asking, given what happens in war, whether he was any different from any other commander in terms of his conduct and performance as a military leader. The Second World War was a total war, but it was also a war of extermination which carried the need for survival at any cost. One side may well be more brutal, but war is rarely based on moral conduct, even when the original aims may be based on such high precepts. Acceptable moral norms during a total war change profoundly. It has been stated that 'we can say that while all sides committed war crimes in the Second World War, some of the combatant nations were far more criminal than others', and some military leaders were more unlawful and more ruthless.[1]

There seems little question that Kesselring was regarded as a sound military leader, especially in the area of defence. Kesselring's first biographer described him as a master strategist, General Bradley admired his military expertise, and Field Marshal Alexander approved of him as an opponent. He was often referred to as 'Smiling Albert' in almost an affectionate way, known in code as 'The Emperor'. In some accounts he appears to be on a pedestal, and after the war some saw him as a potential president of the new Germany, and a person who cared for his old soldiers still in prison. His enemies who referred to him as 'Smiling Albert' held him in regard, and many historians, including his first British biographer, place him on a pedestal, believing him to be non-political.

However, Kesselring's background and later behaviour indicate that he was a prejudiced right-wing nationalist, with an uncompromising hatred of communists, undoubtedly anti-Semitic, and as a professional soldier could be ruthless. In terms of his background, he belonged to a national caste that saw war as a profession, it was in his DNA. He knowingly prepared for an aggressive war, while pretending to have no political leanings, and blindly served an iniquitous regime. He worked throughout the *interbellum* years in the clandestine rebuilding of an aggressive war-machine, never questioning its morality or legality. Kesselring never denied Hitler, never pretended he opposed him, and to the end of his days said nothing against the man who brought such devastation. Kesselring was Hitler's natural disciple, even if he did not sign the Party's membership book.

It was Kesselring's teamwork and expertise behind the concept of *blitzkrieg*, yet he claimed he had no idea Hitler was preparing for war. The nature of German military activity, along with Hitler's political views, made it evident even to an Australian academic in 1937, and some 12,000 miles away, that a major war was being planned.[2] Kesselring was intelligent and informed, and it defies common sense that his cries of ignorance deserve the credibility they have frequently been given.

There is an argument that his bombing policy was only tactical, aiming at military targets, and not the immoral strategic bombing. However, his views may not have been determined by moral considerations. Kesselring frequently stated that he considered high level bombing imprecise, and he saw the tactic as wasteful. The Condor Legion in Spain had caused considerable loss of civilian life without regret by the perpetrators, as had the bombing of Warsaw. It was simply Kesselring's belief that the Luftwaffe was best used as a support for the ground war.

In North Africa Kesselring failed to persuade the Italians to occupy Malta, or to understand the powerful logistic build-up by the Americans, with the ramifications of Operation *Torch*. The egocentric and often dysfunctional personality clashes of Patton, Montgomery, and Clark with the inability of Alexander to control his subordinates, allowed Kesselring's defensive systems to work in a terrain which made attack difficult. Kesselring was acclaimed a genius of defence, but this praise helped cover up the inexperience and frequently inept Allied leadership, who used his so-called genius to account for their failings, as they tended to do with Rommel. It is always easier to praise the enemy than blame our own leaders.

Had the war finished with the retaking of Rome, Kesselring's legacy may have been safer. The bitter partisan war in North Italy involving brutal massacres, hostages, and reprisals, as seen at his trial tarnished his reputation. Kesselring's ruthlessness finally descended to sheer brutality, which brought him within the ambit of war crimes, verging on crimes against humanity. While in Italy, Keitel was obliged to send a signal making Kesselring the highest authority because the partisan war was directed by SS *Obergruppenführer* Wolff, but it was only for military appearances. The SS troops were notoriously barbaric, but Kesselring's orders were sometimes no better. His ruthlessness finally descended to sheer brutality, which brought him within the ambit of war crimes and verging on crimes against humanity. The massacre at Marzabotto was ten times the size of Lidice, and yet Kesselring dismissed it as a mere war operation. The SS were barbaric, but Kesselring stated that 'anti-guerrilla warfare must in large measure be carried out by the army', and he was in charge.[3]

It has been tempting for some historians to suggest that because Churchill and Alexander appealed against Kesselring's death sentence, that it implied that he must have been 'decent'. Churchill was the driving force, and his motives were political, to keep West Germany onside during the Cold War. Germany and its aspirations had changed dramatically in nearly every aspect of national life, and Kesselring was almost like a time-warped alien. His association with the *Stahlhelms* was not just poor judgment, but as with his later gaffes he demonstrated an inability to change or adapt to a new world.

However, many historians, especially those with an interest in the military aspects, regard him as a first-class commander, and his reputation as the master of defence still comes before the criticisms levelled at him at the trial and since. He was certainly a respected military commander, liked by his men and officers, and even respected by some of his opponents. When he died at 74 years of age, he was still a right-wing nationalist who remained loyal to Hitler, one of the most wicked political leaders ever born, but his reputation as a master of defence survives to this day.

Field Marshal Erwin Rommel

Reconsidering the Desert Fox

Chapter One

The Younger Rommel

Introduction

When exploring the figure of Field Marshal Erwin Rommel, the huge number of books and articles written about him must be recalled. Rommel is, along with Patton, the only general to be portrayed in a movie, the name (the nickname in his case) being the film's title. This means that whenever examining Rommel's public image, the myths surrounding him have to be understood. Otherwise, there is a risk of swinging the balance to over-criticism, which is as mistaken as over-praising his qualities. Unlike the other field marshals studied in this book, Rommel's military experience is given considerable time because he was known as a 'fighting leader'. This includes detailed information about his battle experiences in both world wars, which made him a natural military commander. Rommel has been acclaimed by friend and foe as heroic, which was based entirely on his military abilities, and therefore detailed time is given to his military conflicts to try and understand the differences between the reality of the man, and the myths which have since accrued.

Some of Rommel's character traits emerged immediately. He was clearly ambitious, willing, and determined to rise above his social status. On every occasion Rommel displayed great energy and willingness and wanted others to follow his example. Rommel was also impulsive, he was not the kind of person who devoted much time to thinking, and his attitude made things difficult for those who worked with him. As a general he was best known for his accomplishments in North Africa between 1941 and 1943, also fighting in northern Italy in 1943, in charge of the 'Atlantic Wall' in 1944 and fighting in Normandy until wounded.

Rommel's involvement or lack of with the 20 July plot against Hitler remains debated, and it is important to explore the reasons behind his eventual *volte face* towards Hitler.

The Young Officer

Erwin Johannes Eugen Rommel was born on 15 November 1891 at Heideheim am der Brenz, near the university city of Ulm. He was the son of Erwin Rommel and Helene von Luz. His father was a high school teacher, later to become a headmaster at Aalen. His mother was the daughter of the head of the local government council. The environment was that of an upper-middle class family born in Swabia, an agricultural area of Germany. From his early youth there were no indications that Rommel would develop a career in the army. His father, who had served his obligatory period of duty as a lieutenant in the artillery of the Royal Württembergs, resigned his commission without considering the possibility of a military career. Furthermore, Rommel's geographical location, in west Germany, did not have the same military traditions as Prussia or of the other eastern German states, and his family had no ties with the armed forces. Rommel was part of a middle-class family in the country, and his siblings somehow adapted to this social background more than he did. His elder brother Karl joined the army in the Great War, eventually becoming an observer with the air force and later served as an adviser to the Turkish Army, but because of a severe case of malaria was invalided out. Gerhard, his younger brother, became an opera singer and acquired some fame, while his sister Helene developed a career as a teacher. In 1906, Erwin just as flying was starting in Europe, built a glider with a friend which could actually fly, if not for long. For a moment he considered the possibility of studying aeronautical engineering, but he was keener on open air activities. Four years after building the glider, Rommel wrote down a curriculum listing the activities he claimed to practice with success: sport, ranging from bike riding to skating, and skiing. Rommel's father was described as pedantic, constantly asking his son questions to check his overall knowledge. Erwin like his brothers and sister felt closer to their mother.

As to who was behind his choice in joining the army, if anyone, remains unclear. As the moment of his conscription was approaching, Rommel's father urged him to apply for an officer's position which would have suited their social needs. This did not mean developing a career in the military, but apparently the young Erwin Rommel promptly pursued this possibility. He displayed ambition from the beginning, but he experienced that it would not be easy. His first attempt to join the army of Württemberg was with the artillery, this branch offering a secure career and a rise to higher ranks. He failed, then attempted to join the engineers, showing he had not lost touch with the technical knowledge that helped him build the glider. He failed again, and eventually turned to the last resort: the queen of the branches, the infantry. In March 1910, Erwin Rommel joined the 124th Infantry Regiment as a Fahnenjunker, an officer cadet, but only after he had a hernia surgically repaired. After this period, he ended his training period at the Officer Cadet School of Danzig where, on 27 January 1912, he obtained his rank which enabled him to return to the 124th Infantry Regiment, now located at Weingarten near Stuttgart as a second lieutenant. As a cadet, Rommel was not outstanding and considered 'average', scoring sufficient points in rifle practice, and considered adequate for such physical activities as marches, horse riding and gymnastics in spite of his build, being defined as thin and delicate. What stood out was his character, described as strong willed and energetic, supported by a great deal of enthusiasm. For the rest, Rommel was the typical soldier: clean, punctual, conscientious, easy in company and supported by a strong sense of duty. Unlike most other cadets, Rommel did not drink or smoke or chase women. All in all, it was considered that he could have made a useful soldier, which is probably what Rommel also thought, and became focused exclusively on his army career.[1]

The irony is that, as Germany went to war, Rommel was detached to an artillery unit. On 1 March 1914, as a second lieutenant he was attached to the 49th Field Artillery Regiment at Ulm, which Rommel considered from that moment his real homeplace. When given the command of a field gun battery, Rommel was not happy with the change, writing in his diary on 31 July 1914, about his desire to re-join the 124th

Infantry Regiment, the unit he had trained with during the previous two years. This did not occur, and the next day Rommel left for the front as Germany attacked Belgium and France. The war revealed a major trait in Rommel's character, namely his charisma, showing great personal courage and a willingness to act, and Rommel soon gained the trust of the entire unit. He undoubtedly possessed great leadership qualities, and his men started to idolise him down to the point of being ready to follow him no matter where it led. Leading by example was a well-known requirement for officers, especially in the German army, and Rommel followed the principle without hesitation. He was the first to take risks and face the enemy, and his men could do nothing else than follow his example. In September 1914, during the battle of Varennes, Rommel was wounded, and for his courage was awarded the Iron Cross second class, and 2 September, was made adjutant to the battalion. After hospitalisation Rommel finally re-joined the 124th Infantry on 13 January 1915, while the unit was deployed in the Argonne Forest. On that same day Rommel was given command of a company. It only took a couple of weeks for Rommel to prove himself again on the battlefield. He took the lead of his unit and crossed about one hundred metres of barbed wire obstacles, eventually reaching a strongpoint. Taking the French soldiers by surprise, he was able to seize four enemy positions, and from there repulsed the counterattack of a French infantry battalion before heading back to the German lines. The operation only cost a dozen casualties in Rommel's unit, which earned Rommel the Iron Cross first class. Significantly, he was the first junior officer of the 124th Infantry Regiment to be awarded this medal.

Rommel was wounded again in July 1915, this time by shrapnel. As he was recovering, Rommel asked to be sent to the Gallipoli front as an instructor. Fate had something else in store for him, as he was given command of a company with the newly formed Württemberg Mountain Battalion, which would become part of the *Deutsches Alpenkorps* (DAK), a newly formed unit organised specifically for mountain warfare. Rommel's battalion, including six infantry companies and six machine gun platoons, spent an entire year training before being sent to Romania to fight the

Russian Army. On 18 September 1915 Rommel was promoted first lieutenant, the last of his promotions for some time. As he wrote in his post-war book *Infantry Attacks*, Rommel recognised at once the importance and the meaning of the promotion:

> Winning the men's confidence requires much of a commander. He must exercise care and caution, look after his men, live under the same hardships, and – above all – apply self-discipline. But once he has their confidence, his men will follow him through hell and high water.[2]

Rommel's experience in Romania was eye-opening, and he soon coupled the requirements of command and leadership with the lessons of the battlefield. The Eastern Front was completely different from the Western, where the war was being fought in the trenches, and any advance had to be accomplished with mass attacks always costly in lives. There was nothing like the trench warfare on the Eastern Front, where units were able to move and manoeuvre against their enemies. This made victories faster, and cheaper in terms of losses. Needless to note, Rommel did not spare himself, and it did not take long before Rommel could put the lessons learned into practice. In the meantime, there had been developments in his personal life. On 27 November 1916, Rommel married Lucia Maria Mollin, whom he had known at the time when he attended the War School at Danzig. The girl was of the same social middle-class extraction as Rommel (something not so common at the time), but she was also very different from him. Her origins were Polish and Italian, the reason for her visit to Danzig had been to study languages. Rommel's relationship with Lucia was solid and happy, despite occasional meanderings. About the same time as he courted Lucia, Rommel knew Walpurga Stemmer, who gave him a daughter in 1913. Walpurga died in 1928, but Rommel had a strong sense of duty, and he supported his daughter after her mother's death. In 1928 Rommel's first son, Manfred, was born.

As the Mountain Battalion was deployed to France in January 1917, Rommel, now first lieutenant, was given command of an *Abteilung*, a mixed unit about the size of a battalion. In July he and his unit briefly returned to Romania where on 10 August, Rommel was wounded for a third time. This time, in all likelihood, by friendly fire, a bullet hitting his left arm. This incident did not prevent Rommel from continuing with his duties for another two weeks, all this occurred just as the entire Alpenkorps were about to be transferred to another front in Italy.[3]

Shaping a Commander

In May 1915 Italy had declared war on Austria–Hungary, hoping that her involvement against Russia could enable a swift breakthrough on the border, with a subsequent advance towards Ljubljana, and its plains. This never happened, and after Germany declared war on Italy, a counteroffensive was launched in the Alps region to the north. By 1917 the two armies were facing one another along the Dolomites, that part of the Alps separating Italy from Austria. The eleventh Italian offensive (initiated like the Allied offensives on the Western Front) failed to achieve the decisive breakthrough. The Italian Army suffered some 400,000 casualties in the period between May and September 1917, and the Austro-Hungarian Army with 240,000. The culminating point of the battle on the Italian Alps had been reached, and the Austro-Hungarian commanders faced a critical choice: either to withdraw, or to launch a counteroffensive to drive the Italians away from the positions they had occupied. Given the weakness of the Austro-Hungarian Army, the German support was deemed essential, and an idea was proposed, which the German Command approved enthusiastically, namely proposing a major offensive supported by the German Army. This proved to be a test. Both sides had been developing solutions in order to break the stalemate at the front, the British with the innovative tank, the Germans with a new tactic which emphasised command and movement.

This German tactic known as *Auftragstaktik*, a term which can be translated as mission command, was not really an innovation. The idea was to have every single commander on the battlefield perform a given mission, not to follow orders from above. The origins of the concept had been established in the 1870–71 war, when Prussia allied with other German states established itself as a unified country. In order to avoid political and moral consequences, the Prussians did not issue specific orders to their allies but rather gave them a mission. This meant that the subordinate commander was left free to see how to accomplish the mission as he perceived it, and without the restraints of a superior commander demanding adherence to a plan. This concept was entrusted to the smaller units, even down to the companies. Officers had to use their initiative, and act independently within the framework of a plan, which the superior command merely outlined without developing details. To fully understand how innovative this concept was, it must be recalled that even in 1914, armies moved on the battlefield in a way not that different from their Napoleonic predecessors: in formation, almost in line, with units at times halting to wait for the neighbouring unit to reach the designated position. The Allied enemy commands had a distinctive style of control, known as 'top-down command'. The plans were detailed, each unit was required to accomplish a mission and was told exactly how. Commanders merely had to obey orders, and personal initiative was curtailed.

The Germans experienced the advantages of the *Auftragstaktik* for the first time in the east. In a fluid situation, having the single commanders and their units to act independently offered many advantages. If a breakthrough were achieved, the local commander could exploit it without waiting for the authorisation of the superior command or even reinforcements. This caused confusion and panic amongst the defenders, who saw their lines pierced, and all too often were unable to react without the proper input from their superior command. The demand was that the German officers were required to possess unique command and leadership skills. Special units, termed 'Assault Troops', were created to break through the enemy lines relying on every possible weapon and technique available. It was their officers who were to make the difference. They were required to analyse the situation first hand, react to any development on the battlefield, and be able to lead their men into battle without hesitation. There were a good many excellent German officers who developed those skills, and Rommel was amongst them.

In September 1917, the entire German and Austro-Hungarian deployment of forces on the Italian front was reorganised, following the activation in the area of the 14th German army which was to lead the offensive. The army, under command of General Otto von Below, was specifically created as a mountain army with experienced and equipped units. The core of the 14th Army was the German Alpenkorps, which was deployed behind the lines and brought forward only at the last moment to achieve maximum surprise. Its task was to break through the Italian positions on both sides of the Isonzo River valley which, after moving in a south-easterly direction, at the city of Tolmin took a south-westerly direction towards Gorizia and of Monfalcone, before reaching the Adriatic Sea. The upper part of the Isonzo, where the 14th Army was to achieve its breakthrough, the town of Caporetto (Kobarid today) faced two mountain ranges. The southernmost one gave access to San Pietro al Natisone, and from there to the cities of Cividale del Friuli and of Udine in the north-eastern plain, dominated by Matajur Mountain which is where the Kolovrat mountain range started. Its main peaks are the Kuk, the Piatto (flat), and the Podklbuc Mountains.

The creation of the Württemberg Mountain Battalion was part of the German response to the appearance on the battlefront of the French Chasseurs Alpins, the French mountain troops which had created problems for the German Army in the Vosges Mountains. Initially, the Bavarian Army in November 1914 created its own 'Snowshoe battalions', grouped later into a single regiment. Other units of the same kind were then created by the Prussian Army, the Württemberg Mountain Battalion was the local contribution to the overall project. The battalion was formed by transferring experienced skiers or climbers, the officers being selected by their proven capability to lead their men in combat. Rommel, who was given command of the 2nd Company, found in the battalion commander, Major Theodor Sprösser, a figure capable of inspiring and motivating. After its initial posting to the Western Front, the Württemberg Mountain Battalion was sent to Romania, and attached to the Alpenkorps for the attack on a series of fortresses dominating the access to Transylvania. Used in a feint attack, the Württemberg Mountain Battalion succeeded in seizing Mount Lesului because of the efficient use of the *Auftragstaktik* tactic. The single companies moved independently even down to their sections, under an efficient artillery fire covering their approach. This accomplishment, which cost Rommel's company the loss of only one man, was followed by the successful repulse of a Romanian counterattack which initially saw Rommel's men being outnumbered, until Major Sprösser came with the rest of the battalion. The experience was followed by a period of leave, which enabled Rommel to marry.

In January 1917, Rommel was back in Romania and given command of an *Abteilung*, a detachment made of two rifle companies and a machine gun platoon, which he led in the seizure of the village of Gagesti, from where Rommel riding forward on a horse faced a group of Romanian soldiers, encouraged them to surrender. This was the last act of the Württemberg Mountain Battalion in Romania, the unit being transferred again to the Western Front where it remained until August when it was moved back to Romania. This time Rommel distinguished himself with the seizure of Mount Cosna by leading the Alpenkorps' attack. On this occasion, Rommel demonstrated his leadership and command qualities. First, he exploited the terrain advancing to the top of the mountain using every gully and creek, which enabled his unit to attack and subdue various isolated enemy positions. Then, having moved about one and a half kilometres behind the Romanian positions, Rommel deployed his unit successfully repulsing a counterattack. On the following day, as the Alpenkorps stormed the enemy positions on the Cosna, Rommel's battalion advanced under cover of machine gun fire. Because of previous reconnaissance, Rommel was able to attack the most vulnerable enemy positions, and after repulsing yet another counterattack, the mountain peak fell into German hands. The Romanian troops counterattacked the Germans for a week, without success until, on 25 August, the Alpenkorps was withdrawn from the front and sent to recuperate in Carinthia, before being deployed to the Italian front. There, on 24 October 1917, the German and Austro-Hungarian attack started. In the lead was the 14th Army, which had the Alpenkorps as its spearhead, including the Württemberg Mountain Battalion with Rommel's own *Abteilung*.[4]

Battle of Caporetto reveals Rommel's Potential

At 2.00 a four-hour artillery bombardment started, hitting all the Italian positions along the Isonzo line. At 6.00, as the artillery stopped firing, the infantry moved forward to attack the same positions, the soldiers marching through pouring rain. The first wave moved forward, and this time the Württemberg Mountain Battalion advanced behind the *Stosstrupp* intended to break through the enemy lines. Facing a terrain similar to Mount Costa, Rommel's men worked through the sloping rocky terrain and dense woods. Soon the battalion ran into the second line of the Italian defences, the first line having practically been obliterated by the artillery fire.

The battalion reached the ridge of Mount Hlevnik, and at 8.00 hours, right after the artillery bombardment ceased, Rommel's men jumped forward to attack the Italian first line of defence, which the artillery fire had already decimated. Immediately, Rommel saw an opportunity and seized it by taking the lead of two rifle companies and one machine gun company, which he led to the summit of the Hlevnik. In doing this, Rommel showed his capability of observing the local terrain and a certain degree of ingenuity. Rommel was joined by Lieutenant Schiellein's detachment, which was put under his command, the first step of the advance had been accomplished.

In the meantime, the Bavarian Life Guards had also advanced, also breaking through the Italian positions. Their next step was to attack the Na Gradu Mount, and for this task the Life Guards commander, Major Count von Bothmer, ordered Rommel to secure their left flank. Evidently, Rommel did not want to play an ancillary role and sent a sharp reply: he only took orders from Sprösser, and he would not play along von Bothmer's lines. The rivalry between different units started to emerge, and it was thanks to the intervention of Major Sprösser that the Württemberg Mountain Battalion was able to secure an independent role. Nevertheless, von Bothmer's order had to be dealt with, and Rommel decided to move his position, which was made possible by the arrival of the rest of the Württemberg Mountain Battalion, under Sprösser's direct command, at the nearby village of Foni. Without endangering von Bothmer's flank, Rommel moved north of the Kolovrat ridge, towards the Kuk Mount with the aim of advancing as an independent unit to break through the enemy defences alone. Most importantly, Sprösser backed Rommel's rejection of von Bothmer's request. The Württemberg Mountain Battalion would not be used in support of the Life Guards or as a reserve unit, but would take the lead in the offensive since this was the best way to use these troops. To oppose von Bothmer's request, Sprösser pointed out that Rommel's troops were advancing which made it impossible to satisfy his request.

Rommel was already on the move. At first light on the 25th his detachment moved from his positions to advance on the side of the Kolovrat Ridge, which enabled them to move in a parallel line to the Italian line of defences, while trying not to be seen. The advance was uneventful, apart from the meeting with a group of Italian soldiers who were captured without firing a single shot. Rommel split the detachment in two, which moved to both sides of Mount Nagnoj, and prepared to attack. The Italian reaction was quite mild, and soon the detachment was able to seize the mountain and break through the enemy defences. The move was made in a textbook style; while Rommel, leading the 3rd Company, advanced seizing several enemy positions, the 2nd Company under command of Lieutenant Ludwig, took the enemy by surprise, thus enabling the two groups to approach the summit of Mount Nagnoj. Once there, the Italian fire compelled the men of Württemberg Mountain Battalion to take cover and stop their advance. This situation could have been lost had Rommel not had an idea. He retraced his steps back to the starting point, in order to join the 2nd Company which had been surrounded by the Italians. As the 3rd Company was moving, the situation was immediately recognised, and Rommel decided to attack the enemy without hesitation. The sudden move took the Italians by surprise, and as the two companies joined forces, an entire Italian battalion surrendered. The next step was to advance with the two companies to the summit of the Nagnoj, this time facing a less determined Italian reaction which, by 9.15, enabled Rommel's detachment to seize the peak of Mount Nagnoj.

The Italian reaction took the form of harassing fire, coming from all directions, but a counterattack never materialised. Instead, the Italians started to dig into their new positions appearing determined to defend.

While the German artillery started pounding the Kuk Mount, the situation soon changed since it was clear that Rommel had hit the enemy defences at a decisive point. At 10.30 another detachment from the Württemberg Mountain Battalion, led by Sprösser, joined Rommel, and was soon followed by the men of the Bavarian Life Guards, who had decided to follow Rommel's route. The units deployed on the Nagnoj, secured their positions, and the next move started to be planned as the artillery bombardment began, and patrols were sent out to probe the enemy positions on the Kuk Mount. One of these patrols took position in the saddle dividing the Nagnoj and the Kuk, then started to climb the Kuk only to face groups of Italian soldiers who surrendered. Rommel was immediately informed of the development, and he decided that a surprise attack could secure control of the peak. He gathered the 3rd and 4th Rifle and the 2nd and 3rd Machine Gun companies, instructing them to follow the same route taken by the patrol. There was some risk in taking such a step, but the promise of success. If Rommel had estimated the situation properly, the enemy would be taken by surprise enabling a prompt seizure of the Kuk.

Because of the fire coming from Mount Nagnoj, the group led by Rommel advanced without problem taking the Italians by surprise, facing no resistance at all. This convinced Rommel to try advancing along the western slopes of the Kuk, while the Life Guards followed his steps having noticed this young officer's capabilities. By noon, the detachment led by Rommel reached the village of Ravne, which was stormed without hesitation. The Italians were taken by surprise, failing to react. They were all taken prisoner, making Rommel's responsibility heavier and propelling him to make another crucial decision, namely, to move forward beyond the Kuk in order to prevent the enemy from counterattacking and reinforce their positions. Taking the 4th Rifle and the 3rd Machine Gun companies, Rommel moved towards the road connecting the Kuk to the Mrzli vrh and Matajur mountains, the road being reached at 12.30. Captured food supplies were necessary because Rommel's advance had cut him off from his supply lines.

The Italians attempted to counterattack, but this move was to Rommel's advantage. The roadblock was approached by a column, some 2,000 strong, which attacked but was soon mowed down by Rommel's well-placed machine-guns. After brief fighting, the Italians surrendered leaving Rommel with an enormous number of prisoners and many vehicles, one of which Rommel used to reach the village of Livek. There he met Spr̈osser, who had also advanced with the rest of the Württemberg Mountain Battalion and the 2nd Bavarian Life Guards, who also had taken advantage of the seizure of the Mount Kuk. Feeling that the German positions were safe, Rommel decided to act without hesitation, and having noticed that the enemy were reinforcing their defences of the Mrzli vrh and of the Matajur, he decided on another surprise attack. Rommel boldly suggested to Spr̈osser that he moved against a peak with the aim of dominating the Matajur, and with a prohibition on firing, thereby encouraging the Italians not to send any further reinforcements. At the same time, Rommel with his detachments were to try and seize the Matajur's dominating peak. Spr̈osser agreed to the plan, and he put under Rommel's command the 3rd Rifle and the 3rd Machine Gun companies which Rommel had on the move immediately.

The weather was sunny, and the men suffered from heat fatigue, Rommel himself was exhausted, but he continued making his men walk. The observations made after these events were pertinent in understanding the man Rommel. He had the charisma of a leader, and he was the first to endure the fatigue providing his men with his example, but as any good commander knows it could not last for long. As they approached the Italian positions on the Matajur, Rommel granted some much-needed rest to his men while he started planning his next move. Because of information one of his officers had supplied, Rommel prepared to attack the village of Jevscek by night, his concern being the possible arrival of enemy reinforcements. At night, the village was seized without a fight. The Italians had not realised the enemy was so close, and they were caught unawares by the speed of Rommel's advance. This enabled

Rommel to take a risk, and at 5.30 on 26 October, he took two rifle and two machine gun companies with him advancing towards a peak (1096), with the aim of seizing it before Sprösser. The advance was uneventful but, as Rommel and his men approached the enemy defences, they were met with a hail of fire which compelled them to take cover. Rommel immediately sent the machine gun squads to take position behind the troops moving towards the village, then he rushed in support of the other German troops who had been pinned down by the Italian fire. The plan worked. The German machine guns caught the Italian troops advancing towards the village in a crossfire, compelling them to withdraw. At this point Rommel decided that the only way to seize a peak was with a frontal assault, which he successfully led, with almost an entire Italian regiment surrendering. It was not enough for Rommel who pressed on again, moving his troops along the road leading to Glava and the next target, but taking a serious risk. Almost every officer in command of his detachment had been lost, either killed or wounded, their posts having been taken over by non-commissioned officers. This was not unusual in the German army, but it revealed the extent of the losses and the fatigue of the men under Rommel's command.

The march was again exhausting, but Rommel reached Mount Nagnoj which was seized using the same tactic, which was an attack moving at the same time against the flank and the rear of the enemy positions. From the summit of Mount Nagnoj, Rommel's men were able to see the peak of the Mrzli vrh which was just two kilometres away. His detachment was dispersed over a wide area, and Rommel should have waited to regroup and to rest. He decided not to, and at about 10.00, he gathered the men still available and put them on the march again. It was a composite force with the strength of about two rifle and one machine gun companies, which was much weaker than the enemy forces ahead. Nevertheless, the group advanced along the Matajur road soon meeting Italian troops and they became engaged in close combat. Fighting against the odds, Rommel resorted to ingenuity. He deployed his men so that they could fire in a way that would make the enemy believe they were facing more opponents than they thought. The Italians were taken by surprise, had a moment of uncertainty and eventually decided they could not cope with the enemy forces. Rommel gambled and took a white handkerchief, starting to move towards the Italians. As he walked waving the improvised white flag doubts crossed his mind, but they were soon dispelled, as the Italians decided they had had enough and started to surrender *en masse*. Again, an entire regiment surrendered, enabling Rommel to continue with his advance towards the Matajur.

As he approached the Italian positions, the reaction he faced was different. The intense fire coming from the defences of the Matajur compelled Rommel to take an alternative route, which led right behind the enemy positions. After having seen for himself the next peak and the vast number of prisoners taken, Sprösser decided that the enemy resistance was now stiffening and ordered Rommel to withdraw. Rommel obeyed, but he kept with him a hundred men along with six machine guns, he was determined to attack the Matajur. It was another dangerous gamble, because it was possible the Italians might be more determined to resist. However, Rommel could not help resorting to his old experiences of determination, boldness and decisiveness which could achieve results despite unfavourable odds. Without facing resistance Rommel and his men seized the point south of the Glava, before moving up to the peak of the Matajur to face an enemy defence position, which was being held by an Italian regiment some 1,200 strong. They might have easily defeated Rommel and his weak group, but being taken by surprise, they surrendered. Rommel resumed his advance, only to find that the Italians defending the summit of the Matajur were determined to fight back. Facing the Italian fire, Rommel outflanked the enemy defences attacking them in the rear. This was made possible due to the patrols sent by the 12th German Division, which in the meantime had been attacking the Italian positions on the northern side of the mountain. Rommel pushed his men to attack, and they succeeded. The peak was seized on 26 October, which was just two days after the offensive had started. From the top of the Matajur Rommel and his men could now see the Tagliamento River valley and the town of Cividale, the promised land with the opportunity for a decisive breakthrough which might lead to the final defeat of the Italian Army.

This would not be the task of the Alpenkorps which, as the Italians started to withdraw, was moved to the right flank of the 14th Army, a mountainous area where Rommel and the men of the Württemberg Mountain Battalion fought a series of delaying actions leading, on 7 November, to the clash at Klautana Pass, some 20 kilometres east of the town of Longarone. Acting in his over-confident way, Rommel attacked the Italian positions but only to see his men being repulsed. The attack had failed, even though the Italians soon abandoned their positions, leaving the road to Longarone and the Piave River valley open to Rommel and the Württemberg Mountain Battalion. As Longarone was approached, it was found full of Italian troops on the move or trying to create some sort of defence. Once again, Rommel's relatively small detachment was isolated from the rest of the Württemberg Mountain Battalion, which did not deter Rommel from attempting yet another isolated attack. The Italian reaction was prompt and determined, the attackers being showered with a huge volume of fire which left Rommel with no other choice than withdraw. Before Sprösser and the rest of the Württemberg Mountain Battalion could reach Dogna, about a thousand Italian soldiers counterattacked wiping out isolated German positions, and almost taking Rommel himself prisoner. It was only on the next day that Rommel succeeded, playing the 'white handkerchief' trick again. He submitted an ultimatum to the local Italian commander who, unaware of the real situation, decided there was no point in resisting and surrendered. This would be the last German success. The Italian commander in chief had ordered a defence line along the Piave River, reinforcements were sent and the worn out German and Austrian troops were no longer able to take the Italians by surprise. By 8 November, the battle of Caporetto, which was to become one of the landmarks of the Italian defeats, was over. Rommel's composite *abteilung* had achieved some real successes, at minimal cost. Up to the Matajur he had lost six killed and 30 wounded, Longarone added another six killed, two severely and 19 others wounded, and one missing.*

---

* Fraser, *Knight's Cross*, pp. 61–78. Butler, *Field Marshal*, Chapter 2 (electronic edition). There is an ever-growing literature on Rommel and the Caporetto battle. See, amongst others: John Wilks, Eileen Wilks, *Rommel and Caporetto* (Barnsley: Leo Cooper, 2001). Peter Lieb, *Wüstenfuchs und Bluthundin den Alpen. Erwin Rommel und Ferdinand Schörner in der Schlacht von Karfreit 1917*', *Militärgeschichtliche Zeitschrift* 77:1 (2018) 78:107.

Chapter Two

Rommel Grows in Recognition

Analysing Rommel

There are considerable insights into Rommel in the Caporetto battle. The confusion in the battle led other units to claim the seizure of Mount Matajur, for which the commander of the 14th Army had promised to award the coveted *Pour le Mérite* decoration. It was only later Rommel discovered that the merit of the success, along with the medal, had gone to Lieutenant Walther Schnieber of the Infantry Regiment 63. This was a mistake, the Infantry Regiment 63 had seized Mount Colonna, which in the 14th Army report had been incorrectly reported as Mount Matajur. However, it was clear that Rommel and the Württemberg Mountain Battalion had been robbed of their success and Rommel, without hesitation, started making sure that his protest was heard. Naturally, Schnieber could not be deprived of his *Pour le Mérite*, but matters were soon rectified. Both Rommel and Major Spröser were awarded the medal, and their successes were acknowledged, but Rommel had learnt a lesson.

The actions at Matajur and in the Caporetto battle display Rommel at his best. He was able to move in a terrain which was familiar, having already fought in a similar context in Romania and on the Vosges, and he swiftly appreciated the situation. The Italians could be easily defeated, as they were not used to dealing with unexpected situations. The battles had offered the promise of success, and Rommel was clearly determined to grasp such occasions.

This was part of Rommel's character, which would emerge later revealing his personality. He was evidently ambitious, and his determination was aimed at satisfying his personal motivation. It could be said that once he saw an opportunity, he would sink his teeth into it like a dog with a bone. There are moments in war when the situation becomes uncertain, and both commanders and soldiers know little about what is happening. This is called the 'fog of war', which describes the uncertainty following the first moment of the attack when, in the heat of the battle, no one can say what is really happening. In such a situation action can be determined by the roll of a dice. If the commander is lucky, the enemy will crack, and the fight will be won. If not, the enemy will resist, or even react leading to disaster. It could be claimed that on many occasions Rommel was lucky, and as such he won the day.

Nevertheless, it would be unfair not to acknowledge that Rommel played a sound part in creating his own good fortune. Whenever possible he would seek – and often find – the best way to outflank the enemy positions. This enabled him to push forward, with the aim of taking the enemy by surprise and minimising the possibility of resistance, knowing that swift movements and shock would reduce the enemy resistance. In order to achieve this Rommel did not hesitate to push on, relentlessly. He demanded much from himself, and in turn asked the same of his men who were willing to follow him because of his undeniable leadership capabilities. Stress and fatigue took their toll, but by making himself an example, he rarely realised that most of his men were bound to crack at points, which tended to be well below Rommel's personal limit. In many cases Rommel had to face his own units breaking down, mainly because he had been asking too much from them.

Rommel's determination to achieve his goal and his own efforts, regardless of the fact that his men could not deal with excessive strain, became one of Rommel's noted peculiarities. In some cases, success simply covered the actual extent of fatigue he had imposed on his own units, at other times failure would highlight the situation. This often meant that Rommel's success was in many cases the fruit of luck and determination, but it is impossible to define which was the most decisive factor. However, Rommel's approach on the battlefield often proved to be correct, as future experiences were to prove. Fast movement with deep drives into the enemy positions were the keys to success, and Rommel resorted to them more and more, until their ultimate failure. At times he openly disregarded orders and the general situation. Rommel was not inclined to take instructions from those he did not value, and the case of von Bothmer was demonstrative of this attitude. Whenever facing an order which did not match his own aims, Rommel was inclined to disregard it seeking support from others, in this case from Sprösser, and in some other cases from other commanders, mainly at the top. At Caporetto, Rommel never sought to acquire a picture of the overall situation, and his determination led him to act in accordance with his own plans. It was this attitude which made him disregard von Bothmer, then even Sprösser's order when facing the top of the Matajur. Rommel would not let an order block him, and whenever necessary openly disregarded them even if he could not rely on the support of some superior commander. Once again, luck was of the essence. Had Rommel been defeated, his lack of respect for the orders he had been given by superior officers might have proved fatal to his career. But he was successful, and this led many to ignore the fact that the success had been achieved despite given orders.

Rommel's attitude in battle can be compared to that of the proverbial bull in the china shop. He set his aim and went for it, ignoring everything else, which included estimating essential components such as supplies. Rommel's swift and deep advances into the enemy lines had his unit cut off from supplies, a shortage often made good by resorting to the captured resources of the enemy. Had Rommel not been blessed with success, the supplies could not have been captured and his unit would have soon faced starvation and ammunition shortage. Determination is one thing, reckless behaviour is another, and it might be claimed that on many occasions luck, once again, made the difference for Rommel who, like a good many German officers, merely saw supplies as a burden. It was considered something the field commander should not be concerned about, being a matter for the quartermaster officer who would be required to exercise the same kind of efforts Rommel exhibited. These efforts could be unrealistic, and his men had their limits too, with which Rommel rarely bothered himself. This does not imply he did not understand, or even value the need for supplies or support, which he considered like other commanders. As such, he had the classic attitude, taking them for granted, relying on the work of some staff officer or some other commander, who were supposed to work up to Rommel's own demanding standards.

Rommel was a field commander who acted well when leading a relatively small unit which he could shape to meet his needs. Caporetto provided an opportunity for him to be at his best, with a unit he knew well and men willing to follow because of his charisma, a suitable terrain and an even more suitable enemy who was not inclined to fight. Caporetto also provided Rommel with yet another lesson: he had to make his point of view known from the start, shouting out loud if necessary. It was not by chance during the Second World War he developed the habit of taking pictures, writing down the achievements on the battlefields, and producing well illustrated works which were simply meant to outline what he and his men had done. There would be no other Lieutenant Schieber to take his merit, and his point of view would be made clear and put on paper. All this turned the field commander into more of a literate man and generated a huge number of records for historians to study, while being cautious of his exaggerations.

The Path to Generalship

At the beginning of 1918 Rommel went on leave and, on 11 January, was appointed aide to the staff of LXIV Army Corps, the headquarters commanding the Württemberg army units. We do not know much of Rommel's activities as a staff officer, but on 18 October 1918, Rommel was promoted Captain, less than a month before Germany surrendered. He was home by Christmas 1918, and he entered the 100,000-men army of the Weimar Republic, obviously because of his achievements and the *Pour le Mérite*. This was not an easy period because Germany was in turmoil and close to a civil war. Rommel did not appear to have been involved in the fights against the Communists, never coming close to the paramilitary Freikorps formations. He simply carried on as he had done before, serving as a career officer, called from time to time to deal with the unrest that plagued post-war Germany. On 25 June 1919, he was given command of a company of the 13th Infantry Regiment based at Stuttgart. This would be Rommel's military home for the next ten years, being posted on 8 December 1921 to serve as a staff officer with the headquarters of the I Battalion, 13th Infantry Regiment, before being posted on 1 July 1924 to the office of the regimental welfare staff. On 1 October 1924, Rommel again took command of a combat unit, the 4th Machine Gun company of the 13th Infantry Regiment.

Rommel's personal life was more eventful, with his son Manfred being born on 24 December 1928, and on 1 October 1929, Rommel was then posted to the Infantry Training School at Dresden. Rommel was not part of the group of officers involved in the mechanised revolution, men such as Heinz Guderian, but his position enabled him to revive the accomplishment that secured his career. Teaching small unit infantry tactics to junior officers, Rommel was once again a leader and a commander. Relying on his book *Infantry Attacks*, a book of memoirs on his experiences during the Great War, Rommel taught the young officers to win by boldness, relying on speed and surprise, which would be the main characteristic of the new German Army. He was promoted major on 1 April 1932, and on 1 July 1933 Rommel left the Infantry Training School being posted to Dresden as *Kommandantur*, the local army command. It was only on 1 October that Rommel returned to command a unit, the III Battalion of 17th Infantry Regiment at Goslar. He was promoted lieutenant colonel on 1 March 1935, and he had his moment on 15 October the following year when he was posted to take the lead of an officers' training course at the Potsdam War School. There was a certain irony in the posting, Rommel having never attended the War School since he failed in passing the necessary exam. In fact, the new posting seems to have been not just the consequence of Rommel's skills as a leader and commander, or as an instructor, but rather of his rubbing shoulders with the new regime which had taken over in Germany at the end of January 1933.

Hitler on the Stage

On 30 September 1934, Rommel met for the first time Germany's new chancellor, Adolf Hitler. The occasion was Hitler's visit to Goslar for the local Harvest Festival, which included a review of Rommel's unit. The story of Rommel clashing with the commander of Hitler's personal bodyguards is probably apocryphal, and the comments made on it by Rommel's biographers seem more interesting than the story itself. Some judged the clash as a sign of how little Rommel valued the people of the Nazi apparatus, others at times claiming that Rommel met Hitler for the first time in 1938. Nevertheless, the fact is that it appears that Rommel's rapid rise coincides with Hitler's elevation to power. In a few years Rommel would be in charge of Hitler's personal headquarters, which made the so-called clash not only hardly believable but inconsistent. The notion that Rommel had little interest in politics, and therefore did not become involved with the Nazi regime was more a post-war creation than the truth. In 1935 Rommel met two other Nazi leaders, Hermann Göring and Joseph Goebbels. There seems to have been a deep dislike between Göring and Rommel; on the other hand, Rommel was appreciative of Goebbels. One can be certain that Rommel disliked some of the components of the Nazi regime, like the brown-shirted *Sturm Abteilungen* (SA) and others, but he seemed appreciative of Hitler. One comment he allegedly made to his wife was 'why is Hitler surrounding himself with people of this sort?' Implying that he might have disliked some of the Nazis, but he appreciated Hitler. One thing is certain, Rommel did not hesitate to work with the Nazis, even if he did so just for the sake of his career. Thus, on 25 February 1937 (which is less than three years after meeting Hitler and just two after meeting Göring and Goebbels), Rommel also served as liaison officer to Baldur von Schirach, the Hitler Youth leader. The appointment came after Rommel between 15 and 23 January 1937 attended a National Socialist Training Course for the Wehrmacht, which at least indicated an acquiescence of Nazism. Rommel's task was to provide the Hitler Youth with a military training, which made sense given his past appointments as an instructor.

However, the idea of training youngsters indicated Hitler's aims and the true nature of the Nazi regime. Rommel did not serve in this position for long, the reason for his departure was to attempt to have the army take over the military training of the Hitler Youth, and his appointment to Wiener Neustadt in November 1938, which, incidentally, came not long after Rommel met Hitler again. On 9 November 1938, Rommel was seconded from the Potsdam academy to command the task force protecting Hitler during the celebrations of the Beer Hall Putsch. The appointment also saw Rommel in charge of Hitler's personal security in early October 1938, during the German occupation of the Sudetenland region of Czechoslovakia following the Munich agreement.

The story usually narrated is that Hitler asked for Rommel after reading his book *Infantry Attacks*. However, it was unlikely the first time they met, or that Rommel dealt with the Nazis. It is also worth noting that Rommel's career started moving at a faster pace. This could also have been the consequence of Hitler's decision to start the German rearmament in 1935, by transforming the *Reichswehr* into the *Heer*, the German Army. On 1 October 1937, Rommel was promoted colonel, and on 10 November 1938, he was sent to command the War School at Wiener Neustadt, in the newly annexed Austria. Some observers have regarded this as Rommel's decisive step towards the Nazi regime. Between 29 November and 2 December Rommel attended for the third time the National Socialist Training Course, this time a place reserved for senior officers. After listening to Hitler giving a speech on 1 December, Rommel wrote to his wife reporting his words: 'the soldier today must be political because he must always be ready to go into action for the new politics.' If not an enthusiastic supporter, Rommel was at least more than willing to work along with the new regime and its leader. In March 1939, Rommel was once again in charge of Hitler's personal security during the seizure of the rest of Czechoslovakia. This came shortly after Rommel had been promoted to major general, on 1 October 1939. A few days later, Rommel took over command of Hitler's military unit assigned to his personal protection. To the contrary of other newly promoted generals,

Rommel's achievements in the interwar years were limited to instructing and to protecting Hitler, which he often did in wartime.

Two days after the German invasion of Poland, on 3 September 1939, when France and Britain declared war on Germany, Hitler left Berlin in his special train which as customary, when he was on the move, using it as his temporary headquarters. Rommel was part of Hitler's retinue, and he witnessed first-hand the war in Poland. There was not a single doubt in his mind, rather his admiration for Hitler which seemed to have established deep roots. On 10 September, Rommel wrote to his wife remarking that he had been allowed to attend some of Hitler's situation conferences, usually restricted to Hitler's closest advisers, during which he was even allowed to speak a word. Nine days later, in yet another letter to his wife, Rommel remarked with some enthusiasm how Hitler had allowed him to chat for almost two hours about military problems, noting 'he is extraordinarily friendly towards me.' Hardly anybody adverse to the Nazi regime would have made such comments, nevertheless, this did not necessarily mean Rommel was a keen supporter. The point with Rommel's character is quite simple if the traits of his behaviour are linked. Rommel was ambitious, and he knew one thing only, namely the army, his real home. Drawing close to Hitler naturally served his ambition, and the rise to generalship is proof that Rommel did what he did because he wanted to secure his career in the army. On the other hand, it is difficult to believe that Rommel ever considered discussing or thinking of anything other than military matters. Rommel's descriptions of the ruins of Warsaw exposed how he simply looked at the matter from a mere military angle. He described the city as destroyed, without water, food, or anything else, but showed no understanding of the miseries of its population, as he paid little or no attention to such detail. All that mattered to him was the military success on the battlefield, which made him a supporter of the Nazi regime, and to an extent of Hitler himself, to secure his own career.

Rommel had no experience with armoured or even mechanised warfare, his time spent in the inter-war army had been entirely devoted to his First World War experience. Infantry warfare was all he knew, and at a relatively low-level. Not surprisingly, as he put forward his application for commanding a Panzer Division, the Army Personnel Office rejected it, undoubtedly relying on the fact there were other junior generals better fitted for the task. Rommel would have served better if put in command of a Mountain Division, which was the most obvious choice. Nevertheless, Rommel had sensed that the Panzers offered the best chance of success, and he turned to Hitler. The details are not known, but it is clear that Rommel pleaded with Hitler and secured his support for the required command. Rommel had risen to the point of being one of Hitler's favourite generals, and this was the way Hitler had to please him. On 15 February 1940, Rommel was given command of the newly formed 7th Panzer Division, whose staff he greeted with a 'Heil Hitler' and the Nazi raised arm salute. Rommel might not have been a Nazi himself, but evidently, he did not dislike having to deal with them as long as it was necessary.[1]

Chapter Three

An Important Commander

The Panzer Commander

Rommel's characteristic personal traits emerged soon after joining the new command, first ridding himself of officers he rated unsuitable for the job. His attitude of being over-demanding of himself clearly clashed with the attitude of some soldiers not so keen on personal sacrifices. On the other hand, Rommel started training the 7th Panzer Division in a highly professional way, soon showing he may not have been one of the commanders whose name was tied to the birth of the Panzerwaffe, Germany's armoured arm, but that he was skilled enough to understand its nature and requirements. Rommel's experiences as an infantry commander would be instilled into the Panzer Division by making bold and swift decisions, the basis of sound command.

The 7th Panzer Division had just been formed from a 'light division', a provisional type of unit used during the war against Poland, including a mixture of Panzer and cavalry. The division was not the best of its kind. Its tank regiment consisted mainly of Czechoslovakian tanks, the Panzer 38, pressed into use by the Germans following the seizure of that country. Other divisions, most notably those part of Guderian's XIX Corps, were equipped with the more modern German tanks and had been given the task to break through the French defences at Sedan, to advance to the west following the course of the Aisne River. General Reinhardt XXXXI Corps was to break through the Meuse River north of Sedan, at Charleville Meziers, covering Guderian's flank. Rommel's 7th Panzer Division was part of Hermann Hoth's XXXX Corps, which had the task of crossing the Meuse between Ivoir and Dinant to form the northern wing of the offensive, as it was to advance south of the Sambre

River along with the 5th Panzer Division. Rommel was part of the main offensive but only in an ancillary role, but events would soon enable him to lead the division as it suited him.

On 10 May 1940, as the German offensive in the West started, Rommel's 7th Panzer Division approached the Ourthe River close to the Belgian frontier. The Ourthe was crossed the next day via a ford, due to a bridge captured intact at La Roche en Ardenne. On this day the first clash with French units took place near Marche, the motorcycle battalion being supported by part of the divisional artillery. In the clash, the division had its first losses: three killed, seven wounded and three missing. It was now facing the French defences in front of Dinant, in a situation similar to that experienced by Rommel in 1917. The division was moving fast, having covered some 90 kilometres in just two days and being 35 kilometres from Dinant, but it had also lost contact with the neighbouring units, in particular the 5th Panzer Division. As events unfolded, Rommel could fight as he was accustomed.

Without hesitation, and without trying to seek contact with the 5th Panzer Division, on 12 May Rommel committed the Panzer Regiment and the 7th Motorised Infantry Regiment, one of the two parts of the division, to attack the French defences before Dinant. The attack started at 7.00, and after three hours of fighting, Colonel Rothenburg's 25th Panzer Regiment had broken through the French defences and advanced towards Dinant, just 27 kilometres away. Rommel's advance had been so fast that General Hoth, the corps commander, decided to put the advanced units of the 5th Panzer Division under Rommel's command. The rest of the division was still moving well behind Rommel's 7th Panzer Division. At 16.45 on 12 May, a tank company reinforced by elements from the first battalion of the 7th Motorised Infantry Regiment reached the Meuse at Dinant. It is worth noting, the leading elements of Guderian's XIX Corps only reached the Meuse at Sedan at 23.00 hours later on that same day. Rommel had not just won the race to the Meuse, but he would also be the first to attack. Guderian had set the main attack at Sedan to start at 16.00 on the next day, 13 May, but Rommel had his division attack across the Meuse at first light. He would only enjoy modest air support, because the bulk of the air units were engaged to support Guderian's effort.

The attack started at 4.30 on the 13th, with the motorcycle battalion and the 6th Motorised Infantry Regiment advancing near Houy, north of Dinant, and the 7th Motorised Infantry Regiment advancing towards Dinant. The French counterattacked with tanks and artillery, particularly against the northern prong of the division, which did not prevent it from reaching the Meuse and seizing a suitable crossing point. In late evening, as the darkness fell, the division started moving its tanks and armoured vehicles across the Meuse using the elements of the pontoon bridge. The first bridgehead on the Meuse had been seized, about the same time as Guderian's XIX Corps broke through at Sedan, at the cost of 60 killed, 122 wounded and six missing. Neither Guderian nor Rommel would rest on their laurels. As the sun rose on 14 May, only the northern and the southern arms of the German armoured drive across the Ardennes had been able to cross the Meuse, at Dinant and at Sedan. Apart from Guderian's XIX Corps, Hoth's XV Corps had only Rommel's 7th Panzer Division across the river, the 5th Panzer Division were still on the move while both divisions of Reinhardt's XXXXI Corps still had to cross the river. This was the decisive moment, the breaking point of the entire battle. No one thought of resting, refitting, and regrouping the forces for the advance. The move ahead was to start immediately, movement and surprise being the key elements of battle. Clearly, Rommel's lesson had produced its effects, and now he was putting theory into practice using the new element of warfare.

The French launched a series of counterattacks against 7th Panzer Division's bridgehead, which were all repulsed. At 19.30 on the 14th, after five days of marches and combat, the division started to advance, Rommel again having given the order to pursue with all weapons. The Panzer Regiment was in the lead, Rommel having joined for the occasion Colonel Rothenburg, who rushed into the assistance of the 7th Motorised Infantry Regiment attacking the town of Morville, about 12 kilometres west of the Meuse. After fierce fighting the town was seized at 22.30, but at a cost: 51 killed and 158 wounded. The bridgehead was now secure, and the advance to the west could continue. The men had some rest, badly needed after their efforts, then at 10.00 on the 15th the division started its advance to the Channel following Hoth's order to attack towards Avesnes. Once again, Rommel put Rothenburg's Panzer Regiment in the lead and joined it, the rest of the division to follow, while the Luftwaffe attacked the city of Philippeville. Before the city was reached, the Panzer Regiment clashed with French tanks and disabled seven of them before engaging the bulk of the French forces. During the battle that followed the 7th Panzer Division was able to inflict severe losses, a recorded total of 12 heavy and 14 light French tanks, before reaching Philippeville at 13.00 and seizing it by 15.40 on the 15th. The rest of the 1st French Armoured Division was left behind, Rommel protecting the flanks of his division with artillery and anti-tank guns.

The situation must have reminded Rommel of Caporetto, because he found himself with the Panzer Regiment, practically isolated from the rest of the division and the other advancing German units. Nevertheless, he decided to continue the advance, which was soon halted by strong French defences about four kilometres west of Philippeville. At this point Rommel took personal command of a reinforced Panzer company, went back to Philippeville to gather any other unit which had reached the city, and having found the advanced element of the reconnaissance unit, turned back attacking the French positions, destroying 13 tanks, and capturing 20 others. Only at 19.00 was Rommel joined by other units from the division, namely a machine gun battalion attached for the purpose, and after deploying it in defence of the ground seized during the battle with the French tanks, he prepared the Panzer Regiment for yet another advance. The day, however, cost the 7th Panzer Division 15 killed and 56 wounded, but a small price compared to 450 French prisoners and a total of 75 enemy tanks destroyed or captured. Rommel was in charge of the leading elements of his division which was itself practically isolated, the 5th Panzer Division was still fighting about 25 kilometres behind. No contact had been established with it, or with any other German unit on the move.

Speed and movement were the key to success, and typically Rommel was determined not to lose the momentum. At 4.00 on the 16th the reconnaissance unit moved forward to pave the way for the attack, which started at 14.30 with Rommel leading the division towards the city of Avesnes, right behind the fortified line running along the border between France and Belgium. By the evening the division had reached Sivry, the last Belgian town on the route to Avesnes, and at 18.00 the division attacked with the Panzer Regiment once again in the lead. Due to the work of the divisional pioneer and reconnaissance units, the road was cleared of obstacles enabling an advanced party, led by Rommel, to move towards Avesnes at 23.00 under the protection of the divisional artillery. As the party reached a position about ten kilometres east of the city it came under intense fire from the French defences, but they were soon silenced. Following this incident, the Panzer Regiment ran into a French mechanised division deployed along the main road, which did not prevent them from continuing their advance, as the German Panzer moved through the enemy vehicles preventing them from reacting by their fast manoeuvre. Taken by surprise the French collapsed, soldiers fleeing the area in some cases after having thrown away their weapons, and thereby enabling the Panzer Regiment to drive through Avesnes and move beyond the city. In the early hours of 17 May, Rommel's 7th Panzer Division captured about 6,000 French soldiers, a success which meant that the aim of reaching the Channel was not only possible, but also feasible in a short period of time. The success had brought Rommel's division to about 45 kilometres ahead of the advancing infantry, Rommel himself having lost any contact with the rear units of his division which were advancing along the main road, in large part still at Sivry.

With the rest of the division some 20 kilometres back from his position, Rommel found himself practically isolated, and in a situation of total chaos and confusion. To give a picture of the situation, on that same day, 17 May, General Hoth gave the 7th Panzer Division the order to seize Avesnes, which Rommel had already taken – a success which enabled him to look at the next objective: the bridge on the Sambre River at Landrecies, some 18 kilometres to the west. Facing at last a French counterattack aimed at recovering the lost positions at Avesnes, the leading elements of the division were able to repulse the attacks because of the intervention of the Panzer Regiment, which at 5.30 on the 17th, moved on to attack the French units to the west of Avesnes. The speed of the German advance was such that these units were caught completely by surprise, and they collapsed like the others had at Avesnes. Eventually, it was the large number of prisoners taken that slowed down the advance of the 7th Panzer Division which, at about 6.00 hours, seized the bridge on the Sambre River intact. The leading elements of the division, two tank battalions and part of the motorcycle battalion, were about 30–50 kilometres to the west of the bulk of the division, with the rest of the Panzer Regiment, the reconnaissance unit, and the motorcycle battalion. This situation compelled Rommel to take a reconnaissance vehicle and move back to Avesnes, finding at last contact with the rest of the division, enabling him to order the infantry and the artillery to move forward to the Sambre River. At this point the corps commander, having been able at last to assess the actual situation, ordered Rommel to seize a bridge on the Sambre 13 kilometres north-west of Avesnes, at Berlaimont. This meant diverting the 7th Panzer Division from its route, but also enabling (if the attack were successful) the other divisions to advance at a faster pace. Rommel, whose leading units were some 30 kilometres ahead of the neighbouring 5th Panzer Division, did not personally involve himself in this task, which was given by the divisional operations officer to a battle group which seized the bridge intact. In the meantime, having secured communications with the corps command, Rommel asked for air attacks along the road to Cambrai with the clear aim of bringing even more chaos and disorganisation amongst the French troops.

At 19.00 on 18 May General Hoth ordered Rommel to move towards Cambrai, before ordering him to shift the axis of advance to support the 5th Panzer Division, in order to surrender the divisional route (along with the bridges captured intact) to allow the neighbouring division to advance more rapidly. Apparently, Rommel did not receive the order and used the 7th Motorised Infantry Regiment to attack on two sites along the Sambre, while the 6th Motorised Infantry Regiment mopped up the French military in the area. It was possible that some rivalry was starting to emerge with the 5th Panzer Division, as Rommel appeared not too eager on helping the neighbouring division to link up with his own pace of advance; it was also a matter of supplies. Having moved so fast, Rommel's Panzer were now facing shortages of fuel and ammunition, and using what was left available to pave the way for the advance of the 5th Panzer Division, which would also have benefited from taking over the roads used by the 7th Panzer Division, which could be regarded as a waste. At 17.00 on 18 May, Rommel resumed the advance, now with two battle groups one of which (with the Panzer Regiment, the motorcycle battalion and one infantry battalion) advanced along the main road towards Cambrai. The other (the 7th Motorised Infantry Regiment) moved to the south before starting to advance towards Cambrai and approached it from a southerly direction. The French resistance started to collapse, the Panzer Regiment approached Cambrai at about 21.00, enabling Rommel to divert the motorcycle and infantry battalion to move to the north of the city, with the aim of seizing the bridges on the L'Escaut Canal. They managed this successfully, just as the Panzer Regiment found resistance into Cambrai and had to move to the east of the city, which was practically surrounded, the 7th Motorised Infantry Regiment having advanced to the south and to the south-east of Cambrai. Still fighting, the French counterattacked at Cambrai and at the bridgeheads on the Sambre, which was successfully defended due to the intervention of corps troops, and of the divisional artillery under command of the divisional operations officer.

At this point the front was characterised by two bulges: to the south the bulk of Guderian's XIX Corps which had moved to the west of St. Quentin, at Peronne, and was close to Amiens, to the north Rommel's 7th Panzer Division across the L'Escaut Canal at Cambrai. All other German units were still dragging behind the leading elements of the German attack, which had penetrated the enemy lines for about 50 kilometres. They soon discovered that their opposition had not yet been defeated, the enemy reaction materialising with two main counterattacks to the north and to the south, and Guderian was the first to repulse the counterattack by General de Gaulle's 4th Armoured Division from the south on 17–19 May.[1]

Rommel appeared to have moved faster than Guderian even though the latter was temporarily halted by Hitler's order, but it remained a necessity in order to allow some rest for the units, and for the supplies to reach the leading elements. Rommel also spent the 19th resting, while regrouping and planning the further advance of his 7th Panzer Division. In late evening, as the 7th Motorised Infantry Regiment established a bridgehead on the L'Escaut Canal to the south-west of Cambrai, the 8th Panzer Division advanced reaching a position about five kilometres to the south of the city. Rommel was completely free to advance, in the direction of Arras. This forward thrust was resumed at 1.40 on 20 May, the division moving along two routes from the north and the south of Cambrai using the bridgeheads on the L'Escaut Canal. Rommel led the northern combat group, built around the Panzer Regiment, reaching the Canal du Nord at about 3.00, the last obstacle before Arras. However, the bridge was blown-up, compelling Rommel to search for another crossing point to the south, as the divisional bridging units were still far behind. An intact bridge was seized at Marquion, enabling the Panzer to cross the Canal and advance towards Arras. Three hours later the leading elements were some three kilometres to the south of the city, Rommel ordering the advance to halt, because the rest of the division was far behind. Back in his armoured car, Rommel drove in search of the rest of the division only to meet a group of French tanks which destroyed both his armoured car and the escorting tank. Rommel had to seek for safety in a ditch, being saved by the leading elements of the division which reached his position later on that same morning. Having approached Arras, the 7th Panzer Division now faced a series of counterattacks, which were repulsed because of the intervention of a Waffen-SS unit from the 3rd Division, which had been requested by the divisional command. On 20 May a bridge was built on the Canal du Nord, but the renewed French resistance did not deter Rommel from planning a further advance to the coast, which was now less than 90 kilometres away. This was the order given on 21 May by the XXXIX Army Corps, which was now in control of the

7th Panzer Division, the movement starting, as scheduled at 10.30, with the Panzer Regiment in the lead followed by the infantry units on both flanks. After advancing for about ten kilometres, at 15.30 the division faced the strongest Allied counterattack of the entire campaign. A force of 74 British tanks, mainly heavy Matilda Infantry Tanks, followed by 70 other French tanks attacked the positions held by the 6th Motorised Infantry Regiment, supported by the light howitzers of the artillery regiment. The German regiment was partly overrun, the British tanks driving through the positions held by the I Battalion whose anti-tank guns proved useless against their thick armour. A defence was set up using the 88 mm anti-aircraft guns, along with the heavy howitzers and all the available anti-tank guns. Rommel personally intervened, directing the fire of the various guns against the advancing enemy tanks, while the Panzer Regiment attacked their northern flank. Nine Panzers were lost in the attempt, but the Panzer Regiment succeeded in breaking through and reached the rear of the Allied forces which, by 23.00, decided to call the counterattack off. The hardest day of battle for Rommel's 7th Panzer Division cost 89 killed, 116 wounded and 173 missing, along with nine medium and four light tanks for the loss of at least 43 enemy tanks. This was the last obstacle on the road to the Channel, which Guderian's Panzer had reached the day before. It was not the end of the campaign, nor of Rommel's personal achievements.

With his typical exaggeration, making frontline reports of units unreliable, Rommel stated that he had repulsed a counterattack made with hundreds of tanks. It is likely that his report suggested to Hitler the idea of the new halt order issued on the 24th, even though the idea of halting the Panzer units before Dunkirk was probably the combination of a series of factors, not in the least the need for them to rest and refit. Either way, Rommel had learnt a lesson, and on 27 May, as the 7th Panzer Division advanced towards Lille, he remained behind with the bulk of the division to prevent the Panzer Regiment from becoming isolated. The advance was successful, Lille was reached and the line of withdrawal of the British 2nd Division being cut, with its units needing to scatter. On the 28th Rommel's division repulsed a counterattack led by the French

25th Division and by the colonial (Moroccan) 2nd and 5th divisions, which were attempting to break through the encirclement. On the next day the 7th Panzer Division was pulled out from the front for a much-needed rest and refit, its Panzer Regiment only having a handful of tanks in running order. The division prepared, with the others, for the second part of the campaign: the attack on the Somme–Aisne line aimed at bringing the German forces deep into France. This would be yet another success for Rommel.[2]

Summing up the 1940 Campaign

Rommel may not have reached the Channel with his 7th Panzer Division, but he had still accomplished a successful campaign, for which his superiors gave him full credit. On 2 June Hitler visited Charleville, where Rommel met him presenting a summary of his division's accomplishments. He omitted the clashes with the neighbouring 5th Panzer Division, which had accused him of appropriating its units for his own purposes, and he made no mention of losses. Rommel ensured that he wanted to keep on the safe side and his account known.

Rommel was not given a main role in the new offensive. This would go to Guderian's Panzer Group (formed from the XIX Corps) which was to attack across the Aisne and advance east of Paris, behind the Maginot Line defences. Panzer Group Kleist was to attack across the Somme pointing toward Paris and to the west of the city, where Hoth's XV Corps would be advancing along the coast. The corps, part of the 4th Army, which formed the westernmost wing of the German deployment intended to advance to Rouen, crossed the Seine River while seizing the French coast along the Channel. Rommel's 7th Panzer Division was part of this, with the 5th Panzer and the 20th Motorised Infantry Division. After reaching their 'jump-off' positions on 3–4 June, the attack started at 4.30 on the 5th soon facing a strong and unexpected French resistance, which Rommel did not experience. His division was able to cross the Somme and establish a bridgehead without facing excessive resistance, this was the result of losses suffered by the French Army which could not create a continuous line of defence. A degree of good fortune arose because the 5th French Colonial Division which, having just been deployed to the area, failed to destroy two bridges which fell into the hands of the 5th Panzer Division. Strong resistance was met only at the village of Hangest, which was seized with a strong attack supported by the Luftwaffe. Given the situation, Rommel deployed his division as an 'armoured box', all fighting units advancing in open formation over an area more than 3 kilometres wide and 18 long. The Panzer Regiment was in the lead followed by the infantry and the artillery with the reconnaissance unit protecting the flanks, something which was made possible by both the terrain and the slackening enemy resistance. In order to proceed with speed, villages and towns were outflanked and bypassed, leaving their seizure to the infantry moving behind.

By 7 June the XV Corps, now moving with all of its motorised divisions abreast, had advanced so fast that it cut off the French IX Corps from the rest of the 10th Army, thus endangering not only the coast but also the possible crossing of the Seine. Attempts to relieve the isolated corps ended by facing defeat, Rommel's 7th Panzer Division easily repulsed a counterattack by the French 17th Light Division. On the evening of 7 June, the division had reached its objective, the Paris–Dieppe Road. On the next day the French 10th Army began to withdraw moving towards Rouen, which was now Hoth's main objective. In the attempt to seize an intact bridge on the Seine, Rommel moved his division forward at full speed clashing with a British unit before reaching Elbeuf. However, a *coup de main* aimed at seizing the Elbeuf bridge on the Seine failed during the night. Another attempt to seize a bridge intact also failed, but Rommel was not the only one to face such a situation, the 7th Panzer Division reorganised in the Tourville–Souteville area now faced the task of preventing an Allied breakthrough to Le Havre. At 4.30 on 10 June, Rommel sent the vanguards of the 7th Panzer Division towards Le Havre, soon intercepting the French 31st Division which was trying to reach the city. In the early afternoon the leading elements of the division reached the Channel, isolating most of the French IX Corps and part of the British 51st Highland Division, which had sent a unit towards Le

Havre to try and maintain the link to reach the city using its harbour for evacuation. Facing the road to Le Havre which was blocked and knowing that Dieppe's harbour could not be used because of demolitions, both French and British troops headed for St. Valéry, a town between Le Havre and Dieppe, with the aim of embarking. On the 11th Rommel sent the Panzer Regiment, with infantry support, towards St. Valéry which it reached despite the resistance set up by the 51st Division. Overlooking the harbour, the Germans prevented any embarkation by day, and Rommel submitted an ultimatum to the divisional commander, who refused to surrender. Facing this situation Rommel tried to penetrate the town, but the attack was ill conceived and the enemy resistance too strong, with the result that the attempt failed. Only the German artillery fire and the night rain prevented the British troops from embarking at St. Valéry, even though other harbours were used. Only on 12 June, after a failed attempt to embark troops at St. Valéry, the commander of the 51st British Division, General Fortune, backed by the French IX Corps commander decided to surrender. The seizure of Le Havre meant Rommel held a total of some 46,000 prisoners, along with huge quantities of vehicles and materiel.

At Rouen, Rommel's 7th Panzer Division fought against the men of the 53rd Mixed Infantry Regiment, a unit composed of Senegalese soldiers who fought tenaciously against the Germans. Rumours have circulated for years about the treatment of the Moroccan soldiers, who, it is often claimed, were shot on the spot after having surrendered, but no details nor any evidence has ever been found. Many have tried to link Rommel with the alleged war crimes, a coup for any historian or journalist, seeking scandal rather than the truth. Rommel's name is such that any involvement in war crimes is likely to alter the image of the 'clean soldier' which has been built over decades.

Even though the seizure of Le Havre was not part of the main effort which led to the defeat of France, Rommel's 7th Panzer Division (and the entire XV Corps) had performed so well that it was chosen for an important task along with the 5th Panzer Division: the seizure of Normandy and of the Brittany peninsula. The latter was to drive across the Seine towards Rennes and Brest, Rommel's 7th Panzer Division was to advance towards Cherbourg. The order came on 17 June, just as Marshal Philippe Pétain asked for an armistice. It was just a race against time, and Rommel's division performed at its best. Facing no resistance from the enemy units, which were already under the impression that the war was over, Rommel was able to advance towards Cherbourg without problems or anything which might have slowed down his advance, the leading elements of the division approaching Cherbourg on the 18th. Rommel again offered the chance to surrender, but this was refused, and the attack started on that same evening, to continue on the following day until the French garrison commander decided to surrender. Much to Rommel's dismay, they surrendered to Colonel von Senger und Etterlin and not to himself. However, this was not the end of the campaign, and Rommel's division having proved itself was chosen for the last action, namely the drive along the coast which aimed at establishing a link with Spain. The armistice caught Rommel's division at Saintes, the campaign having cost the loss of 2,592 men (of which 457 killed) and of 52 Panzer in return for the capture of thousands of prisoners, a thousand vehicles and huge quantities of materiel and ammunition. For his achievements Rommel was awarded the Knight's Cross, the equivalent of the *Pour le Mérite*.[3]

Later, when Rommel achieved his fame as the Desert Fox when fighting in North Africa, this overshadowed his accomplishments in France as commander of the 7th Panzer Division. In less than three months Rommel had gained complete control of his division, managed to acquaint himself with its different components, using them on the battlefield in the most efficient way. Hitherto, Rommel had only commanded a battalion-sized unit on the battlefield and had no experience with armoured warfare. The accomplishment must be recognised for what it was, namely the success of an outstanding field commander able to adapt his own style of command to a new type of armoured warfare. Rommel had proved to be an exceptional division commander, even though his achievements were gained in some of the most favourable conditions which, as at Caporetto, he never hesitated to exploit. He relied on movement and manoeuvre to catch the enemy forces unbalanced, and thereby exploiting a local superiority. Even when defending, as at Arras, Rommel had shown the qualities of a leader and a commander solving the crisis by his personal intervention. It would be curious to ponder what would have happened had Rommel continued his career in command of the 7th Panzer Division.

To North Africa

In putting the 'Desert Fox' in context, it is necessary to consider how Rommel was eventually selected to take command of the German forces in Libya, and why. In the summer of 1940 Hitler considered sending a Panzer Division to support the Italian offensive into Egypt, with the aim of seizing Alexandria and thereby closing access to the Royal Navy. General Wilhelm von Thoma was sent to examine the situation, returning with an unfavourable report. The area was unsuitable for armoured warfare, the Italians were poor allies (von Thoma knew them during the Spanish Civil War), and the overall impression was negative. Hitler eventually abandoned the idea of supporting the Italian offensive, but soon sent German troops to Libya in February 1941, because of the Italian collapse and General Wavell's offensive. He had two motivations; first, there was a strategic concept behind the idea, and secondly, it was more of a political notion. Had Libya fallen into British hands, the political and strategic repercussions would have been too much for Italy's position, and her attitude towards the war might have been badly influenced. General Hans von Funck, commander of the 3rd Panzer Division (selected at first for this deployment in North Africa), was sent to evaluate the situation first hand but returned with a negative report. Hitler might have considered abandoning the Italians to their fate, but he looked for a commander who, in his opinion, could be able to deliver what he wanted, namely preventing the Western Desert Force seizing the whole of Libya and so preparing the ground for a subsequent Axis offensive.

In a matter of days Hitler's attitude changed, as he realised that sending a relatively small brigade sized unit, would not have been enough to prevent disaster, and he decided to send an entire corps. The newly formed *Deutsches Afrika Korps* would include the original 5th Light Division, formed with elements from the 3rd Panzer Division and corps troops, and the newly formed 15th Panzer Division. The aim was to redeploy these forces to Libya, having the soldiers acclimatised while preventing a British advance, and prepare for a subsequent offensive intended to destroy the enemy forces in North Africa. Considering that transports across the Mediterranean imposed a delay, it would have taken at least three months before the bulk of the *Afrika Korps* reached Libya. By taking other plans into account (the attack in the Balkans, due to start in April, and Operation *Barbarossa*, which was to start in June), Hitler was making plans for the future as he perceived it should be. It was understood that Rommel was not intended to start an offensive until early 1942, which was to be after the Soviet Union had been defeated, and Germany would have been in the condition to focus on the war against Britain. This would also provide the men of the *Afrika Korps* time to acclimatise to the tropical conditions and acquaint themselves with the environment and the enemy.

Rommel was the perfect choice for the task. He had proven himself on the battlefield as a capable commander, who could learn on the spot and was used to applying his methods of warfare in different situations. In addition to this, his energy and enthusiasm undoubtedly counterbalanced the negative view offered both by von Thoma and Funck who, like most of the 'old school' army generals, might not have found the appointment to their liking. This is why Rommel, who had been promoted major general in August 1939, was promoted again just six months later, on 7 February 1941. Rommel, now lieutenant general, was put in charge of the newly formed *Afrika Korps*, without taking into consideration that Rommel's experiences of command on the battlefield were limited to leading a battalion strong unit in 1917 and a single division in 1940, for a period not exceeding six weeks of war. This appointment was also done without considering that Rommel had no experience in tropical warfare or dealing with an ally like Italy. Nevertheless, Rommel's star was on the rise, and this influenced his future decisions once he arrived in Libya with his troops.

High level meetings came one after another, a clear signal of the importance of the mission he had been given. On 6 February Rommel met the Commander in Chief of the Army, who instructed him to assess the situation, wait for the arrival of all the German troops (the 5th Light Division was to be completed by mid-April, the 15th Panzer Division was to arrive in Libya by the end of May), and limit his activities to reconnaissance until the deployment was completed. The next step was Rome where Rommel, accompanied by Hitler's chief military aide General Rudolf Schmundt, met Mussolini. On 12 February 1941, Rommel arrived at Tripoli, a mere five days after the remnants of the 10th Italian Army had been defeated at Beda Fomm, and a few weeks before the Italian commander in Libya, Field Marshal Rodolfo Graziani, was officially relieved of command and replaced by General Italo Gariboldi. Rommel never met Graziani, but somehow managed to deal with his hosts who were clearly relieved by the arrival of the German troops. As the units were disembarked along with their vehicles and guns, parades were held at the centre of Tripoli with all the top-ranking personalities attending. Apocryphal stories have it that Rommel had the Panzer Regiment of the 5th Light Division circuiting around the town and parading more than one time to give the impression of a greater strength than the real one, but this is probably just part of the Rommel myth.

What is not part of the myth is how Rommel faced the situation. The first combat units of the 5th Light Division, which had just landed on the 14th, were immediately sent to the east and deployed at Sirte, soon seizing the position at the height of the Gulf of Bomba known as the Mugtaa defile. At the end of February, a frontline had been created, some 700 kilometres east of Tripoli and just 25 kilometres away from the nearest British positions. Historians would, and still are, debating whether General O'Connor might have seized Tripoli before the arrival of the German forces. This was another aspect of the Rommel myth. Many, if not most of the British generals who opposed him in North Africa have been criticised for their lack of skill and capabilities in handling the war, excluding Montgomery. This did not mean they were less capable than Rommel, probably just lacked his good fortune.

Reports from the frontline units were positive, as they showed that in front of them there was only a screening of enemy troops who lacked any aggressive intent, Rommel started planning to attack Tobruk, wanting to do so by 8 May. This plan required more transport capacity, which was simply not available. All Rommel could obtain was the permission to move the defensive front forward, and thereby exploit any favourable situation should the British forces present themselves as an easy target. However, Hitler did not inform Rommel that Germany was about to attack Greece (and Yugoslavia, a last-minute change of plans), and above all the Soviet Union. Only after the latter had been defeated would the necessary transport capacity be put at Rommel's disposal. For the time being no large-scale offensive was to take place in North Africa. No one had recalled that Rommel was not inclined to be idle, or let a chance be wasted. To try and make his view clear Rommel went to Germany for a series of meetings at the Army Staff, which proved to be unsatisfactory. Back in Libya on 24 March, after yet another meeting with Mussolini and General Gariboldi, Rommel was informed that the Italians did not want any advance into Cyrenaica, the easternmost province of Libya (the front approximately ran at the line dividing Tripolitania from Cyrenaica), because of the related supply issues, and because their own units were not ready for an offensive of any kind. In the meantime, General Streich, the commander of the 5th Light Division, carried out a series of armed reconnaissance which revealed that the positions before him had been vacated by the enemy troops. As Rommel returned to Africa, the 5th Light Division had advanced as far as Maradah, already reaching the limits of advance imposed by both the German and the Italian leaders and commanders.

The German 'mission command' style of warfare gave the local commander ample latitude with a certain degree of freedom of action, mainly because the commander on the spot was able to evaluate the situation first hand, by obtaining a better analysis than his superior commanders. There were limits to this freedom of action, since even the 'mission command' style of warfare required that local actions were carried out within a larger, and at times more complex, strategic, or operational framework. By imposing a limitation on Rommel's action both Hitler and the Army Staff were looking at the overall picture. The aim was to prepare and carry out a major offensive aimed at the Suez Canal, which was to link up with another attack aimed at the Middle East, and Vichy France Syria in particular. Such a double pincer attack would have permitted an invasion of the Middle East, with many consequences for the British Empire, with a possible advance towards the Far East. Any local action was considered premature, and likely to jeopardise the strategic planning. Needless to note, Rommel was not informed of the strategic situation, and all he could see was an opportunity which could not be missed. As he had done in the past, he tended to ignore orders which prevented him from seizing any favourable opportunity.

On 31 March, the 5th Light Division attacked the British positions at El Burayqah, which were seized after heavy fighting. The divisional reconnaissance unit went in pursuit of the retreating enemy, only to discover that its retreat seemed more extended than anticipated. The reconnaissance unit approached Adjdabia, and Streich had the entire division (or what was available) following it, seizing the town on 2 April with Rommel's consent. The opportunities were starting to develop, and Rommel asked for an Italian division to be put under his command. This led on 3 April to a sharp argument between Rommel and Gariboldi, who was strongly opposed to any further advance, on the grounds that the supply situation made it impossible. Rommel simply ignored him as he had done with the message from the Wehrmacht High Command instructing him not to advance, unless 'it can be determined beyond any doubt that the enemy is withdrawing most of his mobile units from Cyrenaica.' By adapting the directive to suit his needs, Rommel was able to confront Gariboldi claiming that he had been given freedom of action. In a matter of days, the roles reverted. If Rommel were intended to command a reserve unit at Italian disposal to defend Tripolitania, a task to be carried out until the arrival of the *Afrika Korps* had been completed, now he managed to take the lead and practically impose his decisions to the Italian commander, to whom he was formally subordinated. All this was aimed at securing another success on the battlefield.

The British Forces in Cyrenaica were not strong, the Commander in Chief Middle East, General Wavell, having had to send two divisions to

Greece to support the country facing the German attack. This situation was not considered serious because no main action from the German side was expected until May, when the two divisions in the area would have been completed and trained. As Rommel seized Adjdabia the commander of the 2nd Armoured Division facing him, General Gambier-Parry, ordered a retreat which was sanctioned by General Wavell, who had the 9th Australian Division deployed facing the *Afrika Korps*. It was clear that Rommel aimed at seizing Benghazi, which had already been considered given the situation. To make matters worse, Wavell complicated the situation with his decision to replace the XIII Corps commander, General Neame, with the more experienced General O'Connor who, in turn, persuaded him to keep Neame in command, having served as an advisor to the Middle East command.* The unavoidable chaos which ensued suited Rommel who, in the aftermath of the seizure of Adjdabia, on 3 April decided to attack with the aim of seizing the whole of Cyrenaica, which he managed, relying on his familiar style of command. Pursuing the withdrawing enemy and trying to keep the pressure constant, Rommel formed two groups. One, with the reconnaissance unit in the lead followed by the motorised elements of the Italian Brescia Division, which was to advance along the coast towards Benghazi while another, mostly formed of Italian units, was to advance inland with the bulk of the forces, consisting of the 5th Light Division and the Italian Ariete Armoured Division. What eventually occurred was a repetition of Rommel's experiences at Caporetto and in France, but in the unfamiliar and hostile desert area. Rommel was constantly on the move, trying to keep the units moving in the right direction and urging them to advance. This was a necessity never experienced in these conditions. The Western Desert was not the Italian Alps or France, lacking roads or even sound reference points. The result was that units lost their bearings, some becoming stuck in sand and others running out of fuel and supplies. This was a problem Rommel had not considered, focused as he was on the opportunity for a success.

---

* This was the designation adopted for the Western Desert Force at the beginning of January, the corps being de-activated in mid-February when all the units in Cyrenaica fell under direct command of the Headquarters Cyrenaica. The designation has been kept for simplicity.

The Italians had to come to help with their transport columns, while the 5th Light Division had to send all its motor vehicles back to pick up the much-needed supplies, only to remain immobilised for an entire day. A column with some 800 lorries was formed on 5 April to send supplies across the desert. Most of them reached their destination, some were lost in the desert, and the last one to be salvaged took a week.

Realising the danger, General O'Connor sent the 3rd Indian Brigade to Mechili to defend a large supply depot and block the road to Tobruk. Gambier-Parry withdrew from Msus too early, having destroyed the supply depot, which contributed to the loss of all the tanks of the 2nd Armoured Division which was supposed to support the Indians at Mechili. To make matters worse, both General O'Connor and General Neame, the 2nd Division commander, were taken prisoner by chance near Derna, which was seized on 8 April. As the Brescia Division reached the town, Rommel gave the order to reconnoitre the terrain to Tmimi and Tobruk, while forming a battle group with the units of both the 5th Light and the newly arrived 15th Panzer Division to attack Mechili and advance towards Tobruk. This was where elements of the 7th and 9th Australian Division were already withdrawing. In a week Rommel had seized Western Cyrenaica with no intention of stopping. By 10 April Rommel was convinced that the enemy was in full retreat, and his intention was to prevent any breakout from Tobruk while advancing to the Libyan–Egyptian border with the aim of reaching the Suez Canal. The 5th Light Division's reconnaissance unit was then sent to bypass Tobruk via Acroma and reach Bardia on the eastern side of the Cyrenaica bulge, which it managed by 12 April. After a brief attempt to halt the German advance at El Adem, the British forces withdrew to the Egyptian border leaving the Australians to garrison Tobruk. With the whole of Cyrenaica in his hands, all that Rommel had left to do was to seize Tobruk. For this task he calculated that the Brescia and 5th Light Division would suffice, ignoring another reality, namely the complete lack of knowledge of the Tobruk defences. This was something the 15th Panzer Division commander experienced first-hand when, driving unknowingly into an Australian field of fire, he was killed. The impromptu attack carried out on 11 April by elements of both the Brescia and the 5th Light Division clashed with a fortress defended by more than 24,000 well-armed and determined soldiers, who easily repulsed the enemy with losses. This was just the beginning of the battle for Tobruk.

Attacking an enemy stronghold is substantially different from attacking an enemy line of defence. The latter, once broken through, enabled the kind of warfare movement which suited Rommel. The former required careful preparation and study because it was only by locating the weak spots of the enemy defences and concentrating all the efforts against them, that a fortress like Tobruk could be seized. Rommel, as experienced at Cherbourg, had neither the patience nor the determination to prepare the attack against Tobruk. Above all he would not listen to advice, such as given him by General Heinrich Kirchheim. This general, aged 59 at the time, had served in German Southwest Africa for ten years since 1904, and was one of the few German experts on colonial warfare. He had been sent to Libya with the task of studying the environment and its requirements, only to be pressed by Rommel into taking over command of the battle group made up of elements from the Brescia Division. Relying on his experience, Kirchheim warned Rommel that the soldiers needed to familiarise with the environment before attacking, making it clear this was not Europe and that Africa had its peculiarities. Rommel simply ignored him and attacked Tobruk as planned on 13–14 April, only to realise that Kirchheim had been right. The 5th Light Division's Machine Gun Battalion 8 crossed the anti-tank ditch marking the outer Tobruk defence perimeter, and they defended its positions until the Panzer Regiment 5 attacked in the morning. However, lacking reference points and facing the unexpected Tobruk defences, the two groups soon lost contact, the tanks having to withdraw after the loss of 17 of them, and the Machine Gun Battalion soon found itself out of ammunition, having lost 280 men and forced to withdraw. Rommel blamed the weak commander of the 5th Light Division for the failure, ignoring all other factors such as the Tobruk defences. The Tobruk bunkers were simple underground shelters with a ground level opening, enabling the soldiers to fire at the enemy after surviving the artillery bombardment. The Australians learned that the ground opening could be concealed with tarpaulins, wood, sand, and being invisible would be bypassed by the attacking forces which could then be fired upon from the rear. Needless to say, Rommel later made extensive use of the Tobruk bunkers.

Undeterred, Rommel personally led another failed attempt to attack Tobruk on 16–17 April, also aimed at cutting off the Ras el Medauar bulge from where the Australian artillery could hit the Acroma crossroads, which enabled bypassing Tobruk. The attack failed, just as the Italians rejected Rommel's requests for reinforcements, for the simple reason that their infantry units took time to reach the Tobruk area lacking motor transport. On 23 April the British attacked the German held positions at the Libyan–Egyptian border. Another attack was attempted at Ras el Medauar on 30 April, again with the Machine Gun Battalion 8 and the Panzer Regiment 5 in the lead. Even if it eventually left a dent in the Ras el Medauar bulge, the new attack also ended in a failure for which Rommel blamed General Streich.[4]

The Winter Battle

On analysis Rommel's first experience in North Africa was a failure. Not so much from the military point of view, and both the German and the Italian propaganda used the re-conquest of Cyrenaica to boost the Axis as being again on the offensive, successfully both in the Balkans and in North Africa, which was true enough. Rommel's failure was not related with Tobruk or the failed destruction on the battlefield of the enemy forces, but to his handling of the *Afrika Korps*. Given it was his first time with command of a corps, Rommel simply handled it in the same way he had with his detachment from the Württemberg Mountain Regiment or the 7th Panzer Division. He never fully grasped the different situation and requirements of commanding a corps, which he treated just as a series of units which were asked to perform as he demanded to achieve their aims. Hence the clash with Streich, Rommel being used to exerting himself to the limit, but failing to understand that not everybody else could and would do the same. He would see to it personally, whenever possible, driven by what seemed an endless energy and determination. Thus, any failure could only be the result of somebody else not putting in the same effort and determination, and Rommel was not inclined to acknowledge his own limits, tending to finger-point whenever something did not go according to his plans.

This question of limits was clear to those at the German Army Staff, who acknowledged that the situation in North Africa required a direct intervention. Informed by Rommel of the British attack at the Egyptian border caused alarm, as it requested reinforcements which were unavailable, and the Chief of Army Staff concluded that Rommel was simply not up to the job as a corps commander in North Africa. Not only had Rommel's handling of the various units in piecemeal actions severely impacted on their actual strength, but he also appeared to have no clear idea of their situation and deployment. In order to try and resolve the situation, Halder decided to send his chief of the operations staff, General Paulus, to North Africa for an inspection. The choice was particularly apt since Paulus and Rommel were on good terms, and Paulus was considered the only one who could exercise a personal and direct influence on Rommel, who was regarded by General Halder as having 'gone stark mad'. When Paulus arrived in Libya, he found what could best be described as a disastrous situation. Supplies were chaotic, naval transport from Italy to Libya was being successfully harassed by the Royal Navy and the Royal Air Force, all of which managed to reduce the amount of shipping reaching Tripoli. This port, along with the smaller Benghazi, were the only harbours available for unloading the units and the supplies, and both had limited capacity. The starting point of Streich's attack in March was some 750 kilometres away from Tripoli, which required the use of 750 tons of transport capacity. The advance to the Egyptian border and the siege of Tobruk more than doubled the distances, at the same time the arrival of the 15th Panzer Division also increased requirements. This was all without considering factors such as the limited transport capabilities, the supplies being mainly brought by trucks along the only available paved road, (the *via Balbia* running along the coast), and the fact that a new road had to be built to bypass Tobruk (the 'Axis Road') enabling supplies to reach the border at Sollum and the Halfaya Pass.

Other factors soon emerged, such as the issue of the *Afrika Korps* not being examined and advised before sending German troops to North Africa. The Italians supplied foodstuff and fuel, neither of which met the German requirements. Food was not just a matter of taste, but of nutritional value. The Italian supplies were rather poor, with the result that sickness spread amongst the *Afrika Korps* soldiers. Fuel was also inadequate, the Italians relying on diesel which the Germans did not use. In addition, no provision had been made for desert conditions. Sand damaged the non-tropical developed German air-filters, reducing the lifetime of the engines to half their average capability. Tanks required an overhaul after some 1–1,500 kilometres, which meant that once disembarked at Tripoli they could reach Tobruk or even the Egyptian border, but after that journey they ended up in the repair shop for the much-needed overhaul. In addition to these issues were the quarrels with the Italians about the breaking down of supplies, undermining co-operation between the Axis allies.

When Paulus met Rommel on 27 April the latter described the supply situation as quite satisfactory and insisted on carrying out the attack against Tobruk as planned. Paulus eventually gave his approval with the aim of taking time for a personal evaluation of the situation. At 18.15 on 30 April the 5th Light and the 15th Panzer Division (which had one of its regiments brought in by air transport), supported by the Italian Ariete and Brescia divisions, attacked Tobruk without adequate preparations, or even rest. Kirchheim, temporarily replacing Streich, had carried out his own personal reconnaissance of the ground which enabled his units to advance faster and deeper than the others. As a result, the elements of the 5th Light Division broke through the outer defences of Tobruk, but the 15th Panzer Division did not. Eventually, Rommel had to accept that even this last attempt had failed, and it simply created a bulge in the Tobruk line of defence, where Kirchheim's soldiers remained in the positions they had seized. Paulus, after an initial optimistic evaluation of the situation, soon realised that Tobruk would not be easy to win, and he agreed with Rommel that more units were needed before making another attempt. The decision was sanctioned by the Army Staff, which started planning supplies to help Rommel, who desperately needed help. Opposed by an Australian counterattack, Kirchheim's men faced a shortage of ammunition revealing the extent of the supply crisis to Paulus, who concluded that the key to waging war in North Africa was not Tobruk or the positions at the Libyan–Egyptian border, but supplies. When Paulus reported back to General Halder, the latter just remarked that Rommel could not cope with the situation.

Between May and November 1941, the situation in North Africa remained calm, apart from two attempts made by the British to break through the Axis positions at the border, at Sollum, and at the Halfaya Pass, which were both repulsed, and followed by a German attack (Operation *Skorpion*) aimed at securing the possession of the vital Halfaya Pass, enabling movement along the *via Balbia* at the border. Rommel's staff did not remain idle, working at the same time on a plan for the attack against Tobruk and on another plan, an offensive into Egypt aimed at reaching the Nile. For this effort even more reinforcements and supplies were needed. Rommel was clearly not at ease with this kind of work, and he indulged in a series of inspections of the frontline units, unaware that fortune was going to be on his side again. Following the arrival of the majority of both the 5th Light and of the 15th Panzer Division, the *Afrika Korps* was now a full fighting force capable of independent actions, but still relying on the Italians for a series of tasks, not the least besieging Tobruk. Relations between the Germans and the Italians were not particularly good, and the liaison staff which had been provisionally created was not working well. A more efficient organisation of the available forces was needed, above all a single command was deemed necessary. For these reasons on 15 August Rommel's command was upgraded, creating a new structure, and pushing Rommel's career far beyond expectations. On 1 July 1941, Rommel was promoted General der Panzertruppen, the final rise to full generalship. On 15 August (although the official date was set to 1 September) the Panzer Group Afrika was created in order to take over command of the *Afrika Korps*, and over the Italian corps besieging Tobruk. On this occasion several heads rolled, and new staff officers were brought in, as Rommel had specifically requested. Rommel had moved yet another step up on the ladder after just three months of his last promotion, and four months in command of a corps, incidentally without showing much skill or capability in his handling of the new situation.[5]

By the summer of 1941 the overall strategic situation changed. Since May the British (along with the Commonwealth and Imperial forces) managed to take complete control of the situation in Africa and in the Middle East, first by defeating the Italians in East Africa, then by subduing the revolt in Iraq, and eventually by seizing Vichy-France Syria, thereby depriving the Germans of any real chance of driving into the Middle East. Also, by the summer of 1941 the Germans had to acknowledge that Operation *Barbarossa* was failing, because the Soviet Union could not be defeated in a single campaign. By the end of the year the German plans for the invasion of the Middle East via Turkey and North Africa were shelved, North Africa was left as the only theatre of war where Germany was confronting Britain as an army. Naturally, the German propaganda exploited the situation focusing on Rommel, who was suited to become a 'star' general, which Goebbels exploited to the full. Quite extraordinarily, the fame of the Desert Fox owed much to the British propaganda, which seemed inclined to attribute their failures in North Africa to the great commander rather than to the failure of their own military leaders. As a result, the myth of the 'Desert Fox' was born much to Rommel's pleasure, who probably started to believe what was said about him. The British counteroffensive soon put the newly promoted general to the test.

The British *Crusader* offensive, which led to what the Germans called the 'winter battle', was the first real clash between the two sides since the arrival of the German troops in Africa. The British assault, led by the newly formed 8th Army, came just a few days before Rommel's planned attack on Tobruk, and found the newly formed Panzer Group Afrika in relatively good shape apart from supplies. The British air and naval interdiction had practically halted the flow of supplies from Italy, compelling Rommel to resort to the available stocks. On 18 November large columns of armoured and motorised troops moved inland from the border towards Tobruk, while infantry units attacked the German and Italian positions at Sollum and at Halfaya. The first clash took place on the following day, as the British units approached Tobruk from the south. The Italian Ariete division was attacked at Bir el Gubi and the *Afrika Korps* clashed with the 7th Armoured Division at Sidi Rezegh. In both cases the British forces suffered losses and were compelled to withdraw. On 20 November, as the 8th Army positions south of Tobruk were strengthened, Rommel faced a new situation. The *Afrika Korps* commander, General Ludwig Crüwell, had realised by the 19th that this was not just a reconnaissance in force but a major offensive. Rommel did not believe that until the next day, unable to organise any kind of appropriate reaction given the state of confusion on the battlefield. This situation enabled the 8th Army to attack in the direction of Tobruk with the aim of relieving the siege while the bulk of the *Afrika Korps*, with the 15th and the 21st Panzer Division (the latter formed in August from the 5th Light Division) attacked towards the border before turning west, moving against the British 7th Armoured Division. Since the attempt to relieve the beleaguered Tobruk garrison had failed, the opportunity presented itself for a German counterattack, which aimed at Sidi Rezegh just to the south of the town. Only at this juncture Rommel seemed to have fully grasped the situation, and he reacted as usual. The first result was a clash with the Italians. The Italian motorised corps, led by General Gastone Gambara, was deployed south of Tobruk but was not directly subordinated to the Panzer Group Afrika, and when requested to join forces with the *Afrika Korps*, Gambara replied saying that he could only send part of the Ariete Division. Rommel was not pleased with the reply and directly asked Mussolini to put Gambara's corps under his command, which the Duce did, reminding Rommel that he was subordinated to the Italian commander in Libya. Gambara did not respond as Rommel wanted, but on 23 November developments would bring a change to the entire battle.

On what the Germans called the 'battle of Remembrance Day' (23 November, the day in remembrance of the dead of the protestant church), the 15th Panzer Division led by Crüwell attacked and destroyed part of the 1st South African Division at Sidi Rezegh. Even though the German division suffered heavy losses, the battle was considered a success and the reports, clearly exaggerated, said that the bulk of the enemy forces had been destroyed. Rommel, apart from lamenting the absence of the Italian units on the battlefield, reacted as accustomed, purporting complete success by the destruction of the entire enemy forces. Rommel's reaction to the 'battle of the remembrance' has been analysed in detail and has been criticised, showing Rommel's incapability of leading an army corps on the battlefield. Rommel's plan was the result of a series of circumstances, indicative of his style of command. Rommel had left the headquarters of the Panzer Group to inspect the frontline units, as he was used to when leading in combat. As he had experienced already in France, the result was that he lost contact with his headquarters, which was then led by his chief of staff. One of the consequences of this situation was that Rommel only received summary reports on the 'battle of Remembrance Day', which suggested that the bulk of the attacking force had been destroyed. Basing his plan on these reports, Rommel conceived a daring move, namely, to attack the enemy at the back in the border area, with the aim of destroying his supply bases leading to the complete destruction of the enemy forces. It must be noted that analysing the plan on a purely academic basis, it had its merits. Striking at the enemy when it is weaker is the best way to achieve success on the battleground, and the idea of striking at the very root of the enemy offensive was daring indeed, and if successful, it could have led to a brilliant success. This time fortune would not be on Rommel's side, with the consequences which followed.

In his recent work on the armoured warfare in North Africa, the American historian Robert Forczyk analysed in detail Rommel's 'dash to the wire' (the name of the attack related to the barbed wire obstacle the Italians had put along the border between Libya and Egypt), making some relevant criticisms. Bypassing the divisional command at about 4.00 hours on 24 November, Rommel ordered that the 21st Panzer Division's Panzer Regiment moved towards the Sollum–Halfaya area, without informing Crüwell of his plan until they met. At this point Crüwell objected to the entire plan asking for more caution, pointing out that the two Panzer Divisions badly needed rest, reorganisation, and re-supply. Furthermore, there were some 80 German tanks on the battleground which needed recovery and repair, in order to bring the *Afrika Korps* up to strength. Eventually, Crüwell tried to make the point that the battle of 'Remembrance Day' may have been a success, but that the enemy forces had not been as badly mauled as one might have imagined. Both Rommel's operations and intelligence officer, Colonels Siegfried Westphal and von Mellenthin, agreed with Crüwell, recommending that the *Afrika Korps* be deployed near Tobruk to prevent another attempt to relieve the siege, and pointing out the presence of the New Zealand Division approaching from the east. Rommel was facing a situation where he was asked to act as an army commander, as this was his role at the time, but he simply failed to grasp the realities of the situation and acted in his usual way. As Forczyk commented, Rommel was a man of action, and he was neither used nor inclined to listen to the advice of his staff or of his subordinate commanders, especially when they did not agree with him. Rommel's plan was evidently bold and imaginative, but it lacked the necessary substance required by modern warfare, especially when relying on a motorised force. Rommel's reply to the need for re-supplying was simple, namely capture the British fuel dumps which would provide the necessary resources. He did not add that their actual locations were unknown, which made their capture difficult.

Rommel's demands and expectations hardly differed from those he had made to his subordinates at Caporetto and in France, but this time the situation was very different. The 21st Panzer Division could be refuelled using its own limited resources, but it was only ready to move at 9.00 followed by the 15th Panzer Division at 12.30. Gambara's motorised corps, which had only been given sketchy instructions, started its march half an hour later. Rommel, with incredible speed, reached the Egyptian border with the leading elements of the columns at 16.00 hours, but without realising that the *Afrika Korps* was now a spent force. The more than 100 kilometres march had reduced the actual number of tanks in running order to a few dozen, which by then were lacking fuel. Rommel even refused to use the divisional repair companies to recover the tanks lost or abandoned along the route, using them instead as a combat formation. Rommel had some luck when at night, he and his chief of staff's vehicle broke down, the two were accidentally found by Crüwell whose vehicle was not able to cross the barbed wire obstacle. As a result, the three, namely the commander of Panzer Group Afrika, his Chief of Staff and the commander of the *Afrika Korps* spent the night in the open, surrounded by enemy troops. Only at dawn was the group able to rejoin the bulk of the German forces, probably unaware of the risk they had faced. For the next two days, until 26 November, the battle turned into a series of small unit actions which brought no result at all to the Axis side, while the surrounded Tobruk garrison managed to break through the surrounding forces and link up with the advancing New Zealand Division. Informed of these latest developments, on the night of the 26th Rommel ordered that the *Afrika Korps* return to the Tobruk area the next day. This was a belated reaction, unlikely to change the course of the entire battle. The German official history described Rommel's actions this way:

> His thrust did not even relieve the pressure on his own troops on the Sollum front, but it did lead to senseless losses of irreplaceable troops and equipment, especially as a result of the efforts of the Royal Air Force, which was able to attack the Africa Corps with impunity after the New Zealanders captured the airfield used by German fighters at Kambut [Gambut]. The Africa Corps was so exhausted after returning from its unsuccessful raid that it was not able to change the situation in Germany's favour.[6]

Forczyk's analysis pushes the criticism of Rommel's command even further:

> As a commander, Rommel consistently sneered at logistic issues, but his decision to prioritize supporting isolated frontier garrisons over his support units was another serious mistake. Finally, Rommel's 'dash to the wire' antics inflicted further damage upon his worn-out tanks and exhausted crews for no real gains.[7]

As Forczyk pointed out, Rommel's command during the 'Winter Battle' indicates that he remained ignorant of the technical and logistical requirements of modern armoured warfare, which some of his officers knew better than him.

Rommel's attitude towards his subordinates was well known, but in this case, he pushed matters to the limit. For about a week the battle raged in the Tobruk area, the encirclement having been broken and the Axis forces being unable to restore the situation. Eventually, on 5 December, Rommel opted for the only available solution, withdrawal. This was also the consequence of the latest news from Rome, which informed him that no supplies or reinforcements would be brought by sea until January 1942. The withdrawal was limited to the Gazala line to the west of Tobruk, which led to another complication. Rommel had a meeting on 7 December with General Ettore Bastico, the Italian commander in Libya who had replaced General Gariboldi. Rommel managed to have all the German and Italian troops in Cyrenaica put under his command, while insisting on withdrawing further to the west, in which he faced opposition from Bastico and General Gambara. A serious clash ensued with Gambara, who strongly objected to Rommel's idea of a complete withdrawal from Cyrenaica and insisted on defending the Gazala line. Bastico's opposition was more due to political reasons because he knew that Mussolini did not want to face the loss of Cyrenaica again, and Gambara's reaction was more practical. He understood that the Italian units were 'foot-slogged', and as such could not move with the same speed as the German units. The danger was that the advancing 8th Army had destroyed the bulk of the slow-moving Italian units, while the *Afrika Korps* had sought safety at the border between Cyrenaica and Tripolitania. The argument had its merits, but Rommel was determined to withdraw. Amongst the consequences of this move was to leave the Italian Savona Division, along with German units, isolated at Bardia, Sollum, and the Halfaya. The isolated garrisons could not be resupplied, and they were attacked one after the other by the 8th Army until the last one, the Halfaya Pass garrison, surrendered on 17 January 1942. The overall losses amounted to some 10,400 Italian and 4,300 German soldiers taken prisoner. Rommel's clash with Gambara reached a critical point in January 1942, when the Italian Chief of General Staff General Ugo Cavallero was forced to intervene. The eventual result was the removal of Gambara, which effectively put Rommel in charge of the operations in North Africa. By 13 January 1942 the *Afrika Korps* had withdrawn to El Agheila, which was the same starting position of Streich's attack in March 1941. For the first time in his career, Rommel had faced a personal defeat on the battlefield.[8]

Rise to the Top

On 5 January the first convoy bringing reinforcements and supplies arrived at Tripoli, with Rommel wasting no time with formalities. By the 18th Rommel warned that, given the temporary superiority on the field of the Axis forces which had been ascertained by his intelligence, attack was necessary in order to destroy the enemy forces deployed before the Axis lines. On 20 January, as Rommel was informed that he had been awarded the swords to his Knight's Cross, the Wehrmacht High Command was informed of the attack plan. At 8.30 on the next day the attack started, taking the 8th Army completely by surprise. By the 22nd, Adjdabia was seized, again paving the way for a further advance. Unexpectedly, Rommel faced opposition from his own side. On 23 January General Cavallero visited Rommel to inform him of Mussolini's concerns about the offensive, which in his view was premature given the precarious supply situation. Rommel found himself facing a wall of concern which included, apart from Mussolini, figures such as Cavallero and Field Marshal Albert Kesselring, the newly appointed Luftwaffe commander in the Mediterranean. As was his custom, Rommel simply ignored both the orders and the arguments claiming that, given his promotion to Colonel General which had come the day before (in fact it was announced on the 24th, the actual promotion being dated 1 February), only Hitler could actually make him change his mind, reminding them that the bulk of the troops engaged were in fact German. Adding further weight to Rommel's argument, on 20 January 1942 the Panzer Group was officially renamed Panzer Army Afrika. It may be assumed that this was not a blatant way to ignore the orders he was given, nevertheless, Rommel took the opportunity to circumnavigate them to make his point. He was intimating that he was the one in charge in North Africa, all were subordinated to his will. Eventually, the bulk of the Italian troops were left at the Mersa el Brega position, mainly because of Bastico's personal intervention, while the *Afrika Korps* continued with the attack destroying near Adjdabia 117 enemy tanks and taking some 1,000 prisoners, while the bulk of the British forces withdrew east towards Msus. It was this success which enabled the *Afrika Korps* to set off in pursuit and reached Msus on 25 January, while along the coast the advance of the 90th Light Afrika Division (which had arrived in Libya in 1941) was also starting. On the 27th the group deployed at Msus split in three, moving with two columns east, north-east and to the west, towards Benghazi. The two columns, from the east and south, seized the harbour town on 29 January as the German forces approached Marawa, the town on the *via Balbia* at the gates of the mountain range at the top of Cyrenaica. As the 8th Army withdrew east, the pursuit continued to Mussolini's concern, because of the possibility of a British counterattack. This potential problem transpired to be exaggerated, as on 2 February the leading German column reached the village of Berta, which opened the way to Tobruk. Two days later the column moving along the coast had approached Gazala, which was reached on the 6th by the other columns forming a line before the Tobruk front. This time Rommel did not try to attack the enemy defences or to seize Tobruk, but instead he formed a line facing the 8th Army defences along the Gazala–Bir Hakim line. For the next three and a half months, both sides were facing one another preparing for the attack. In the meantime, Rommel was to discover that as he faced the opposition of the 8th Army there were other issues.

In December 1941, facing the critical supply situation in North Africa, Hitler had decided to send to Italy reinforcements of air units along with Field Marshal Albert Kesselring, who was given the title of Commander in Chief South. Curiously, the title was not as it sounded, as Kesselring only commanded the German air force units in Italy, which in the Mediterranean area had the task of preventing the Royal Air Force and the Royal Navy from attacking the naval traffic between Italy and Africa.

Field Marshal Albert Kesselring. (*Polish Digital Archives*)

Kesselring at the controls of his aircraft. (*Bundesarchiv, Bild 146-1981-066-21A/CC-BY-SA 3.0*)

Kesselring with Wilhelm Speidel and Göring, c.1940. (*Bundesarchiv, Bild 146-2006-0107/CC-BY-SA 3.0*)

A formal portrait of Kesselring. (*Polish Archives*)

Smiling Kesselring in North Africa. (*Polish Archives: Photographer Krempl*)

Kesselring and Rommel in debate, August 1942. (*Polish Archives, Narodowe Archywum Cyfrowe*)

Kesselring as usual visiting the frontline in Italy, 1944. (*Bundesarchiv, Bild 101I-316-1195-04/Demmer/ CC-BY-SA 3.0*)

Kesselring with Westphal to his left visiting the Italian front, January 1944. (*Polish Archives: Photographer Dreesen*)

Kesselring as witness at Nuremberg Trial. (*Truman Library: Photographer Charles W. Alexander*)

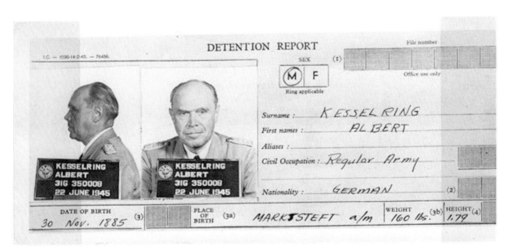

Kesselring's detention papers. (*US Museum of World War II*)

The young, ambitious Rommel. (*Wikimedia*)

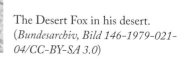

The Desert Fox in his desert. (*Bundesarchiv, Bild 146-1979-021-04/CC-BY-SA 3.0*)

Rommel in North Africa.
(*Bundesarchiv, Bild 101I-443-1589-09/ Ernst A. Zwilling/CC-BY-SA 3.0*)

Rommel and General Fritz Bayerlein in the Sd.Kfz. 250/3 command vehicle. (*Bundesarchiv, Bild 101I-784-0238-06A/Moosmüller/CC-BY-SA 3.0*)

Rommel using binoculars in the desert. (*Bundesarchiv, Bild 101I-784-0238-06A/Moosmüller/CC-BY-SA 3.0*)

Kesselring and Rommel always in debate. (*Bundesarchiv, Bild 101I-786-0306-37A/Moosmüller/CC-BY-SA 3.0*)

Rommel. (*Bundesarchiv, Bild 183-J16362/ Winkelmann/CC-BY-SA 3.0*)

Rommel with officers inspecting defences on a French beach. (*Bundesarchiv, Bild 101I-719-0243-33/ Jesse/CC-BY-SA 3.0*)

Rommel with Sepp Dietrich in France. (*Polish Archives, Narodowe Archywum Cyfrowe*)

Model on the frontline. (*Public domain*)

Model with his Fieseler 156 Storch, 1943. (*tormentor4555 via Wikimedia Commons*)

Model with Rundstedt and General Hans Krebs (right). (*Bundesarchiv, Bild 146-1978-024-31/CC-BY-SA 3.0*)

Model on the frontline. (*Public domain*)

Model and Guderian on the frontline. (*tormentor4555 via Wikimedia Commons*)

Model speaks with Lieutenant Buchterkirch on the eastern front. (*Bundesarchiv, Bild 183-2005-1017-519/ Fritz Lucke/CC-BY-SA 3.0*)

Model planning next move at frontline of Aachen. (*Bundesarchiv, Bild 183-1992-0617-506/Scheerer (e)/ CC-BY-SA 3.0*)

Model checking western defences. (*Polish Archives, Narodowe Archywum Cyfrowe*)

The grand title was mainly to ensure Kesselring's position with regard to Mussolini and to the Italian General Staff, the 'Comando Supremo'. In order to ensure German independence and influence over the Italians, Hitler had put Kesselring under Mussolini's direct command, but with Kesselring responding directly to Hitler himself. This way Mussolini was compelled to sign all the directives issued by the General Staff which involved, directly or indirectly, Kesselring and his forces. The appearance of Kesselring on the scene came as an unpleasant surprise to Rommel who, on the other hand, was still formally subordinated to the Italian Commander in Chief in Libya, which was one step below Kesselring, and he had no formal ties with Hitler directly. The reply given by him to General Cavallero on 23 January was simply indicative of how little Rommel felt having to deal with Kesselring, whose position he envied, as it indicated a direct link with Hitler that never existed. Rommel attempted to put himself in the same position of the Commander in Chief South, but in the months which followed it became clear that co-operation between Rommel and Kesselring would be immensely difficult.

The major issue of the war in North Africa and the Mediterranean in 1942 was Malta, and whether Malta could actually be seized posed serious questions. On paper the problem was simple. Malta represented the main obstacle to the naval traffic between Italy and Libya, and as such it posed a hurdle for the operations of the Panzer Army Afrika. A solution was found by diverting at least some of the routes to Greece, the ships facing a longer but safer journey, in transporting troops by air, and in 'neutralising' Malta with a series of air attacks. This made it possible to increase supplies for the troops in North Africa, but it was clear that the solution was short-term. Kesselring knew that the air campaign against Malta could not last forever, because Hitler had made it clear that by June the air units deployed to Italy would be needed for the new offensive against the Soviet Union. The seizure of Malta with a sea and air-borne assault offered a more permanent solution, which would have secured supplies for North Africa indefinitely. Rommel agreed to the idea, but he was barely involved in the planning and in the dealing with the Italians. This was Kesselring's task, who supported the plan and dealt with Mussolini, Hitler, and their general staffs. Rommel's only focus was on the offensive against Egypt, which he was determined to carry out once Tobruk had been attacked and seized. As the German historian Klaus Schmider pointed out, it is highly doubtful that Rommel could achieve a 'decision in the Mediterranean' even if he managed to reach the Nile and advance across it into the Middle East. In 1942 the entire area was firmly in British hands following the successful reaction to the Iraqi revolt and the seizure of Syria. The German forces could not, as it had been planned, drive into the Middle East from the north, either via Turkey or from the Caucasus, simply because there were not enough for the task. Had Rommel advanced to the Suez Canal, the only practical result would have been to drive the Mediterranean Fleet away from Alexandria. An invasion of the Middle East would have been a spectacular propaganda success, without any practical results. It would have taken one year at least, before the oil from the Middle East wells could be transported either to Germany or Italy and given the weakness of the forces at Rommel's disposal, no further advance would have been possible. From a strategic point of view, the Mediterranean was now a secondary theatre of war where the Axis could only prepare themselves to face the incoming American attack.

It is obvious that Rommel rarely considered these strategic issues at all, his attention was focused on the Nile and the Suez Canal, because reaching them meant concluding a successful campaign, which was all he wanted. As such anything else had to be subordinated to his own aims. The Italians had examined the Malta problem in 1939, concluding that in order to seize the island, the entire battle fleet had to be committed. Being neither prepared nor willing to take such a risk, they simply decided that in case of war against France and Britain, Libya would have been isolated and made their plans accordingly. The idea of seizing Malta was resumed at the end of 1941 by General Cavallero, facing the growing supply situation of North Africa, but it was not until early January 1942 that the project was seriously considered. Kesselring attempted to take control of the entire plan, but the Italians secured their own influence and started to ask for German support. This included troops, such as the paratrooper division which had seized Crete, and a large number of weapons and materiel, including landing craft. On 11–12 April Mussolini gave his consent to the plan, but this time it was Hitler's turn to be sceptical. Doubting that the Italians could carry out such a task, he was clearly reluctant to commit any German troops, let alone deliver all that the Italians were asking. Somehow, Rommel may have influenced Hitler's decision. By early 1942 the Panzer Army was in a delicate situation facing a solid line of defence held by the 8th Army, which could rely on Tobruk for the supplies, while his southern flank was open and the lines of supply uncertain. Rommel realised he was running a race with his enemies, believing the one who attacked first would in all likelihood be the victor. For this reason, he advocated the seizure of Malta before he attacked Tobruk, in order to secure the lines of supply. Meeting Kesselring on 7–8 April, Rommel agreed that in order for the attack against Tobruk to succeed, it had to be launched at the end of May or in early June, which created problems with air support. As Kesselring noted, the Luftwaffe units in the Mediterranean could not support at the same time the assault on Malta as well as the attack against Tobruk. This required that the Malta assault be launched after Rommel had attacked and possibly seized Tobruk. By mid-April both Mussolini and Hitler had agreed to the assault against Malta, which was given the final go-ahead after they met at the Obersalzberg on the 29th. The idea of attacking Tobruk first then starting the assault against Malta was agreed, but because the preparations for the latter were still ongoing, the delay made the operation impossible until June–August. All this was agreed without considering the contradictory plans which the Italian and German staffs were preparing. The situation was such that Hitler, after being informed of the situation by the commander of the German paratrooper force General Student on 22 May, lost any interest in the plan, because he decided the Italians were simply not up to the task. The Italians lost interest as well, and after a series of postponements and constant requests made to the Germans for the supply of troops and materiel, eventually gave up the entire plan. Following the seizure of Tobruk, General, now promoted Field Marshal Cavallero, had already decided that the plan had to be discontinued since early July.

Despite the bickering between Rommel and Kesselring, the latter continuing with his views even after the war, even though the two had no decision to make as it had been entirely in Hitler's hands. Once Tobruk was seized, Rommel's request to continue with the offensive into Egypt had little to do with the planned seizure of Malta, which was not likely to be carried out at all. Rommel's real decision was more of an operational nature, to continue with the offensive relying on the fact that the enemy had been defeated, and to reorganise before advancing into Egypt. This was Rommel's aim, and the concept at the root of plan *Venezia* was merely intended to pave the way to the 1941 attack on Egypt, which the staff of the Panzer Army resumed at the same time. The plan was a classic 'hook' into the enemy lines, aimed at the destruction of the forces deployed along the defence line to pave the way for a subsequent attack and seizure of Tobruk. The entire mechanised force, which included the *Afrika Korps*, the Italian Ariete Armoured and Trieste Motorised Division, were to bypass the Gazala line of defence turning north and be deployed between Tobruk and Gazala. Then the German and Italian troops would attack the line on both sides, a seaborne landing was intended to take place along the coast while the back of the encircling force was to be secured by the 90th Afrika Division. The plan itself revealed that Rommel was too fatigued to grasp the realities of desert warfare, an encirclement of this kind was better suited to the European than to the African terrain, where units could move almost at will despite the threat of being surrounded. Rommel had also not learned the lesson of the 'Winter Battle' and insisted on leading the mechanised force, putting the northern assault formation under command of General Crüwell. In this case, fortune would be on Rommel's side.

The attack started in the night between 26 and 27 May, the German units advancing as planned due to the help of specialised navigators trained to use the stars as a reference, some Italians shifting north and clashing with the enemy forces. In the meantime, Crüwell attacked the main defence line in the north, approaching it but not breaking through. As the outflanking force halted for rest and refuel, at about 19.00 hours, the presence of strong enemy formations in front of the *Afrika Korps* was reported, leading Rommel to issue the variant to the plan which envisaged a wider movement to the south and to the east, the only way in his opinion to encircle the bulk of the enemy forces. At 21.00 the entire attacking group advanced to the south of Bir Hakeim, along a front some 50 kilometres wide. Without encountering any enemy forces, not even reconnaissance, the attacking group moved as planned, and after another rest-pause and refuel, at 4.30 on 27 May, they turned north and eventually made contact. At 7.00 the 15th Panzer Division clashed with the British 4th Armoured Brigade, which effectively stopped its movement. This led the neighbouring 21st Panzer Division to halt as well, in order to preserve cohesion, while the 15th Panzer Division almost destroyed the 4th Armoured Brigade which withdrew north-east towards El Adem. Rommel's moment of caution did not last for long, and by 7.45 he cancelled his order to hold off, replacing it with the instruction to push on at all costs along the north-eastern direction. By 10.00 the *Afrika Korps* had crossed the line Bir Hakeim–El Adem, reaching the vital crossroad behind the Gazala Line known as Knightsbridge, just as the 90th Afrika Division approached El Adem. At 12.35 Rommel ordered the last step of the drive forward, the advance to the coast, but as he made his appearance at the headquarters of the *Afrika Korps* at 14.15, he realised that the plan was not going as he anticipated. The 21st and 15th Panzer Division were being attacked from all directions, and they were unable to move forward. Even this did not prevent Rommel from ordering them to resume the movement at 14.45, an order with which only the 21st Panzer Division was able to comply, as the 15th Panzer Division was not able to move until 15.30. However, this left its right flank exposed, and as the division started to move, it was attacked by the British 2nd Armoured Brigade, joined quickly by the 22nd Armoured Brigade. The threat was only checked due to the intervention of the *Afrika Korps* battle group, and in particular the anti-aircraft regiment which established a three-kilometre line of guns which started pounding the enemy tanks. Even so, a Panzer unit had to be detached from the 21st Panzer Division in order to check the enemy armour and prevent their attack from infiltrating the rear of the 15th Panzer Division. Eventually, at 18.10 the *Afrika Korps* command gave the order to stop and regroup while digging in for the defence, as both Panzer divisions were being attacked again by strong British armoured formations. They were still a long way from the coast. The Italian motorised corps could not come to the rescue, by drifting north it led them into the minefields causing them to be stuck in the Gazala defence line. A first attempt to attack the Free-French held positions at Bir Hakeim failed, and the only success the Italians managed to achieve was to open a clear path along the minefields through the defence line.

As the night fell on 27 May, it became clear that Rommel's plan had been a complete fiasco. Not a single one of the attacking groups had reached the established positions, and the enemy forces were reacting strongly. Clearly, despite the successful march and the swift advance, the enemy forces had not been encircled and were now able to react threatening to surround the attacking forces themselves. As had happened before, the sluggishness of Rommel's enemy forces came to his rescue. The British reaction was slow and led to disruption in the command chain. For a moment Rommel considered withdrawing to the starting line, the entire advance to be reduced to a 'reconnaissance in strength' to save face. However, Rommel realised that he held the advantage because the British armoured formations had been sent to attack piecemeal rather than with a single co-ordinated, and concentrated strike which showed their weakness, suggesting they could be reduced in strength much more than his defending forces. In the attempt to regain the capability to manoeuvre, Rommel sent the 21st Panzer Division to advance to the north (the 15th Panzer Division being held to defend its rear as per *Afrika Korps's* command suggestion), with the 90th Afrika Division swinging to the west and joining the *Afrika Korps*, while General Crüwell's forces were asked to break through the defence line. The German advance was halted again, and only on the 29th the attacking forces were able to regroup in the Knightsbridge area. In the meantime, General Crüwell had been captured, his place taken by Kesselring who had been visiting his headquarters. The fact that a field marshal, Kesselring in particular, was being put under his command probably pleased Rommel even in a moment of difficulty. In fact, Rommel had been compelled to face a new situation, his initial order to continue the attack northwards having been rescinded at 6.25 on the 29th given the strong enemy presence in the area. The *Afrika Korps* had now been joined by the Italian divisions, but they were attacked in force by the 2nd and 22nd British Armoured Brigade, the 4th Armoured Brigade being held by a sandstorm. As the attack was being repulsed in a fierce artillery and tank-versus-tank fight, the 15th Panzer Division moved south to consolidate the contact with the Italian Ariete Division, to meet with the supply column moving from the south. Facing this situation, the *Afrika Korps* commander General Nehring, suggested that the entire army be moved south-west along the minefields of the British defence line. This was in order to secure a supply line across the minefields, which would be opened by the Panzer Army along with the Italian Pavia and Trieste divisions. It took some time and three other British attacks before Rommel did what he had never done before, namely, withdraw taking the advice of a subordinate commander. At night the Panzer Army started deploying near Sidi Miftah, east of the positions held by the British 150th Infantry Division. What would be fought now was an entirely different battle.

The move prevented a crisis and enabled the Panzer Army to regroup and be resupplied, with the result that at 6.30 on 31 May, both the German Panzer Divisions reported that they were again ready to attack. The supply crisis was overcome the next day, apart from a shortage of water for the 90th Afrika Division, showing that even Rommel had to change his plans because of logistical needs. The battle which was fought in what the British called *the Cauldron* and the Germans *the Sausage Boiler*, was a battle to open a passage across the Gazala defence line in the 150th Brigade sector. This lasted until 1 June, when Rommel developed a completely different plan. Rather than trying to continue with the attacks to the north, he decided to concentrate against the southern-most tip of the Gazala defence line at Bir Hakeim. The seizure of this area would have effectively broken through the entire southern portion of the defence line, thus providing the Panzer Army with the necessary capability to manoeuvre, which Rommel needed to defeat the enemy forces. It would also enable a Panzer Division to recover the tanks on the battlefield while launching diversionary attacks to the east. Bir Hakim, strongly defended by the Free French forces, was attacked at 6.00 on 2 June by the Italian Trieste and the 90th Afrika Division, supported by all the reconnaissance units of the *Afrika Korps*. They were immediately opposed by strong resistance, helped by the barbed wire and minefields surrounding the Bir Hakeim stronghold. After the initial attack failed, both the Trieste and the 90th Afrika Division had to shift to the defensive and regroup for the next two days before resuming the attack, which, on the 6th, saw the 90th Afrika Division advance to about 700 metres short of Fort Hakim, the core of the stronghold. Halted again by the French defensive fire and by minefields, the attack was called off until another attempt took place on the 8th, this time witnessed by Rommel. It was interrupted at about midday when the British 4th Armoured Brigade launched a relief attack from the east. At Bir Hakeim, having turned into the cornerstone of the entire battle, the 90th Afrika Division launched another attack in the evening, which by 20.00 hours had managed to break through the Fort Hakim defences approaching the last defence ditch, the *ridotta*. The assault group, which was down to about 200 men, eventually had to abandon its attempt to subdue the enemy positions and withdrew. At this point Rommel realised the importance of Bir Hakim, and the fact that the British were either unwilling, or unable to support it as they should have, something even the stubborn French defenders were soon bound to realise. Kesselring was not much help, as he informed Rommel that the situation at Bir Hakim had to be sorted out by using every available means. This was a request prompted by the Luftwaffe's concern that Rommel might want to starve out the fortress using the air force units in order to preserve his ground ones. This was not the case, as Rommel explained, stating there had only been a delay. On 10 June a concentric attack, led personally by Rommel, saw the 90th Afrika and the Trieste Division attack Bir Hakeim along with the *ad hoc* formed Group Baade, which moved against the fortress at 11.00 preceded by a strong air attack. At nightfall the attack, strongly supported by the air and by artillery fire, had managed to seize the hill 186, a commanding position within the stronghold, at the same time the British 7th Armoured Division abandoned the area east of Bir Hakeim, withdrawing to the east and the south. The French defenders eventually realised that no more resistance was possible, and they opted for a breakout. The attempt took place between 22 and 23.00 hours, the bulk of the surviving Free French forces, including their commander, managing to escape from the stronghold and join the British forces to the east. Bir Hakim certainly proved that encirclement in the desert is no more than a mirage, but it also provided Rommel with the success he needed to conclude the battle.

The Gazala Line having been broken, Rommel was able to resume a war of movement, now with the aim of destroying the two enemy forces still relatively intact, the 1st South African and the British 50th Infantry Division. The attack, to start from Bir Hakim, pointed to the south of the Tobruk defence perimeter which, once reached, would have been used as a pivot for the bulk of the Axis units which were to swing north-west and encircle the enemy forces. The attack, started at 15.00 on 11 June, saw the 90th Afrika Division approach almost at once El Adem, which was seized the next day, thus compressing the British armoured forces to the west around the Knightsbridge area. It was then that Rommel started his attack to the north, which by threatening to cut the coastal road (*via Balbia*), eventually compelled the 8th Army to abandon the Gazala line positions. The *Afrika Korps* eventually reached the sea, but did not prevent the bulk of both the 1st South African and 50th British Infantry Division from escaping to the east between 14 and 15 June, proving yet once again that no realistic encirclement is possible in a desert. The British armoured units were now compelled to withdraw to the Egyptian border, all the 8th Army could do was to try and repeat the same situation of 1941, which meant holding the fortress Tobruk while preparing a relief.

This took no account that this time the *Afrika Korps* would be attacking Tobruk at full strength, unlike in April and May 1941. The capture on 17 June of a large stock of enemy supplies at Gambut, fuel in particular, came as a good omen and on the next day the full strength of the Panzer Army Afrika closed in at Tobruk. The defence perimeter was surrounded by the infantry, while the armoured formations regrouped to the south before approaching the enemy positions on the 19th. The attack started in the morning of 20 June, preceded as usual by the Stuka dive-bombers. This time events were to Rommel's advantage, and by 8.30 the leading German tanks had broken through the defence perimeter and approached the anti-tank ditch, only now facing a stiffening enemy resistance. Between 12 and 14.00 hours the German and Italian units reached the *via Balbia*, effectively smashing the Tobruk defences. By 19.00 hours the 21st Panzer Division had seized the town itself, the attack recommencing at 5.30 on the next day now facing only sporadic resistance. This enabled opening the *via Balbia* to the Axis forces, and at 9.00, Rommel accepted the official surrender of General Klopper, commander of the 1st South African Division, forty minutes later. The success was complete, the Panzer Army having taken at Tobruk 33,000 prisoners, destroyed, or captured about 100 tanks, and most importantly, seized hundreds of vehicles and large stocks of supplies.

Often overlooked, if not for the capture of Tobruk and the subsequent decision to advance into Egypt, the battle of Gazala displayed Rommel's strengths. Even though he indulged in leading the attacks himself, thus cutting himself off from the entire front, and still prey to erroneous estimations of the enemy forces, Rommel was able to prove his worth as an army commander on the battlefield. This, despite the fact that his plan, based on speed and manoeuvre, had turned into a miserable failure in just two days. Rommel was now more careful on listening to advice, acknowledging the importance of supplies, and reacting accordingly, at first with the decision to regroup close to the Gazala line, and then with the decision to eliminate the Bir Hakim stronghold. In doing this he exposed the bulk of the Panzer Army to the enemy reaction, and it could be argued that the sluggishness of the British armoured doctrine, and its use on the battlefield were as much use to Rommel as the skills and capabilities of his own soldiers. The seizure of Tobruk was the crowning gem of Rommel's success, but at the same time it led to his ultimate failure.

The fall of Tobruk was first and foremost a sensational propaganda and psychological achievement, which impacted both sides. The Malta option was eventually abandoned for good, General Cavallero, who just a few days before had been insisting with Kesselring on the project, on 20 June drafted a letter then signed by Mussolini which required some 40,000 tons of diesel oil fuel for the Italian navy, and thereby postponed the entire operation to the next August, effectively putting an end to the entire plan. What escaped Cavallero's attention, and some others as well, was the fact that had Rommel been successful and had Alexandria been seized, the importance of Malta would have been greatly diminished with the problem of supplies largely resolved. More to the point, with the Axis now reduced to fighting in order to secure the resources needed to carry on with the war, such a success would have provided a much-needed propaganda and psychological boost, regardless of its actual strategic importance. Hitler had no doubts about this element, and his reply to Mussolini dated 23 June made it clear that carrying on with the offensive into Egypt was a unique occasion, one that could not be lost, and which could be linked to the German offensive in southern Russia, towards the Caucasus. Mussolini, also looking forward to this unique opportunity and a propaganda success, enthusiastically agreed, probably being aware at the same time that the Italian preparations for the seizure of Malta were far from complete, and that the entire plan still presented too many risks.

Acting on the basis of Mussolini's directives, which in fact he had ignored, Rommel was already leading Panzer Army units towards the Libyan–Egyptian border and would cross it before the authorisation arrived. It was on 22 June Rommel asked for the formal authorisation to start the invasion of Egypt. No one objected to the decision, both Kesselring (who would criticise Rommel for the decision in his post-war memoirs) and Bastico agreeing to it on the next day. On 24 June, Rommel was authorised to attack Egypt, just two days after Hitler had promoted him to field marshal, only seventeen months after he had been given command of the *Afrika Korps*.

The question remains as to whether Rommel could have acted in a different way. With hindsight many, first and foremost Kesselring, noted the difficulties in driving deep into Egypt with an army which had been fighting for about a month, and would face strong enemy forces determined to defend their positions. Such criticisms made perfect sense, and one could argue that a more cautious commander should have taken time, rested, and regrouped before trying to march towards Alexandria and the Suez Canal. However, Rommel never had any doubt about his decision, convinced as he was that the bulk of the enemy forces had been destroyed, and that the same success he had achieved in France could be repeated. As no one attempted to persuade him otherwise, this made the events which followed not just a consequence of Rommel's decision.[9]

The Shadow of Defeat

Rommel never really made a choice, the decision to advance into Egypt having already been taken, and it was nothing more than the prosecution of the campaign he had started in 1941. At 19.00 hours on 19 June Rommel ordered the 90th Afrika Division, which had been deployed east of Tobruk to defend the flanks of the attack, to reach the Bardia–Gambut area, and from there to the Egyptian border. The division seized Bardia, reportedly void of enemy troops, on the 20th reaching the border the same day. The next morning Rommel ordered the 21st Panzer Division to follow the same path on 22 June, along with the 15th Panzer Division moving southward in order to approach the wire defence at the border south of Sollum. They were followed by the Italian motorised corps, now with an extra armoured division (Littorio, just arrived in Libya) and by the 90th Afrika Division, which followed the path of the *Afrika Korps* being replaced at the *via Balbia* by the Italian infantry corps. On 22 June, Rommel cancelled the planned three days of rest, and expecting too much from his men instructed the *Afrika Korps* to advance east to pursue the enemy, which was withdrawing, hindering restoring its defences. After deploying in the early hours of 23 June, between 18.00 and 18.40 the *Afrika Korps* moved on to attack the positions at Sidi Barrani, several hours before Rommel was officially authorised to move into Egypt. This was the place where, in December 1940, the British Western Desert Force had attacked the Italian positions starting the process leading to the arrival of the German troops in Africa. The first unit to cross the border and advance into Egypt was the 90th Afrika Division at 18.15, followed by the rest of the *Afrika Korps* as the night fell. The absence of enemy response suggested there would only be a delaying action, which prompted Rommel to start a 'ruthless pursuit' of the enemy. It was all very similar to the situation Rommel once faced at Caporetto in 1917.

Problems arose from the beginning, with the Luftwaffe being unable to keep pace with Rommel's advance, which exposed the German and Italian units to the harassing attacks of the RAF. The transport columns were delayed, resulting in a lack of fuel and a temporary delay to the advance, with the divisions reporting only a few operational tanks (the 21st Panzer Division only had 40 left). On the other hand, the soldiers appeared excited and confident that Rommel would lead them to success. On 24 June the advancing columns had reached the area to the south of Sidi Barrani, still finding no enemy defence. The reconnaissance unit approached Mersa Matruh in the evening of the 25th, and they were unable to report about the enemy and its disposition. Nevertheless, Rommel decided to attack the next day, just as the bulk of the *Afrika Korps* was approaching Matruh. He evidently did not expect anything else than a delaying action. As it transpired, the fortress, similar to an Egyptian Tobruk, was defended by the 10th Indian and the British 50th Infantry Division, while to the south the New Zealand Division was deployed along with the British 1st Armoured Division.

As the Axis forces attacked in the afternoon of 26 June, they had no idea of what they were facing. Purely by chance, the 90th Afrika Division broke through the enemy line south of Matruh, reaching the coastal road and cutting the town off from the rest of the enemy forces. This enabled the 21st Panzer Division to start encircling the New Zealand Division from the north. Only now, Rommel discovered that he was facing an entire enemy army corps which was much stronger than his own forces: almost 160 tanks against the 23 available to the 21st Panzer Division. Its advance halted, the 15th Panzer Division came to the rescue, but was unable to close the pincer movement around the New Zealand Division. On 27 June the British units started to withdraw to the Fuka position, just as the *Afrika Korps* started to run low on fuel and ammunition. Once again, that most of the enemy units managed to escape east proved that encirclement in the desert is not possible, Rommel still having not learnt this lesson.

The remaining 8th Army units at Matruh were attacked on 28 June, the Axis forces meeting a stubborn resistance that lasted until the next day, when the final surrender added some 8,000 extra prisoners of war to the Panzer Army Afrika booty. With another success in his bag, Rommel might have considered resting before continuing with his advance towards Alexandria and the Nile. After advancing for more than 500 kilometres in ten days, the Axis forces started showing signs of exhaustion, their combat strength being reduced to a minimum while supplies started running low, and the Luftwaffe's support was almost non-existent. Other commanders might have taken such a decision, but not Rommel, who relied on momentum and morale to support his advance against an enemy he thought defeated. It was a wrong assumption.

On 30 June the Axis forces approached the El Alamein 'bottleneck', once again totally unaware of the enemy defences. As the Panzer Army Afrika deployed to attack, the comments made in the war diary of the 90th Afrika Division disclosed the prevailing mood. Alexandria was just 130 kilometres away; the enemy having deployed at El Alamein with its last defence line before the Nile. Their hopes evaporated as the *Afrika Korps* faced a sandstorm which delayed its deployment by three hours, opening it to a massive air attack by the RAF. Nevertheless, the 21st Panzer Division managed to seize a defensive box held by the 18th Indian Brigade, taking 1,200 prisoners but losing 18 of its 52 tanks. The first sign of breaching came from the Italians, the unit advancing along the coastal road falling prey to panic as it fell under heavy enemy artillery fire. The attack was renewed at 15.00 on 2 July, the *Afrika Korps* now facing stiff resistance, with an armoured counterattack compelling it to ask for Italian intervention to defend its exposed flanks. The soldiers were showing signs of fatigue, the supply situation had not improved, while the RAF and the enemy artillery relentlessly pounded the German and Italian positions. The concern that Alexandria might be out of reach started to spread, and the Panzer Army Afrika reached its breaking point. On 3 July the German attack again made little progress, while the New Zealand Division counterattacked, partially overrunning the Italian Ariete Division which was panic stricken and had started withdrawing. On that night, foreseeing an enemy counterattack the next day, the Panzer Army was ordered to switch to the defensive, Rommel still believing this to be a temporary measure which would not prevent him from resuming the advance. He was wrong. Between 4 and 22 July a series of fierce engagements put the final end to the advance of the Panzer Army Afrika, and to its chances of breaking through to Alexandria and the Nile. The breaking point was marked by the destruction of the Italian Sabratha Division which was attacked along the coast by the 9th Australian Division. Even though the Sabratha was a division only by name, its overall strength was 3,000 men, the crisis reached its peak on 22 July when two depleted German battalions were also overrun by the 9th Australian Division. After a pause, the 8th Army's final attack on 26–27 July marked the end of the first battle of El Alamein, and the end of Rommel's myth as an invincible commander.

Trying to repeat the same pattern he had learnt at Caporetto and in France in June–July 1942, Rommel brought his own forces to breaking point, and he depleted any chance he may have had of breaching the enemy defences advancing to Alexandria and to the Nile. As the lines at El Alamein switched to the defence for both sides, it became clear that the 8th Army had succeeded in making the Panzer Army Afrika fight a battle of attrition, which it could not win because of its inferiority in numbers, material, and supplies. Soldiers had reached the point when exhaustion made them incapable of fighting, as Rommel's expectations were impossible to meet, with Rommel himself suffering the effects of strain. He was described as poor in health and with strained nerves. As usual, Rommel blamed Bastico for the failure, noting the absence of reinforcements, but it may be assumed that he too realised the reality of the situation. His repeated pleas for reinforcements were satisfied to a limited extent, because neither the Italians nor the Germans possessed the necessary reserves. Furthermore, since Alexandria had not been reached and Malta had not been seized, the supply situation remained critical, aggravated by the distance now separating the Panzer Army from its supply bases which also hampered air support, as the tide had definitely turned to the advantage of the RAF.

Rommel was conscious that the Americans would provide support to the 8th Army and, foreseeing a further strengthening of the enemy, he prepared a last attempt to break through at El Alamein. Before this started, on 21 August Rommel suffered a fainting fit which suggested he had reached the limit of physical exhaustion, with many senior leaders recommending he should be replaced by General Guderian. It was Hitler's refusal which saved Rommel, but it could not prevent him from facing failure. The last offensive started on 30 August, plagued by the shortage of supplies. The battle of Alam Halfa (or second battle of El Alamein) never reached a critical point, the Axis forces faced too strong enemy defences to ever have a chance of breaking through. Rommel realised this, and by 2 September he wanted to switch back to defence. Eventually the fuel shortage, enemy air attacks, the realisation of the enemy superiority, saw the Panzer Army halting its attempts to advance, and pulled back to the starting positions by 6 September. At the end of the battle one name emerged, that of General Bernard Montgomery who was now being praised as the one who had stopped Rommel.

El Alamein marked the end of Rommel's career as a commanding officer. He never considered withdrawing from the Alamein line, rather insisting for propaganda purposes that Alexandria could still be reached, but neither Hitler nor Mussolini ever considered this a possibility. Rommel became involved with a battle he could not win, and in which he could not display any of the skills and capabilities which had contributed to the creation of his myth. The third (or second) battle of El Alamein simply confirmed the situation. Lacking supplies, Rommel envisaged a battle of attrition, which only served Montgomery's purposes even though there was a moment when the 8th Army came close to losing the battle.

Eventually, the order to withdraw given on 4 November simply put an end to Rommel's North African campaign, and all that followed, particularly after the Allied landing in French North Africa four days later. It was now nothing more than the final appendix to a campaign

Rommel had started almost by chance in February 1941. After a long withdrawal across Egypt and Libya, on 2 February the last units of the Panzer Army withdrew from Libya, starting to deploy in Tunisia, along the Mareth line, the 8th Army entering Tripoli on 23 January. Once there, Rommel attempted a last effort, recognising in the green American forces the weak element in the enemy disposition, and attacked them at the Kasserine Pass with the aim of driving behind the enemy lines in Tunisia. The attempt lasted for only four days, between 19 and 22 February 1943, and it marked Rommel's last time he exercised a field command in the war. By then, Rommel's time was over already and practically everybody, from the Italians to Kesselring and even Hitler, no longer wanted him to be in command in North Africa. The 'Desert Fox' had become an encumbrance, Hitler realising that his most famous general could not be associated with yet another defeat. On 9 March 1943 Rommel left his command of the Army Group Afrika, the Panzer Army having been reorganised as an Italian Army, his place being taken by General Jürgen von Arnim. The story of the *Afrika Korps* only survived him for two months.[10]

All that followed is usually glossed over in Rommel's biographies. After a period of rest, in May 1943 Hitler gave Rommel an important task, to prepare the plans for the seizure of Italy in case of their collapse. Acting at first with a reduced staff, Rommel worked along with the staff of the Commander in Chief West to prepare troop movements and deployments, foreseeing an Italian collapse in case of an Allied invasion of the country. The plans were ready in July, shortly after the Allied landing in Sicily, and Hitler thought of giving command in Italy to Rommel. The opposition of Hermann Göring and of the German ambassador in Rome made him change his mind, and Rommel was eventually given command of the Army Group E in Greece. It was not a backwater posting, Hitler being convinced that the Allies, after invading Italy, would move on to invade the Balkans in order to advance into Romania, and then link up with the Soviets advancing along the southern part of the Eastern Front. Rommel never took command of the Army Group E, as he arrived in Athens on 25 July 1943, the day of Mussolini's downfall.

He was immediately recalled home, and he was given command of the Army Group B, which was deployed in northern Italy, at first without disclosing the name of its commander. That Rommel's name still had some worth is proved by the Italian reaction to the announcement that he would be the one in command. The new Chief of General Staff, General Vittorio Ambrosio, hysterically reminded colleagues of the efforts made in February to rid themselves of him in Africa. He asked the government to put pressure on the Germans for his removal. Hitler refused, even considering the possibility of giving Rommel overall command in Italy. The plan was for Kesselring, who was in command of the German forces in central and southern Italy, to withdraw north following the Allied invasion, with Rommel taking over command as the German forces reached the northern Apennines. On 8 September 1943, the Allies landed at Salerno and Italy surrendered, Rommel's Army Group B led the disarming of the Italian Army in northern Italy while securing coastal defences, but Rommel fell ill on 14 September. It is worth noting that, in his postwar memoirs, Kesselring criticised Rommel for having made Italian soldiers prisoners rather than allowing them to return home, as Kesselring had in Rome, which led to the birth of the partisan movement. The truth is that Rommel's first order was in fact to allow the Italian soldiers to return home, and it was changed after the news that they were fighting against Kesselring's troops in Rome. Regarding Kesselring's reactions it should be recalled that he had no other option, and could hardly take the Italian soldiers prisoner, given the lack of forces at his disposal, especially in comparison with the Italian numbers in Rome.

However, on 4 October, Hitler was uncertain about the strategy to adopt in Italy, which in short was divided between Kesselring's idea of a prolonged defence of the southern part of the country, and Rommel's plan for a withdrawal to the northern Apennines where the German forces were anticipated to defend. Eventually, the Allied strategy pushed Hitler to his final decision. Since it was clear that the Allies were not trying to invade the Balkans nor intended to land in central or northern Italy, Kesselring's strategy was considered better suited to the situation making him the natural choice for taking over command in Italy.

On 20 November 1943, Rommel left Italy, being temporarily given the task to inspect the coastal defences in Denmark, until the Army Group B headquarters moved to northern France and activated under the Commander in Chief West. Rommel did not take Hitler's decision well, having exacerbated his rivalry with Kesselring and feeling like demotion, if not a lack of trust. Rommel is often described to have been at this time depressed, and deeply imbued with a sense of defeatism. This may be true given his situation, but at a closer look, Hitler's decision was entirely in his favour. Kesselring was chosen to command a secondary theatre of war where hardly any decisive battle could take place, whereas Rommel was given a command in the most important theatre of war, having to prepare to face an Allied invasion, which both sides believed could be the potential decisive turning point of the war. It would also be Rommel's own pivotal moment.[11]

Chapter Four

End Days

Facing Decisions

Field Marshal Gerd von Rundstedt, the Commander in Chief West, once described Rommel as a good divisional commander and nothing more. There was a certain degree of truth in this remark, as it described Rommel's qualities and outlined those he lacked. Rommel excelled in commanding units on the battlefield, relying on his own physical courage and strength. In North Africa he excelled whenever capable of leading on the battlefield, even though he sometimes made critical mistakes such as the 1941 'dash to the wire'. As it was, the command in North Africa suited Rommel, because the army he was leading was reduced in size, and there were no real strategic decisions to make. Even in Italy, Rommel had a secondary role to play, and his units were mostly involved in disarming the Italians or fighting the Yugoslav partisans at the border. The task Rommel was given in France was something completely different, as it no longer offered the opportunity of leading the units on the battlefield, but involving staff work, along with a series of strategic choices to make. In this area of command Rommel was particularly weak. The plan to defend Italy along the northern Apennines was partly borrowed with a strategic analysis of the situation made at the end of 1942 by the German Army Staff. Rommel's ideas were soon rebuffed by his subordinate commanders who, after inspecting the line which was to be defended, pointed out its weakness and the fact that it would require too many divisions.

Even Rommel's activity in France, where other than being in command of the Army Group B, he was also inspector of the coastal defences, which indicated all the limitations of his capabilities as an army group commander. Admiral Friedrich Ruge, the naval liaison officer to his staff, wrote in his memoirs of Rommel's relentless activity in improving the coastal defences which, until then, had only been developed in the main harbours. Rommel developed a belt of strongpoints along the coast, the positions protected by bunkers capable of covering one another with their defensive fire. The shore was covered with obstacles intended to halt or destroy the enemy landing crafts, which would either cripple the attempts to land, or compel the enemy to come ashore with the low tide, thus having to cover a large stretch of unprotected land under fire. Rommel's ingenuity cannot be criticised, but his lack of overall view can. Several commanders commented how his continuous requests for working on the shore obstacles actually prevented their soldiers from training, which they also desperately needed, because in most cases the units deployed in France were either new or second rate. Rommel's defences mainly worked at Omaha Beach; the Utah Beach defences were untested because the landing actually came ashore to the south of the projected area. The British beaches (Gold, Juno, Sword) did not experience any level of resistance comparable to the American ones, and neither the beach obstacles nor the coastal strongpoint ever prevented the enemy landing. Rommel also made another error, this time of a theoretical and psychological nature. He argued that the first 72 hours following the start of the invasion would be decisive, and therefore undermined the morale of his own soldiers who, three days after the invasion, started to wonder whether the enemy could be defeated at all. The American writer Cornelius Ryan would be the only one to take advantage of Rommel's claims for the so-called 'decisive day'.

More importantly, Rommel's concept of how to deal with the invading forces turned out to be a complete mistake. The idea of deploying the Panzer Division close to the coast to face the Allied landing was not entirely his own, the same suggestion having been made in 1943 by Guderian, who claimed that this was a necessity given the limited supplies available, and it would severely curtail their redeployment in other areas. On 6 June 1944, the new 21st Panzer Division, which had been rebuilt after North Africa, counterattacked the British forces in very much the same conditions that its predecessor had attacked the enemy defences in

Egypt: having no idea of the actual strength and disposition of the enemy forces. Needless to say, the idea of an immediate counterattack against the enemy landing forces turned out to be a major mistake. Also, by deploying the Panzer Division to face the Allied advance inland caused another crisis. By the end of June 1944, it became clear that, unless relieved by infantry divisions which were not available, the Panzer Division could not be extricated from the frontline in order to regroup and to prepare for a major counterattack. It would be wrong to put all these mistakes on Rommel's shoulders alone, but they demonstrated what the British commented about him in Normandy, namely his presence was not felt at all, and it was as if he were not there.

Rommel believed his theory that the first 72 hours would have been decisive. It did not take long before he started to realise that the battle being fought in Normandy was a losing one, and that the only way to reverse its outcome was to bring new forces in to counterattack *en masse* the enemy. However, this was not possible because Germany no longer had such resources. Rommel's behaviour was curious. On 1 July, during a meeting with the commander of Panzer Group West, General Leo von Schweppenburg, Rommel revealed that during his recent meeting with Hitler the latter had admitted that an offensive in the west was no longer possible. This view left only the 'reprisal weapons', namely the V-1 and V-2 (flying bombs and rockets), as an instrument of war which might compel the Allies to start negotiations. On 17 July, Rommel sent a report to Hitler outlining the precarious situation in Normandy, openly stating that 'we must expect that in the foreseeable future the enemy will succeed in breaking through our thin front, above all, Seventh Army's, and thrusting deep into France.' Given the lack of reserves and despite his noted fighting spirit, Rommel ended the message by urging 'for the proper conclusion to be drawn from this situation.'[1] It is curious what sort of reaction Hitler might have had in reading this message, which some have interpreted as a form of ultimatum, but Rommel was wounded two days later by a strafing British Spitfire. The request for a 'solution' raised another element of Rommel's character and story.[2]

Rommel's ties with the anti-Hitler resistance have been largely exploited in the creation of his post-war myth, with the intention of transforming him not only as an exceptional commander, but also in the anti-nazi conspiracy. However, there is little if any evidence of Rommel's involvement with the anti-Nazi resistance 20 July plot to assassinate Hitler. Most informative was the file which eventually led to Rommel's own end. On 28 September 1944, Martin Bormann, Hitler's secretary, put together a series of events suggesting that Rommel might have been involved in the 20 July plot. This file started with a simple statement: many of those involved, including some which had been put under trial and hanged, had mentioned Rommel who 'was in the frame', who had supposedly said that he would put himself at the disposal of the new government in the aftermath of the attack. The names included Rommel's chief of staff General Stülpnagel and Field Marshal von Kluge's nephew Colonel Rathgens. The claim was read somewhat sceptically, Bormann recalling Rommel's service as commander of Hitler's headquarters and the many ties with Hitler and the propaganda ministry. However, Rommel's defeatist attitude in Italy could not be ignored, and Bormann (who also had cast doubts on Rommel's achievements as a military commander) noted that Rommel had never been a Nazi. Most importantly, Bormann highlighted some traits of Rommel's personality. His ambition, which made him grasp any opportunity to be photographed along with Hitler, and his vanity which made him remove his glasses when photographed. A further proof of Rommel's attitude was his critical remark towards the conduct of the war, as reported by Gauleiter (district leader) Murr. This comment, which attracted the attention of Himmler's security, was explained as a complaint about Hitler's absence from the Western Front, and criticising his colleagues, such as von Rundstedt, von Kluge, and Göring, all of which amounted to mere hearsay but also possible heresy.

The critical point is that no actual evidence of Rommel's involvement was ever found, even though Hitler compelled him to commit suicide allowing some, after the war, to automatically enlist him in the anti-Hitler movement. General Speidel's post-war memoirs sanctioned this, only to be challenged by David Irving's biography whose thesis was that

Rommel never opposed Hitler, not knowing of the attack, all of which was resumed later by David Fraser and Hans Georg Reuth. Others argued that Rommel was in fact aware of the anti-Hitler opposition, like other top-notch commanders such as von Manstein and Guderian, but they were opposed to killing Hitler. The simplest explanation is that Rommel was too close to people involved in the 20 July plot not to have been sounded out. Almost certainly he knew of the anti-Hitler circle and of their plans to overthrow his regime, even though he may not have been informed of the actual 20 July plot. Undoubtedly, Rommel would have been available and more than willing to put himself at the disposal of the new government, an attitude he certainly shared with the other generals who merely kept a 'wait and watch' attitude, waiting for the conspirators to take their steps. From the evidence claiming Rommel was an anti-Nazi, or that he even opposed the regime is too much of a leap. Rommel's ambition was probably the real driving force behind his successes and the reason behind his failures, and also explained his attitude towards the anti-Nazi movement and the 20 July plot. Rommel's words to General von Schweppenburg on 1 July are enlightening in so far at that point, even the last illusion of reversing the course of the war had disappeared. Rommel had arrived at the point where he faced the choice of remaining loyal to Hitler and his regime, which meant going down with him, concluding his career as a defeated general, or to try and take this position in order to save himself. If given the choice, Rommel would have probably preferred to be some form of a traitor but at the same time become Germany's president, rather than remain loyal and end in a prisoner of war camp. This probably explains why he was compelled to commit suicide, while others, including his accusers, survived thanks to the lack of proof. Hitler was certainly aware of Rommel's ambition, but he could not risk facing him at the moment of crisis knowing that the myth he had helped create had a popular influence amongst German soldiers. In a way, Rommel's myth which he himself helped to create, and which he unquestionably enjoyed was also the reason behind his eventual downfall and death.[3]

Rommel in the Contemporary Views

Propaganda Minister Joseph Goebbels on 22 February 1941 incorrectly wrote that on Rommel's arrival in Libya, Mussolini had given Rommel full powers and that he had three armoured divisions at his disposal to re-conquer Benghazi. Almost a month later, on 21 March, as Goebbels noted the award of the oak leaves to his Knight's Cross, he wrote that Rommel was a marvellous officer whose narration of the difficulties of the war in the desert made a deep impression. According to Rommel, the Italians represented a hurdle as they were not a warmongering people. They wanted the besieged garrison of Jarabub to surrender, but Rommel opposed the idea. The comment was that the Italians should have been happy to see the German motorised troops arrive in Africa, Hitler certainly was, as he was determined not to abandon the continent to the British. Not surprisingly, on 9 April Goebbels happily noted down Rommel's seizure of Derna, which came just as the German invasion of Yugoslavia and Greece was making progress. Goebbels clearly exaggerated the German successes when he wrote a week later that the British were withdrawing in North Africa even though they still held Tobruk, with Rommel now having at his disposal eight Panzer divisions which, having already reached the Egyptian border, should have enabled him to follow the British withdrawal to Mersa Matruh. This flow of incorrect information was such that, on 29 April, Goebbels noted that Rommel was still advancing while the Luftwaffe was striking at Mersa Matruh.

It was only on 11 June that Goebbels' notes provided a more accurate view of the situation in North Africa, as he recorded the hard fighting for Tobruk, and above all, Rommel's position between the Germans and the Italians. He described Rommel as a truly legendary character for both the German and the Italian soldiers, and his having to deal with the inferior quality of the Italian officers which he did without hesitation. Goebbels' 16 July diary entry revealed the strong connection existing between Rommel and Goebbels, as the latter noted down the arrival of a letter from Rommel, thanking him for the propaganda efforts in favour of the soldiers fighting in North Africa. Goebbels took care to note that he would make more efforts to ensure that the German soldiers in that theatre of war would not be overshadowed by the war against the Soviet Union. The link between Goebbels and Rommel was a Lieutenant Alfred Berndt who had joined the propaganda ministry in 1936, but after joining the army in 1939, became the staff officer for the propaganda of the *Afrika Korps* in 1941. Rommel used his influence with Hitler's aide Rudolf Schmundt to have him fast-tracked for promotion, Berndt rising to the rank of captain in 1943. On 8 September 1941 Berndt, on leave in Germany, met Goebbels and gave him a proper picture of the situation in North Africa. The supply convoys were attacked and sunk, with the result that soldiers suffered from the shortage of almost everything: from ammunition to proper food which, because of the lack of vitamins, caused the widespread transmission of disease. The concern was now for a possible British counteroffensive which, along with the situation caused by the lack of supplies, had become a reason of concern for the German soldiers, and also because of the attitude of the Italian soldiers and their officers. The only certainty was Rommel's belief that he could deal with a British offensive and hold the line, regardless of the situation. Based on this, Goebbels portrayed the picture of a commander who spent his time with the soldiers, who loved him. Even the replacement of the Italian commander in Libya, General Gariboldi, with General Bastico was not good news, Bastico being known as 'bombastic'. Rommel had taken the necessary steps with Hitler, who in turn lent on Mussolini to have Bastico grant a free hand to Rommel.

Goebbels' 22 November 1941 diary entry, (referring as usual to the day before) is particularly revelatory, as he noted Hitler's appreciation of the situation just after the start of the British operation *Crusader*. Hitler, who (according to Goebbels) saw the situation as it was, evaluated the British offensive in a more realistic way than the generals of the army staff, but despite his concerns, he had great hopes in Rommel. He saw it as the only chance to secure a proper result in North Africa, given the limitations imposed by the shipment of reinforcements and supplies. Foreseeing a defeat, Hitler asked Goebbels to set the propaganda tune in such a way to deny Churchill any prestige achievement. Goebbels was aware that the British Prime Minister was anxious to gain a prestigious victory in order to demonstrate that Britain was in fact supporting the Soviet efforts against Germany. Three days later, after a meeting with Field Marshal Keitel and General Jodl, Goebbels noted that whenever the fight in North Africa was discussed it was necessary to portray Rommel as the 'people's hero', which was a necessity for the army since the Luftwaffe already had its heroes, unlike the former. Keitel and Jodl wholeheartedly agreed, and they suggested making the most of Rommel's fiftieth birthday, to celebrate a commander who had done marvels with the limited forces at his disposal. Goebbels noted 'we can make use of men like these.' As Goebbels noted on 30 November, the day after meeting Hitler, that the latter considered Rommel a very energetic and circumspect commander, capable of managing a demanding situation. Hitler's attitude towards Rommel was a clear determinant in creating the myth, Goebbels noting on 19 December the two most remarkable commanders the army had were General Eduard Dietl and Erwin Rommel. Rommel was a man who could be trusted, and one had to be happy to have him in North Africa. The withdrawal from Cyrenaica did not ruin such an ideal image, especially if compared with the situation on the Eastern Front, and developments proved these observations right. On 20 January 1942 (again after meeting Hitler), Goebbels noted that Rommel was considered the most capable general of all. Hitler, who had noted his capability of standing fast, had commented that with the newly arrived tanks, Rommel had claimed not just to be able to hold the positions but to start a new offensive. He had now decided to take him out of North Africa as soon as the situation stabilised, replace him with General Crüwell and put Rommel in charge on the Eastern Front.

Goebbels and Hitler were not the only ones to hold Rommel in high esteem. On 24 February Goebbels remarked that, thanks to the British propaganda, Rommel had become the most popular general across the world, which was good for Germany. Rommel was such an excellent man and a remarkable commander that propaganda could do him no harm at all. The praises following Rommel's counterattack and the seizure of Benghazi proved this comment right, and it was something Rommel had to be granted. Not surprisingly, news of Rommel's offensive in North Africa made its way promptly to the foreign press, even though it was not clear whether Rommel had launched an in-depth reconnaissance or a proper offensive. As Goebbels noted on 28 May, one could expect that the British acknowledged Rommel's success even if he just seized Sollum by claiming this was his aim. Goebbels could not help noting that Tobruk should have been seized, and if anyone could do that, it was Rommel. On 5 June Goebbels would note down Rommel's success in North Africa with great rejoicing. The situation was such that Rommel could exploit it making things difficult for the British in North Africa. This delusion did not last for long, as already on 9 November, as the Allied landing in North Africa was noted, Goebbels had to comment on how the British were rejoicing over the demanding situation Rommel now faced. Three days later, noting the clear enemy aim to link Montgomery's advance in Egypt with the Allied landing in French West Africa to seize the whole of North Africa, Goebbels practically acknowledged that Rommel was no longer the 'miracle man'. A few days later, the entry in Goebbels' diary illustrated the new situation: Montgomery was the new star, acclaimed by the press as he claimed he could do with Rommel all he wanted. The only positive remark was that, had the Americans had a Rommel in Tunisia, the situation could be much worse.

Nevertheless, Rommel was held in high esteem, and on 14 January 1943 Goebbels noted that Rommel had clear ideas on how to restore the situation in Tunisia, by attacking again, in spite of the difficulties created for him by Bastico, and above all by Kesselring with whom a noticeable series of different opinions had become known. Kesselring was an optimist, but it was Rommel who had to answer for the actual situation while Kesselring could describe it in his optimistic view, without having to bear the brunt. It was only at this stage that Hitler, who still had complete trust in Rommel, explained that he wanted to give him a command in the Caucasus probably with the aim of having him lead the invasion of the Middle East from the north. This did not happen, and Hitler decided to keep Rommel in charge in North Africa, now believing he should have been given overall command in Tunisia. It was not just the Italian opposition, but also Hermann Göring's (as Goebbels noted on 2 March) which prevented this happening, the overall command organisation of Rommel, Kesselring, von Arnim, the Italian Comando Supremo, all clearly influenced his decisions, and this eventually caused Rommel to fall ill. As such, Hitler took him out of Africa and ordered him to rest and to recover his health. Despite the fall of Tunisia, Rommel was still highly regarded in Hitler's view, and on 9 May Goebbels noted that he was the right man to deal with the incoming Allied attempt to establish a foothold in Europe. Suggesting Rommel could do that even with the limited forces available, was an attitude made clear in Goebbels' 27 July entry. In this he wrote of Hitler's reaction to Mussolini's downfall and his decision to give overall command in Italy to Rommel. The opposition from Keitel and Jodl prevented Hitler from having Rommel replace Kesselring in the first instance, and eventually Kesselring was given the task to deal with the situation.

When posted to northern France, Rommel seemed to produce marvels again as Goebbels noted on 18 April 1944, that his work had been exemplary, his open encounters with the British and the Americans having clearly pushed him to do the best; Goebbels wrote that 'Rommel is again the old combatant.' Hitler was certain of this, and relied on Rommel to deal with the invasion which was considered the decisive moment for the war in the west. All was praise and confidence, despite the opinion of the SS General Josef Dietrich, once commander of Hitler's personal bodyguard, who considered Rommel more a drummer than a commander. As Goebbels noted on 6 June Hitler's remark that Rommel had fully met his expectations, the Allied landing in Normandy still had to happen. However, on 4 July even Goebbels had to admit that Rommel had failed in meeting the expectations one had placed on him. On 31 August Goebbels noted, in the aftermath of the attempt to kill Hitler, and following the first round of trials against the anti-Nazi conspirators, that both von Kluge and probably Rommel as well were heavily involved. The star of the Desert Fox had fallen for the last time.[4]

The Historians and the Rommel Myth

As noted by Goebbels, Rommel's myth was not just created by the German propaganda but also, if unintended, by the British as well. Not surprisingly, his myth came to a new life after the war due to his former enemy starting a new kind of propaganda. Rommel's figure offered many advantages, at a time when German generals were being put on trial, and the first attempts were being made to re-create the German armed forces. First, Rommel was a fallen hero who could in no way face the risk of being put on trial. Secondly, Rommel had not been in the least involved in the 'dirty war' on the Eastern Front, his successes having only been achieved against the British (and Commonwealth) and the American forces. His war in North Africa could be described as the 'clean war', not in the least because the absence of civilians prevented any sort of accusation of crime. As such, Rommel was the ideal figure to represent the 'good side' of the German Army, the one who fought for the country against odds, and with valour led by a commander who could be seen as the people's hero. Thus, without amplifying the valour of the enemy, the achievements of Montgomery who defeated him were also seen as more important than they actually were.

The start to the new 'Rommel myth' was given in 1950 by Desmond Young's biography, followed three years later by Basil Liddell Hart's edition of the 'Rommel Papers', in fact a mixture of his memoirs *Krieg ohne Hass* (War without Hate) and of the letters to his wife. The stunning success of both publications also started the creation of Rommel's myth as a resistance fighter against Hitler, which, albeit still lacking a shred of evidence, also suited the needs of the new Desert Fox image. He was portrayed as a commander willing to fight for his country despite his personal disdain for the Nazi regime, with Rommel attempting to bring Hitler down, and so paying for the attempt with his own life.

It is interesting to note how Rommel's characterisations in movies portrayed him in a completely different light to how he is usually described by those who fought and stood alongside him, particularly in North Africa. While the true Rommel is described as brusque, hard to deal with and inclined to barracks' slang, the on-screen Rommel is usually a mild mannered, calm, and rational commander, if not some sort of upper-class personage. This was James Mason's characterisation in the 1951 movie *Rommel: The Desert Fox* from Young's biography, taken to its extremes, even from an historical point of view, as it exacerbated Rommel's involvement in the 20 July plot. Christopher Plummer in the short scene he plays in the 1967 movie *The Night of the Generals*, based on Hans Hellmut Kirst's novel, (Plummer is seen smoking a cigarette, Rommel notoriously disliked smoking) did the same. Thus, just to consider the most successful movies, the Rommel character made appearances in several others such as the 1962 *The Longest Day* from Cornelius Ryan's book.

This popular image of the Desert Fox was continued by Ronald Lewin in his 1968 book *Rommel as a Military Commander*, remaining unchallenged in David Irving's 1977 book *The Trail of the Fox*, and in David Fraser's 1993 *Knight's Cross: A Life of Field Marshal Erwin Rommel*. It took German historians to start challenging the myth, at first Maurice Philip Remy's 2002 book *Mythos Rommel* (The Rommel Myth), followed then by Ralf Georg Reuth's 2004 *Rommel. Das Ende einer Legende* (Rommel, The End of a Legend). The fact that all sort of books on Rommel are still being published regularly, such as the recent collected series of essays edited by Ian F. W. Beckett *Rommel. A Reappraisal* (2013) reveals the fact that the myth of the Desert Fox is still alive and popular, and although Rommel was a controversial character, his figure is bound to leave a permanent mark in history no matter what.[5]

Final Thoughts

It is this author's personal opinion that Rommel without doubt possessed exceptional qualities of command and leadership, which with his personal courage and determination enabled him to prove himself and the units he led on the battlefield, whenever the occasion suited and permitted favourable developments. Rommel was an excellent commander at Caporetto, also proving himself as the 7th Panzer Division's commander by taking over the division in a brief period of time, leading it on the battlefields on the Western Front in 1940. Rommel's problems were caused by two major reasons. The first was his relentless ambition, which prevented him from self-criticism and self-evaluation. The second was his meteoric rise in command, which was not substantiated by an adequate background. Put in command of the *Afrika Korps*, Rommel could not resist from exploiting the opportunity which was offered to him, despite the fact that he had no experience as a corps commander, nor had he any experience of tropical warfare. Had he followed Hitler's instructions and taken time before starting his offensive, and had he used the time available to become acquainted with the task in hand and the unfamiliar terrain, the course of events may have developed differently in North Africa.

In evaluating Rommel his ambition should always be considered. This was the prevailing pressure which pushed him not to miss any opportunity, and at the same time the reason he reacted badly whenever facing a tricky situation or even defeat. Clearly driven by ambition, Rommel tried to exploit every opportunity either on the battlefield, or when dealing with the powers to be. It would be pointless to try and reason whether Rommel was a fervent Nazi or not, since this hardly ever interfered with his command or even his career. More than likely, he became a supporter of the regime whenever this suited him, only to try and draw a line between himself and Hitler when he realised that he was no longer on the winning side. As such, Rommel is probably best described as an opportunist. Somebody who would exploit every chance, whether on the battlefield or not. Naturally, Rommel's capabilities evidently diminished as the situation in North Africa degenerated and he no longer faced favourable opportunities.

Rommel's career can be divided in two parts, the first starting at El Alamein. Having missed the opportunity (assuming this ever existed) of reaching Alexandria and the Nile, Rommel started to react to the situation he faced, influencing it to suit his needs. Secondly, the subsequent appointments in Italy and in northern France merely reveal that, having risen in rank but not in experience or knowledge, Rommel had been given commands which no longer suited him and acted accordingly. His involvement with the anti-Nazi conspiracy and the possible involvement with the 20 July plot are probably just the consequence of the combination between Rommel's ambition and the opportunity he was offered. From here to claim that Rommel was an anti-Nazi means taking a giant leap, his attitude being probably just the same as he had when the regime was on the rise, only in reverse. Rommel's myth represents at the same time a good opportunity for the historians to study him, but at the same time it also poses relevant hurdles in the search for the truth as it makes it difficult to place the Desert Fox in his appropriate place in history.

Field Marshal Walter Model

The Firefighter

Chapter One

Early Life

Strictly speaking Model was not Hitler's last field marshal, others were promoted after him until April 1945 as the Third Reich faced its end. He was, however, the last commander with a solid reputation and a name to support his promotion, which would make him a first-class leader in the later years of the war. All too often he was depicted as Hitler's 'firefighter', given that he was deployed at the most difficult areas of the front, and one of the field marshals closest to Hitler. Walter Model was undoubtedly a good field commander and a man who followed the assumed laws of the Prussian military tradition to the last. Although not one of Germany's most known field marshals, his career followed the ups and downs of the war until he found the position which suited him best, namely, the man who could deal with the crises whenever these occurred.

The Reluctant Soldier

Walter Model was born on 24 January 1891 at Genthin, near Magdeburg in Prussia. His birthplace was a small provincial town of just some 5,000 inhabitants, nevertheless, a community making progress with its local factories, a tribunal, and two main schools: a gymnasium and an Evangelic seminar. Walter's parents, his father Otto Paul Moritz Model and mother Maria Wilhelmine Pauline Demmer belonged to the middle-class, with no military tradition. Otto was a schoolteacher, and in the spare time a chorister. Maria's grandfather owned a *Gasthaus* and claimed to be the owner of the finest horses in the area. This proved to be Walter's juvenile passion, horses. Although engaged in his mother's family line of work, Walter did not follow the family tradition of teaching and choir singing. Even with the remote connection of Walter's birthday coinciding with the birth of Frederick the Great (which was rescinded in Prussia by the date of 27 January celebrating the birth of the Kaiser Wilhelm II), there appeared no military leanings. Despite their background, the Model family (who had another son, Otto, in 1884) lived in quite austere conditions and the father sought better circumstances elsewhere. In 1906 the family moved to Weissenfels where his father taught at the local seminar, moving again two years later to Naumburg. This move was, as it transpired, decisive. Unlike Genthin and Weissenfels, Naumburg was a garrison town for a battalion of Jäger, the light infantry, and one of artillery, and many retired officers were living there. This was also a time when the military career, as is well-known, was seen as the best possible way to establish oneself a place in society, being an officer was socially acceptable and one of the best ways to climb the social ladder. As Model started attending school, he found himself surrounded by sons of army officers, such as Hans-Valentin Hube who was the son of a colonel, and Walter was invited to witness the local drills of an infantry unit.* It appears that this did not suit Walter's personality, who was not interested in physical activities including sport, but he was keen on studying classics. Apart from showing an aptitude for Latin and Greek, he also studied history and poetry and eventually joined a literary society. These interests certainly helped him, and in February 1909, he was selected as one of the candidates to join the Abitur, the first years in the classical studies Lycée. His friend Hans Hube did not try and follow his steps, but rather, following the family's traditions, joined the army. However, it remains a mystery as it did for his family at the time, as to why eventually Walter opted for the military career even though his position was far from being perfect. This lack of being an ideal situation derived from having no military ties, and there

---

* Hans-Valentin Hube was a future General in the Second World War. Hube, after commanding the 16th Infantry Division from June 1940, which was transformed into the 16th Panzer Division the following September, fought on the Eastern Front and in September 1942 was given command of the XIV Panzer Korps. Surrounded at Stalingrad, he flew outside the pocket once only to return and had to be evacuated again on Hitler's personal order. After overseeing the rebuilding of the XIV Panzer Korps, Hube fought in Sicily and at Salerno before being given command of the 1st Panzer Army on the Eastern Front in February 1944. He distinguished himself during the battle for the Korsun pocket, when his army managed to escape the Soviet encirclement. He died on 21 April 1944 in an air crash.

was no possibility of support from his parents. They realised that joining the army as an officer was not easy, and they preferred Walter to follow in his brother's steps, becoming a law school student. In order to make things easier for Walter, his Uncle Martin intervened.

Martin Model, a reserve officer in an infantry regiment, used his contacts to lead Walter to being interviewed for an officer's position. This, however, had a pre-condition, namely, Walter had no other choice than joining the army in the same regiment as his uncle, the Regiment von Alvensleben No 52 (once it was mobilised and inserted within the army framework), or the 6th Brandenburgisch Regiment. Accompanied by his father, the 18-year-old Walter went to Cottbus to be interviewed by the regimental commander (the regiment had two battalions at Cottbus and one at Crossen), and Colonel Henseling decided to take him on as an officer cadet. Walter was unaware this would be his hardest experience, not least because of his physical condition. He was short in height and had a myopic eye-condition, which was of no help at all, and consequently his training sergeant had to shout at him, telling him that 'you haven't got the hardship required by a soldier'. For a brief time, he had the idea of giving up the military career, and it crossed Walter's mind that he should train as a physician. However, training sergeants are not just to criticise you, and with the help of a training non-commissioned officer Model was eventually able to overcome his shortcomings, learning not only to face and overcome his own physical limitations but to train and lead soldiers himself. After serving with a non-commissioned officer's responsibilities, he was eventually promoted ensign. He had learnt the lesson of his life, and he made the firm decision to continue with the military career. Thus, in November 1909, he went to the *Kriegsschule*, the military school at Neisse where he was able to show his improvements. He sailed through the courses which were necessary for the final appointment, returning to his old regiment as a second lieutenant on 22 August 1910. Having achieved this rank, he was sent to the third battalion of his regiment at Crossen where he developed a friendship with a Lieutenant Barnick, with whom he shared the same enthusiasm for hunting and for horses. Once in the military, Model showed very high levels of proficiency because he was showing signs of becoming an enthusiastic and efficient officer, who loved riding horses and could be depended upon. For this reason, in 1912 Model was selected by Major Martin Reymann to be a First Lieutenant and the Battalion's aide, to take over his position. A lucky break came in that same year, as although the regimental commander Colonel Henseling had shown no interest in this young man, Colonel von Jacobi, having noticed Model's activities as a battalion aide, picked him up to become his own aide, (similar to an aide-de-camp). This was the type of position which often paved the way to a very successful army career. It is interesting that, as his career progressed and his position improved, Model started adopting some of the Prussian officers' attitudes and mannerisms, including the accent, and the classical monocle. However, he never abandoned the work ethic of a middle-class person.[1]

As the 1914 war broke out Colonel von Jacobi, who Model held in high esteem, was moved to another unit being replaced by a Colonel Fromm who, in Model's eyes, did not match the figure of his predecessor. Nevertheless, as the unit was moved to the Western Front, Fromm was to give a positive report on Model which undoubtedly helped his career. As regimental aide Model found himself with a baptism of fire on 23 August 1914, as his regiment conducted a frontal attack against the British Expeditionary Force at Mons and were repulsed with heavy losses. By the following month the war had changed its pattern, and the regiment was bogged down in trench warfare with Model, as regimental aide, living in the trenches, thereby soon becoming very popular amongst his soldiers. He was promoted to first lieutenant on 25 February 1915, and he was to make his name during one of the classic frontal assaults which characterised the Great War. In Champagne, on 21 September 1915, Model's regiment faced a major French assault preceded by a massive three-day long artillery fire, which was followed by the infantry attack repulsed with heavy losses. In the aftermath, Model sent a short message to Colonel Prince Oskar von Preussen, the brigade commander, summarising the conditions of his regiment (which had suffered 60 per cent losses) and the need for reinforcements. This simple, calm, and rational message greatly impressed von Preussen, who realised Model was a dependable officer who could be relied upon at a time of crisis. It was because of such observations that Model was recommended to attend the general staff course, while as a young officer he was awarded the Iron Cross 1st class for his behaviour during battle. Model was wounded by a shell fragment in his shoulder on 3 November 1915, spending six weeks in hospital, and shortly afterwards rejoined his unit, but he was sent in early 1916 to attend the staff officer training course at Sedan. By then, the staff officer training courses had lost much of their original selective nature, and they were attended by more and more officers, as the German army needed them. Although this was no longer the pre-designated path to a future career as a superior officer, it came as a great help to Model whose own career path was clear. He was wounded again on 25 April 1916, and at his return to the front Model was made brigade aide-de-camp by von Preussen. He demonstrated such good attitudes and skills that, on 7 June 1917, he was selected to serve as orderly (an aid-de-camp) with the Army Supreme Command, at first at Bad Kreuznach, as part of the operations branch, then from February 1918, he attended the Great General Staff Course (the real general staff course, reserved only for the proper career officers bound to rise to generalship) upon the recommendation of the Army Staff officer Hans von Seeckt (the future chief of army staff) and von Preussen. After attending the one-month shortened course again at Sedan, Model was given the position of supply officer of the Garde Division, which took part in the spring 1918 *Richard* offensives, then to the 36th Reserve Division from 30 August 1918. It was in this position that Model faced the November 1918 revolution in Germany, the surrender, and the end of the monarchy. As he faced the possibility of leaving the army, Model thought again of studying medicine or to start a career in banking. His fate, in the person of General von Rantzaus, was to influence him again.

Chapter Two

Interbellum Years

Nature of his work

As General von Rantzaus arrived at Koblenz along with his division, which had behaved commendably in those tragic times, he gave a final comment on the young officer who had served in his staff. Captain Model (promoted in August 1918) had provided through his actions and accomplishments an excellent image of himself, so much so he was selected for future employment in higher positions. In December 1918 Model was transferred to the staff of the XVII Army Corps, whose operations officer was Major Edwin von Stülpnagel, the brother of Otto von Stülpnagel who had been Model's former superior officer on the Western Front. As the corps faced an insurrection in Danzig, von Stülpnagel knew he could rely on an officer of such good qualities as Walter Model. His behaviour also impressed the corps commander, General von Petersdorff, and his successor General Otto von Below. As the corps was deployed along the eastern border to secure the area, Model was officially given the position of staff officer between 19 January and 10 July 1919. This would secure his transition into the small, 100,000 strong Reichswehr which took place in November 1919, after he had taken part in the disarming of the 'Baltikum' volunteer formations, which had been fighting against the Communists in the Danzig area. Now under the command of General von Cramer, Model again gave a good impression of his qualities as an officer. In November, after joining the Reichswehr, he was posted to the 14th Infantry Regiment at Konstanz, near the Swiss border, before being posted as staff officer to General von Gillhausen, the commander of the security troops in the demilitarised part of Germany along the Rhine. Model did not find this appointment to his liking, as he considered von Gillhausen's activity (clearly attempting to defy the Allied authorities) too unsafe and requested to be returned to his troops. His request was granted, and he became the commander of a machine gun company with the 'Hacketäuer' Freikorps battalion, in reality the I battalion of the 14th Infantry Regiment which was under orders from Major von Falkenstein. In mid-March 1920 there was a Communist uprising in the city of Elberfeld, and after the insurgents opened fire against the police, Model's unit was sent there to repress the uprising. Model's battalion, some 600 strong, faced for the very first time the bitter taste of civil war, and during this repression, killed some 1,000 insurgents (mainly workers), suffering the loss of two officers and twelve soldiers with another 100 wounded. This was not an entirely sad affair for Model, who had a stroke of luck. Quartered at the house in Moltke Strasse 6 he met there Herta Huyssen, who was to become his wife. Model's battalion was then redeployed and sent to Münster, but in that summer Model had other things to think about.

The Huyssen family were wealthy, with ties to the Deutsche Bank, the Krupp firm, and with activities in the Netherlands. Herta took an instantaneous liking to his 'caviar sandwich', the nickname she had given to the young Captain, and within a year the two were married. The ceremony was held on 12 May 1921, at the Lukas Church in Frankfurt. Other than his family and colleagues, the relatives of Herta attended as well as General von Rango. Model was given a week's leave and the couple settled in an apartment in Gerichtstrasse 4 in Münster. The two had three children, two daughters, Hella first, a sister Christa, followed by a son, Hansgeorg, who would follow his father's steps and have a career in the military. While in Münster, Model worked for General Fritz von Lossberg, who at that time was the local military area commander. Von Lossberg was not just a skilled tactician, who had developed the concept of the 'defence in depth' during the war, but he became a mentor to the young captain who was greatly impressed by the defensive theories von Lossberg had developed.

By 1925 the situation in Germany was stabilising, and Model had to face the customary shift from the staff officer duties to the field troops command. On 1 October 1925, Model was reassigned to the 9th

Company, III Battalion of the 8th Infantry Regiment in Görlitz, whose commander was the future General Stumpff. His family followed him, and they settled in Number Two Gutenberg Strasse, the barracks being conveniently situated within the old city ring. However, Model was not idle, as he put his men to work, training them relentlessly with exercises on defence, withdrawal, and sudden counterattack against the rear of the enemy lines. Since the Reichswehr was not granted the use of tanks, the so called 'tank dummies' were created. Mock ups carried around using whatever vehicle at disposal, from cars to bicycles. At the same time, Model had the task of forming the non-commissioned officers who were divided into three groups, for future employment as officers. Model also took care of his men: because many were unable to live off their pay, he created a company support fund to help them. It was at this time that an incident took place with the regimental commander, Colonel von Schenckendorff. As he was passing Model's 9th Company in review, the young Captain failed to make his report. The truth was that von Schenckendorff was five minutes earlier than he should have been. Without flinching, as Model was asked for the report he waited, took out his pocket watch, checked the orders, then replied only after five minutes had passed. During this time Model also worked on military history under the direction of General von Cochenhausen, contributing to a major work with an essay on Gneisenau. On 30 September 1928, Model's time as company commander came to an end, and he was sent to Berlin again to work as a staff officer with the 3rd Division. This was a particularly lucky period for him, not only because of the birth of Hansgeorg in 1927 and of Christa in 1929, but also because he was detached to attend a 'commanders support' course held by Colonel Hans Reinhardt, later to become a general. The course, focused on tactics and military history, followed Model's promotion to major in October 1929, which was attended by a long series of officers who would rise to the top of the German army during the war. These included Adolf Heusinger, Hans Speidel, General Jodl's brother Ferdinand, August Winter, and Ferdinand Rasp. Model's family became close to the family of Hans Speidel, the two usually gathering together at the former house in Moabit, at the Rathenower Strasse 6, which was usually also attended by young and charming women. Model's career was on the rise, and in 1930 he was assigned to the General Staff, the T4 office or the branch dealing with the training of the troops. There Model worked on the preparation of the instruction booklets, and as staff officer, also dealt with the secret defence plans for the eastern border. Under command of Colonel List (the later field marshal), Model found himself close to the very top brass of the German army, List being succeeded in command by Walther von Brauchitsch, who would become the Commander in Chief of the Army.

In August 1931, Model was chosen to accompany von Brauchitsch to the Soviet Union, the group taking part in a six-week inspection trip, from August to October. They went to the military sites in the country to study the developments of warfare while still technically under the restrictions of the Treaty of Versailles. In November 1932, Model was eventually promoted lieutenant colonel. Another troop command assignment followed: Model was given command of the II Battalion of the 2nd Infantry Regiment in East Prussia. His regimental commander, Colonel Kühne, did not take to him but this transpired not to be a problem. In January 1933 Hitler had risen to power, changes at the top of the army took place, and Model was able to rely on his Berlin connections as Hitler re-introduced conscription in March 1935, changing the size and structure of the German army. The old Reichswehr came to an end and became the Wehrmacht. In some ways, this complicated the issues for Model who, in October 1934, had been promoted colonel. The standard practice was that he, as the next step in his career, should have been appointed first staff officer (the position reserved for the operations officers) with a division or corps command, but with the Wehrmacht now expanding, Model's rank did not fit the appointment any longer. After commanding a regiment for one year, Model was to be assigned a new job in the newly created Army Staff, a job without precedent.[1]

From Staff Officer to Panzer Commander

Many officers' careers were built during the period following the transition from the Reichswehr to the Wehrmacht, when the fast expansion of the German armed forces created opportunities that few could only dream about. Several of these careers, like Model's, were to start at the very top, with the Army Staff which was busier than it had ever been overseeing the rapid expansion of the German army. Model, who could rely on his connections, his skills, and the many acknowledgements he had, was lucky and gained a first-class assignment. The Army Staff being led by General Ludwig Beck, a new branch was created to study the strategic possibilities in future wars, which was to research in depth all the technical innovations both abroad and within Germany. This was the task of the 8th Branch of the Army Staff, which had in total a dozen different branches; the technical branch should have been formally under the supervision of the operations branch (the first in the list), which at the time was commanded by General von Wietersheim, and from October 1936 by General von Manstein. It was Colonel Friedrich Hossbach, at the time chief of the Central Branch of the Army Staff and Army Aide to Hitler, who personally selected Model to take the lead of the 8th Branch. He undoubtedly believed that the 1929 Commanders Support Course had paid off, and personally knew Model and acknowledged his activities in the field of training and his writings on military history. Model took over the new assignment on 15 October 1935, Hossbach relying on his fantasy that he would be able to identify the most relevant innovations in the field of warfare. The only problem was Model's lack of technical knowledge, as reputedly he was almost incapable of driving an automobile but known as a skilled and brilliant horse rider. Manstein, who as Chief of the Operations Branch supervised Model's activities, described him as somebody whose work was becoming more and more indispensable within the Army Staff. As a matter of interest, Model did not constrain himself to theoretical work but carried out in-depth research into the most updated technical innovations. This activity put him in touch with another general soon to become well known, namely, Guderian. Model, along with his chief of staff the then Captain Hans Röttinger (who would become Kesselring's operations officer in Italy), contacted him on several occasions professionally. Both Röttinger and Guderian, accompanied by their wives, would frequently meet Model socially at their new residence at Thekla Strasse 9 in Berlin Lichterfelde, with Model's wife Herta showing her skills as a socialite on these occasions. In addition to this, with Colonel Jaschke of the Army Ordnance Branch, Model helped design the first armoured personnel carrier and the new assault gun, with the infantry support vehicle which was known as the *Sturmgeschütz*. Manstein found this idea brilliant and started the creation of this new branch of the army, which was to be part of the artillery which also provided support to other arms. Model also became a megaphone for Guderian's ideas, down to the point that Model almost clashed with his superior, General Beck, who had a more sceptical view on the creation of an armoured branch for the army. Model was no fool, and on inspecting the prototype of a new gun at the well-known firm Rheinmetall, he raised embarrassing questions which soon put an end to an irrational idea. Being told that the new 240 mm gun would require some time to be put in position ready to fire, Model (with the characteristic Prussian, almost snobbish attitude he had developed), put his monocle on and asked how long it would take for the gun to be ready to fire. When he was informed it would take three to four hours, he abruptly replied this was too long. The project was foolish, but Model was not. In any case, in that summer he and his family treated themselves to a holiday in Paris.

In September 1937 the first and only major mass field exercise held by the German army before the war was held at Mecklenburg. Mussolini was also in attendance. This was a great occasion and Model, like others, distinguished themselves with their success. Afterwards he waited for a new assignment, but this took time for various reasons. At the end of December 1937, the cause for this delay became known: Model had been assigned to Spain to witness first-hand the innovations in warfare, while they were being implemented on the battlefields of the Spanish Civil War. In February 1938, Model is known to have been in Avila, but this is all that is known about the period he spent in Spain. When back in Germany, Model was given the task of developing the new 130 mm mortar, which was being developed based on Hitler's ideas. As he was busy with this delicate task, changes took place at the top. In January 1938 the Commander in Chief of the Wehrmacht, General von Blomberg, and the Commander in Chief of the Army General Fritsch were involved in fabricated scandals forcing their resignations. This process of underhand forced resignations enabled Hitler to take command of the Wehrmacht, a new organisation which replaced the War Ministry with the Wehrmacht High Command, with new faces replacing the familiar ones. The Chief of Staff of the Army, General Beck, was removed and replaced by General Halder, and Model's direct superior General von Manstein was replaced and given command of a division. Model was apparently not perturbed by all these changes, as they did not touch him personally. It was evident that Model belonged to the new generation of army commanders, a role he had managed to carve out for himself, and new opportunities arose as the army developed along the new guidelines. Following General Guderian's appointment as Inspector of the Motorised Troops, on 1 March 1938, Model was promoted major general, still in his position as chief of the army technical branch. Model was soon in touch with Hitler who had a deep interest in the development of new weapons. As the American historian Robert Forczyk noted, Model was not just a good officer and an excellent commander, but importantly had had a middle-class background, which was still noticeable, despite his attempts to assume Prussian style mannerisms. This aspect was more than appealing to the Nazi leadership, which wanted to identify itself with this kind of officer rather than the old school, the genuine Prussian ones who were different from Model and his family.

Model met Hitler for the first time, according to available records, as Hitler inspected the development of the new mortar, and gave a speech for this occasion. Hitler made it clear that its content was to be kept secret under all circumstances, and only speculation can propose what he said. Model could not help wondering if this were the signal for an imminent war which, in case of mobilisation, would have seen him appointed as Chief of Staff to the 7th Army. The possible scenario was the planned attack against Czechoslovakia, which never materialised. Instead, Model's new appointment occurred on 10 November 1938 when he was posted to Dresden to be Chief of Staff with the IV Army Corps, under command of General von Schwedler. This was not an easy task for Model who had to supervise the plans for the expansion of the corps in case of full mobilisation, which would see its strength rise from three to nine divisions, six new ones to be formed with the distinct possibility of war. In March 1939 the corps led the German advance into the remnants of Czechoslovakia, the rest of that country after the loss of the Sudeten regions in the aftermath of the Munich agreement. The seizure of the country proceeded without problems, which helped Model to be noticed as an effective commander rather than just a staff officer.[2]

Chapter Three

The Second World War

Poland and War

Model's IV Army Corps took part in the Polish campaign, at first seizing Tschenstoschau then closing, along with other units, the Radow pocket. It was then given the task of marching towards the Vistula and the Bug rivers to close any approach, thereby preventing the escape of the Polish troops. Before the task could be accomplished the Red Army, the Soviet Union having attacked Poland on 17 September, arrived there before the IV Corps. Model developed an unfavourable impression of the Polish Army and population during his stay in the country, the leadership, and the overall organisation which he described as miserable and at a low level. It is not known if Model was aware of the activities against the Jews and the Polish population, mainly because he only remained in Poland for a brief period. By 23 October 1939 he was given the position of Chief of Staff of the 16th Army, a newly formed command deployed along the Moselle River under command of General Ernst Busch. This new appointment provided Model with many tasks, as the staff was newly formed, although with a series of first-class officers who were soon to make themselves known, these included Colonel Gerlach and Colonel Bogislav von Schwerin.

The subordinated divisions had to be amalgamated, and the army faced an important task which required intensive training, which was Model's speciality. The army had an important task as it formed, along with the 12th Army, von Rundstedt's Army Group A which was intended to drive through the Ardennes to attack the French defences on the Meuse River, in particular at Sedan. This was the critical task of the entire attack in the West, and its failure would have brought havoc and ruin to the entire offensive. The 16th Army was committed to the Western Front precisely at 13.00 hours on 9 May 1940, as it received the order to cross the Belgian border at 5.35 the next morning. The army was spearheaded by Guderian's motorised corps which, after crossing the Ardennes, broke through the French defences at Sedan and started its advance to the West. The role of the 16th Army should not be underestimated as it provided the essential defence for the left wing of the German advance, which enabled the Panzer Division to reach the Channel, thereby closing the pocket at Dunkirk. In particular it defended the most important sector of the German southern front, which stretched between the northernmost end of the Maginot Line and the Aisne River, where the French counterattacks concentrated leading to the battle of Stonne. The German victory at Stonne was as decisive as the other victories on the Western Front because a French breakthrough would have endangered the advance to the Channel. It did not happen, despite the French determination and the use of the heavy tanks Char B1 bis, and the German victory secured future events. On 10 June the 16th Army formed the northern pincer of the German attack against the Maginot Line, which came to an end a week later with the entire line of fortification being forced to surrender after it had been surrounded. At the time of the French surrender on 25 June 1940 the 16th Army (along with the other units in the action) had captured 22 French generals, 278 officers and 68,370 troops which demonstrated the role it played in the campaign. Since the army was mostly employed on defensive positions, Model had no chances of witnessing first-hand the German Panzer drive across Belgium and France, and his operational command was still mainly defensive in nature. This did not matter too much, because Model soon had to deal with another task.

    Model and his army spent the summer in Belgium, and in the area of Dunkirk preparing for the planned Operation *Sealion*, the invasion of Britain. This was, once again, a task which required intensive training with the development of new methods of warfare because, it should be recalled, the Germans had no experience of landing on defended beaches. Model and his staff worked intensively, developing ingenious solutions to compensate for their lack of suitable landing equipment, training the troops for the new task. Amongst others, an amphibious version of the Panzer III (named 'swimming Panzer') was developed, though Model did not know it would be used later on another front. Operation *Sealion* was never carried out, and eventually postponed indefinitely in September 1940. Model had little time to rest, as he was posted to another command in less than two months. After the victory in the West, the Panzer Division had acquired a more than prominent role not only in German warfare, but worldwide. Along with the Stuka, the dive bomber which provided effective support to those on the battlefield, such weapons were considered the scourge of Germany's enemies being the most powerful piece of armament in the inventory of her army. Being granted command of a Panzer Division was henceforth a matter of prestige, especially if the division in question was not just one of the many. As it was, in the autumn and winter of 1940, the German army doubled on Hitler's orders, and the number of Panzer Divisions shrank in the number of tanks for each one. This enabled the creation of 20 divisions (a 21st being formed in North Africa in the summer of 1941) out of the original ten, the ten new ones being created out of already existing infantry divisions. Nevertheless, being given command of one of the new Panzer Divisions would have been prestigious, but to be given command of one of the original three divisions whose origins dated back to 1935 was even more so. The 3rd Panzer Division, other than being one of the first to be formed, also had a special role within the German army: its garrison was Berlin, and its troops were all too often used in ceremonial occasions, especially to meet foreign dignitaries visiting the city. The division was part of the city, and its Panzer regiment even adopted Berlin's symbol, a bear, as its own. Needless to say, one can imagine Model's reaction as, on 1 October 1940, he was informed he would be the new divisional commander.[1]

As General Stumpff left command and Model took over, a number of new soldiers joined the division. They would change its social structure as they came from all over Germany, and no longer just from the Berlin area which led those members of the 'old division' to say that it had been 're-modelled'. Several first-class officers and commanders would be under Model's orders, including the divisional operations officer (the equivalent of a chief of staff), Major Pomtow, the Panzer Brigade commander, General Breith, and the Rifle Brigade commander Colonel Kleeman. Model dealt again with his customary habit for hard work. The division, after the campaign in the West and the major reorganisation had to be refitted, and from January 1941 was re-equipped with identical motor vehicles, better than the usual array of mixed vehicles which usually characterised the German divisions. Older soldiers were replaced with younger ones, and in February 1941 the division provided the bulk of the *Afrika Korps* by forming the 5th Light Division, which was sent to North Africa with some of its elements.

On 17 May 1941, the division held a large-scale exercise, attended by Guderian at Marienwerder, which included the crossing of a main river supported by air units. For the occasion the 'swimming Panzers' which had been produced for the planned invasion of Britain, and had been subsequently handed over to the division, were utilised, giving a rather good impression. Model soon became aware of what was going on as he attended the customary map exercise held by the 4th Army staff, led by Field Marshal von Kluge. On this occasion Model became aware not only of the planned attack against the Soviet Union, but also of the task his division was assigned within the framework of Operation *Barbarossa*. By the end of May 1944, the division was at its full complement of men and equipment, ready to face its task. On 25 May Model held a meeting with his officers at the headquarters at Buckow, informing them of the plans. Six days later a secret order was issued instructing the division to leave its barracks on 6 June and deploy within four days close to the Soviet Union border in Poland. As the division left, the Berlin population cheered its men who were going away to win another victory.

Model's 3rd Panzer Division, part of the XXIV Army Corps led by General Geyr von Schweppenburg, itself under command of Guderian's Panzer Group 2, crossed the Bug River, marking the border, at 3.45 on 22 June 1941. On this occasion, as proved during the exercise, the swimming tanks proved to be more than useful even though the infantry actually established the bridgehead. After a clash with the Soviet forces, the division started its advance with Model following the leading units with his advanced command staff. As the various units faced difficulties in moving across the swamps, Model re-addressed the divisional route of advance to the north and by that evening, at 18.45, the southern suburbs of Brest Litovsk were reached. The division did not attack the city-fortress, but it fought against the enemy troops which were withdrawing from the fortress. Model joined the divisional leading unit, the Panzer Regiment 6 which, after some rest and necessary refuelling, again started its advance the next day. The swift progress enabled the 3rd Panzer Division to seize an intact bridge on the Dnepr-Bug canal, swiftly seizing Kobryn. Due to a large suitable road, Model's men were able to advance with unexpected speed, soon reaching the railway line to Minsk. The first Soviet tanks, light ones, were encountered and destroyed, adding even more to the divisional successes. This event did not prevent Model for demanding more. Allowing no rest to his men, he reached the frontline and ordered the pursuit of the enemy without concerns for the flanks, the pace of the advance being slowed down by the occasional pockets of Soviet resistance. Swiftly, the division advanced deep into enemy territory and again Model, clearly unable to stand in the rear, was at the forefront taking personal risks. He took from the 2nd company of the communications battalion a heavy eight-wheeled armoured car, which he used to reach the frontline. Occasionally, when his movements were halted by a road congestion, Model would dismount and personally resolve the problem. As he was doing this, his armoured car was hit by an artillery shell which tore it apart. All of those aboard were killed, Model emerged unscathed from the incident. Following the traditional German system of allowing subordinate commanders to deal with plans as they deemed best leading from the frontline, Model split the division into two combat groups which started their advance deeply into Soviet territory. The first large scale fight took place at Sluzk, the division until then having been advancing along a single road. Model, having split it into two groups and impressed on his subordinate commanders the need for maintaining strict marching discipline to avoid unnecessary waste of time, pushed on. By then his division had advanced some 300 kilometres, covering about one fifth of the distance separating it from Moscow. By the end of June,

Model's 3rd Panzer Division had reached the Beresina River, preparing to cross the Dnjepr. Model, unperturbed by his close brush with death, followed the leading elements of the division and, when the moment of fighting against the enemy positions came, witnessed the combat from the frontline, personally giving orders and directives and looking after the wounded when the battle ended. As the division approached the key city of Bobruisk, Model prepared the tanks for the attack, but having realised that they could not cross the river at night, had the divisional reconnaissance unit recce a detour, which they managed. The road was almost unusable, and a small bridge collapsed under the weight of the heavy vehicles, but the division managed to outflank Bobruisk which was seized the following day, with Model leading the advance himself. Having established a bridgehead on the Beresina, the division was forced to halt because of the road conditions and having spread its elements widely across the advance. It was not helped by the Russian resistance starting to stiffen, and the division now had to fight its way forward. Eventually it started its attack towards Rogatschev, and as the Soviet resistance bogged down the advance, Model reached the frontline to solve the situation by ordering an outflanking movement. By 2 July the 3rd Panzer Division was approaching Rogatschev, even though this time it was facing harder resistance from the Red Army. The city was attacked on 4 July, after establishing a bridgehead on the Dnjepr, the frontal attack being the only possible choice. Not only were Model's troops facing unexpected resistance, on 5–6 July they also faced a Soviet counterattack aimed at breaking the divisional supply lines, which was repulsed due to the timely intervention of the Panzers. Soviet resistance and lack of supplies, fuel in particular, halted the 3rd Panzer Division's advance. It was resumed after they found a suitable spot to outflank the city, and the division was relieved of its positions, because the city was to be attacked by an infantry division. On 11 July the division started its advance towards Mogilew, which was not attacked directly because it was heavily defended. Two days before this advance, Model had been awarded the Knight's Cross. Because the 4th Panzer Division had been able to seize a bridgehead on the Dnjepr, the 3rd Panzer Division was re-directed there enabling it to attack Mogilew from the east. The attack, witnessed again by Model from the frontline, faced strong enemy resistance, failed to seize the city, and the division abandoned its siege on 17 July resuming its advance east. It was eventually relieved two days later because the 4th Panzer Division was now facing a Soviet counterattack. The advance was now bogged down, but this was not a problem for Guderian who, on 26 July, reached the divisional command post for a visit and to congratulate personally Model for the success of his division. The reason for all this was because on 1 August Guderian's Panzer Group managed to resume its advance, the division marching towards Rosslav witnessed by both Guderian and Model. Training and skill came to the fore, as Model's division faced for the first time, on 18 August, the better equipped Soviet units with their T-34 tanks, which the Germans knew nothing about. The almost impregnable Russian tanks were eventually destroyed by the better trained Panzer crews of the 3rd Panzer Division which, as the battle for Smolensk was coming to its end, was directed along with the rest of Guderian's Panzer Group to the south to close the northern pincer at Kiev. The advance started on 23 August, and Model was able to resume the initial pace of advance because the movement had clearly taken the enemy by surprise. After seizing a bridge on the Desna River, the 3rd Panzer Division was halted by Soviet resistance, and it took three weeks before the advance could be resumed. Eventually, the 3rd Panzer Division established bridgeheads on the Sejm and Sula River, which enabled it to link up with the 16th Panzer Division advancing from the south on 15 September. The Kiev pocket had been closed, and 55 Soviet divisions were caught in it after Model had successfully advanced for some 350 kilometres in only three weeks. By then, Model's time as a division commander was coming to its end. The 3rd Panzer Division rested and refitted, ready to play its part in the attack against Moscow, and as it was waiting for supplies near Orel on 9 October, Model was informed that he had been promoted to full generalship. He was given command of the XXXXI Army Corps, another motorised corps which was part of General Georg-Hans Reinhardt's Panzer Group 3. Model took over command on the 29th, just in time to play his part in the attack against Moscow.[2]

The Rise in Command

As he arrived at the XXXXI Army Corps headquarters, Model found an old friend, his chief of staff Hans Röttiger, and met his superior commander, Field Marshal von Bock. Model was an enthusiast, keen on attacking and willing to meet his troops at once. This transpired to be a problem, because at closer inspection it was obvious the troops were not ready for a major offensive as they were short of weapons, vehicles, and men. Nevertheless, Model prepared his plans and by mid-November, as the offensive towards Moscow was resumed, he could attack having been given freedom of movement. Model's central task was simply to protect the northern flank of the Panzer Group 3 and secure a link with the neighbouring 9th Army. As the Panzer Group advanced towards Knin, Model was to maintain the front while advancing his men eastwards, in the area of Kalinin along the Volga. For this task, he could only rely on the 6th Panzer Division, which was not a first-class unit. As December came the situation at the front became harder than it had ever been, as temperatures dropped to minus 20° C, supplies became scarcer and the Soviets not only offered fanatical resistance, but also counterattacked. Model never lost his optimism and decided to advance further, his 6th Panzer Division supported by the 23 Infantry Division. Von Bock, having noticed his determination, decided to make his XXXXI Corps the spearhead of the offensive towards Moscow, just as the Soviet winter offensive began on 5 December 1941.

The German offensive was halted, and for the first time the German army was to fight on the defensive, Model proving himself particularly suited for the task. Model's XXXXI Corps withdrew in good order, but the Panzer Group 3 position was exposed, the advance had created a huge bulge aiming at Moscow with the flanks virtually undefended, and the chaotic withdrawal of other units soon made the situation worse. Facing this crisis, Model did not lose his nerve, and proved to be a reliable commander capable of dealing with the situation making decisions on the spot, just as he had when his division had advanced. Once, as he had found that the vehicles of his division were blocking an area as they had run out of fuel, he ordered them to be pushed off the road to make room for the vehicles of the withdrawing 1st Panzer Division. On 8 December Field Marshal von Kluge took command of the entire sector to the north of Moscow, the crisis reaching its peak on 19 December, when Hitler dismissed the Commander in Chief of the Army, Field Marshal von Brauchitsch, and took command of the army himself. By then most of Model's corps, along with the bulk of Panzer Group 3 motorised divisions, had been encircled by the advancing Soviet troops west of Klin. The Soviet lack of experience and the German determined counterattacks enabled these forces to escape the trap, and on this occasion, Model was able to enhance his reputation as a field commander. While others asked for permission to withdraw, Model would protest whenever ordered to do the same because his positions had been endangered by somebody else's withdrawal. It was not uncommon for him to be at the frontline, pistol in hand, enforcing discipline and giving orders to maintain calmness and prevent collapse. Soon, the troops in the rear areas started calling him *Frontschwein* (front-line pig), meaning he was the kind of soldier who could not accept anything else but leading from the front. Losses were heavy, both because of the Red Army and of the weather, but this did not prevent Model from conducting a tenacious series of rearguard actions which, by January 1942, secured a relative stability to the forces in what had become the Rzhev salient. On 10 January the Soviet offensive struck the 9th Army's sector penetrating deeply into the German lines, and soon the Red Army started to advance along the Smolensk-Vitebsk area between the positions of the Army Group North and the Army Group Centre. Only a man like Model could save the situation.

It might have been Stalingrad *ante litteram* (before its time) as the Army Group Centre withdrew along the Dnjepr River with the Red Army driving deeply into its rear areas between Velikiye Luki and Smolensk, the German defences being reduced to a small series of strongholds all too often manned by rear area troops. The situation was such that the 9th Army commander lost his nerve, and he broke down leaving the army without command.[3] The Army Chief of Staff considered this the most critical sector of the entire Eastern Front, and on 16 January, just two months after he had taken command, Model was summoned to Hitler's headquarters to be given command of the 9th Army to deal with the situation. Hitler was impressed by Model, remarking that while trusting him as a commander he would not serve under him at all. When Model had been given the command, it was nothing more than the remnants of an army, the dozen divisions now under his command had been reduced in strength and morale, and with little left of their weapons, vehicles, and equipment. Model, unimpressed by the crisis, stunned his staff as he asked for an immediate counteroffensive, with the aim of rescuing the forces trapped in the Olenino pocket. The staff reacted with a series of vigorous protests, but Model would not listen. Comments also followed from the units at the frontline, which claimed not to be ready to attack within the strict schedule set by Model. The new Soviet offensive, this time to the south of Model's 9th Army at Wyzma, was dealt with by the arrival of reinforcements, including an infantry regiment which he had brought in by air from France.

The moment came when Model's greatest concern was not the Red Army, but Hitler himself. After taking over command of the army first hand, Hitler started micro-managing the situation at the front and, as the reinforcements were sent over to Model's army, he asked for a counterattack to relieve the Olenino pocket. Model, far from being intimidated by the situation, asked for an immediate audience, and confronted Hitler with a simple question: who was in command of the 9th Army? Hitler, clearly surprised by such an extraordinary attitude, granted Model freedom of movement, and started to respect him more than ever. No matter what, Model decided to keep to the plan and the scheduled attack, which was not postponed, started on 21 January with him, the commander, being at the frontline, as was his custom. The counterattack was a success, despite all the forecasts. The Soviet penetration into the German lines was halted, the Rhzev gap was closed, and Model earned the promotion to colonel general. Foreseeing the Soviet counter-manoeuvre, Model was also able to forestall the new Soviet attack and, as the front stabilised and the crisis was beyond its peak, on 17 February 1942, he launched his own counterattack, which definitely cut off the enemy penetration on the Rzhev area taking some 5,000 prisoners. On 23 May, flying over the enemy lines in a Storch plane, Model was wounded by ground fire and had to be hospitalised because of the loss of blood. His place at the top of the 9th Army was taken by General von Vietinghoff.

It took time for Model to recover from the wound, and as the new German offensive started towards Stalingrad and the Caucasus he was still in Berlin with his family. There, suddenly, on 2 August 1942, he was summoned to Hermann Göring's private residence at Karinhall to discuss a delicate matter. A German staff officer had taken with him during a reconnaissance flight the plans for the offensive, codenamed Operation *Blue*, and these had fallen into Soviet hands after the plane had been shot down. The superior commander was blamed for the incident, and Hitler wanted him to be court-martialled. Göring wanted to ask Model for his opinion on this matter and offered him an opulent lunch, which Model practically refused by stating that, as a soldier on leave, he was to rely on his ration cards. We are not given to know what was said on that occasion, but the officer in question, General Stumme, was relieved of command but eventually posted to North Africa where he served under Rommel.

Model's reputation had definitely been put to good use, which was something which usually happened for him when at the front. Model's somehow innovative defence tactics have been analysed in depth by the American historian Robert Forczyk, who noted how he was able to deal with an unexpected situation by developing new doctrines which suited the situation. The standard German defensive doctrine was based on movement, and the commanders were required to allow the enemy to advance, recognise the focal point of the enemy offensive and strike back at that moment in order to restabilise the situation. The Soviet counteroffensive in the winter of 1941–42 caught most of the German commanders by surprise. They were unable to manoeuvre, given the lack of forces available with the shortage of supplies, and could not prevent the Soviet drives into their rear areas by threatening the flanks and the rear of their units. Model showed an uncommon capability to adapt to the situation, as he forgot the standard German army doctrine and developed a new one. First, he created units capable of moving in the snow-covered terrain by putting together all the available reconnaissance forces. He had them re-equipped in such a way that a mobile brigade sized cavalry unit could be formed to support the Panzer units, which could not move because of the lack of fuel. He formed ski-battalions and grouped all the available artillery under a higher artillery command, to be able to concentrate the available firepower whenever needed. A rigid defence, based on the creation of strongpoints based on the key places in the area, prevented the Soviet advances from creating a stable front, and he kept the main lines of communications in German hands. It was basically an adaptation of the First World War defence doctrine, which Model adapted to the situation. Facing a serious shortage of infantry, Model took a step further reducing the manpower of the headquarters and rear area units in order to reinforce the frontline. This would become a standard practice in the German armed forces in 1943–44. However, it did not make Model a popular commander amongst his troops, the *Frontschwein* was all too willing to take risks and wanted his soldiers to do the same. Nevertheless, Model was able to restore a critical situation, and did it without losing his nerve.

Model returned to the headquarters of the 9th Army on 7 August 1942, only to face another Soviet attack at the Rzhev salient. In fact, the new Soviet offensive against the Army Group Centre had started on 30 July swiftly driving a deep wedge to the south of Rzhev, which was followed by a southern thrust at Vyazma with the clear aim of encircling the 9th Army. To make things worse, all the available reinforcements had been sent to the south and Model's army, as well as the entire Army Group Centre, were suffering a dire shortage of men, weapons, and equipment. The situation was restored soon after Model's arrival back at the army headquarters, the Soviet attacks having been halted with Rzhev still in German hands. Model could rejoice, but he had next to no time left to rebuild his army. In November 1942 the Red Army started a series of offensives, the most well-known being the one leading to the encirclement at Stalingrad. It is not as well known that several offensives were also launched in the other sections of the front, such as the area held by the Army Group Centre. They might have had potentially disastrous repercussions, just as the

Stalingrad offensive. Taking advantage of winter and of the offensives in the southern part of the front, the Soviet commanders thought it possible to crush the Rzhev salient once and for all, trapping and destroying in the pocket Model's 9th Army. The plan, codenamed Operation *Mars*, had been prepared for a long time which, incidentally, enabled Model's staff to discover the plan and in turn to prepare the countermeasures. Model started reinforcing the threatened areas of the salient, forming double lines of bunkers and strongpoints protected by vast minefields, which he inspected himself before the enemy attack started. Supplies were stored to prevent shortages during the battle, and the troops were prepared for immediate counterattacks. This was the 9th Army's critical weak spot, since Model could only rely on three Panzer Divisions which had been badly mauled during the previous battles and had never been fully rebuilt, so that on the eve of the battle they fielded just some 150 tanks between them. This time Model insisted on having reinforcements, and his request was granted, but only if further Panzer units were actually needed in the 9th Army sector. On 25 November 1942 the Soviet attack started, with four different places being hammered by intensive artillery fire before a mass of 800,000 troops supported by 2,000 tanks moved to attack. On both flanks of the salient the Red Army managed to break through the German defences, which enabled a commitment of reserves to pursue the success and close the pincer. Without hesitation, Model asked for the necessary reinforcements while his troops handled the situation to their best. A local counterattack against the westernmost Soviet penetration into the salient managed to halt the enemy advance, while the positions on both sides of the Soviet wedge were held and reinforced. The eastern pincer was also counterattacked, which halted the Soviet penetration into the salient just after about a dozen kilometres. Without waiting for the reinforcements to arrive, Model decided to counterattack at once, and he had his three Panzer Divisions move against the flanks and the rear of the Soviet eastern penetration. The Soviet forces were surrounded, and eventually destroyed putting an end to the threat in that area of the front, and in general to the threat of encirclement. Model then used the reinforcements to halt the Soviet advance in the north-western part of the salient, enabling a counterattack to cut off the entire western Soviet prong which was destroyed. The final operation completely restored the front before the Soviet offensive by 9 December, an offensive which enabled Model to command the situation to his best. Helped by his sharp intelligence, he succeeded in evaluating the situation and dealt with the Soviet penetrations one after another, as they further threatened his defensive positions. The German defences, the Soviet sluggishness and Model's command had turned what could have been another Stalingrad into a German victory. While the 6th Army was being trapped at Stalingrad, Model had succeeded in inflicting about 335,000 losses to the Red Army, which was about 40 per cent of the forces that had been committed to Operation *Mars*. Furthermore, the Germans claimed the destruction of about 1,800 enemy tanks in spite of their numerical inferiority on the battlefield. Model's success was made complete when he reported to Hitler about the situation, and the incredible happened. Hitler, who always refused to allow a withdrawal from the Rzhev salient, was persuaded by Model that this was the most viable action, which would also free a certain number of divisions which could be used to create a reserve. On 6 February 1943, Hitler authorised Model to withdraw, the operation being coded *Büffel* (buffalo), but he did not create an operational reserve. Instead, he decided to use the newly made available divisions to counterattack the Soviets in the newly created Orel salient, which had emerged following Model's 9th Army withdrawal.

The 1943 winter crisis on the Eastern Front was followed by a quiet period, which coincided with the planning and the preparations for Operation *Zitadelle*, the attack against the Kursk salient. The discussion and the planning for the offensive was mainly prepared at the highest level, namely, Hitler, his General Inspector of the Panzer Troops General Guderian, the Chief of Army Staff General Zeitzler, and the two army group commanders involved, Field Marshal von Manstein and Field Marshal von Kluge, respectively commanders of the Army Group South and Centre. Model, despite his lower rank, was involved in the planning not just because his 9th Army was to provide the northern prong to the pincer movement around Kursk, but because Hitler trusted him as a loyal and efficient commander. Of all the commanders involved, Model, along with his superior von Kluge, approached the plan with the most realistic view and a full awareness of the situation. Concerned that new Soviet offensives could materialise in the summer, they wanted to use the forces spared due to the withdrawal from the Rzhev salient to create a reserve, which could deal with these offensives. Instead, most of Model's 9th Army divisions were redeployed all along the Army Group Centre front, leaving him with just six divisions to attack at Kursk. Model was all too aware of the state of his units, which were mostly down to half of their proper combat strength, and that the insufficient Panzer Divisions at his disposal only had a few tanks available. In such conditions he was required to attack a fully manned, well established and completely fortified sector of the front in enemy hands. He had to do this with forces greatly inferior to the enemy, rather than the three to one, the normally required strength deemed necessary to break through an enemy fortified front. The Soviets reckoned that his attack would deplete the scarce 9th Army forces, thus enabling a counter-manoeuvre against the northern part of the front at Orel, but Model (who reckoned that *Zitadelle* had scarce chances of succeeding) was also the only commander who wisely prepared for its failure and for the eventuality of a Soviet offensive. Outlining the situation as it stood, Model succeeded in convincing Hitler to complete the necessary preparations for the attack, even though this led to a delay in the start of the operation. Soon, Hitler would share Model's pessimistic view even though he decided to carry on with the planned offensive. Without asking for authorisation, and different from Field Marshal von Manstein who had refused to carry out any preparation for defence in case of a failure of *Zitadelle*, Model prepared for the attack while, in the meantime, prepared to defend the Orel bulge. A defence line was prepared, and two Panzer Divisions were kept in reserve ready to deal with contingency cases.

Model's attack plan did not aim at seizing terrain, which would have been a clear consequence of a German victory on the battlefield. His purpose was to inflict as many losses as possible on his opponents, while seeking for the best place to achieve a decisive breakthrough. Rather than committing his forces to a frontal all-out assault, he created a series of attack groups which had to feel out the enemy defences, and search for the best place to commit all the available forces in order to achieve a breakthrough. The idea was to try and have the enemy commander to commit their forces against the attacking German units which, relying on their superior tactics and methods of warfare, should have been able to inflict severe losses on the enemy, thus enabling Model to deal with the opposition from a more favourable position. This was a different approach to the battle than that of von Manstein. It was made necessary by the need to keep all the options open in order to be able to react to any kind of possible development at Kursk or elsewhere. Model knew he had to do this because he was relying on scarce forces, since only two of the infantry divisions at his disposal could deploy six infantry battalions and relatively few new tanks. Almost all the new Panzers (which included the Panther and Tiger tanks) had been sent to von Manstein's Army Group South. Model's 9th Army had only been reinforced with a single Tiger tank battalion (which started the attack with just two out of the three companies on call) and with some of the new, long barrelled gun and increased armour Panzer IV, which constituted the main attack force of his army. Apart from 274 of these tanks, he also had at his disposal 202 outdated Panzer III tanks of which only 89 were armed with the relatively powerful 50 mm gun, almost useless against the Soviet T-34. The 327 assault guns Sturmgeschütz III, represented the only complement to Model's scarce armoured spearhead, along with the rather impressive, but also scarcely efficient Ferdinand tanks which were hardly mobile and could only be used on good roads. The 9th Army attack on 5 July failed to take the enemy forces by surprise, and time was needed to clear the vast minefields laid in front of the German units. Model's eight infantry divisions, using the new demolition vehicle Goliath, cleared the minefields and succeeded in breaking through the enemy positions while under cover of heavy artillery fire. As the Panzers moved forward, the heavy Ferdinand and Tiger tanks moved onto a minefield with the result that some of them were immobilised, even though others managed to move forward. By the end of the first day Model could be satisfied with the progress, despite the many enemy defences. On the next day the attacking divisions spent the morning reorganising, the attack achieving a series of successful breakthroughs on the left wing of the 9th Army's front, which were soon halted by the Soviet troops. The German advances were rather modest, between two and four kilometres, and there was still no sign of a Soviet collapse. This prompted Model to start a new attack with the aim of breaking through the Soviet third line of defence, which he deemed necessary as long as the forces needed were still at his disposal. On 7 July the Germans attacked the strongly fortified village of Ponyri, resulting in a three-day battle which was considered the northern prong's equivalent to Prokhorovka. The attack failed in seizing the village, and an all-out assault was started on 10 July all along the front which failed to resolve the holdup. By the end of the day *Zitadelle's* northern wing had merely dented the Soviet front for about fifteen kilometres, and there was no sign the 9th Army could achieve a breakthrough and link up with the Army Group South at Kursk. Losses had been heavy, the army suffering the heaviest casualty rate of the entire Eastern Front to that date, and neither replacements nor reinforcements were available. As *Zitadelle* was being called off, on 12 July the Soviets started a counteroffensive against the 9th Army's eastern front, which was slowed down by well-prepared defences, despite the huge Soviet numerical superiority. By 13 July, as he had foreseen, Model had to commit two of his Panzer Divisions to deal with the Soviet attack which was still advancing towards Orel. On 21 July the Soviet advance was approaching Orel, just as the Soviet attack started, as on 12 July in the northern area of the 9th Army's front it had started to achieve a breakthrough which threatened the entire German line of defence. Once again, skilled defence and the prompt intervention of the reserve Panzer Division prevented this attack from turning into a major defeat, but it was clear that it was only a matter of time. By the end of July Model had succeeded in re-establishing a continuous front in fending off the Soviet breakthroughs, but it proved impossible to halt the Soviet advance despite the heavy losses inflicted by the skilled German defences. Model could now rely on only eight out of the 16 Panzer Divisions on the Eastern Front, but their condition was no match for the

Soviet armour. On 31 July Hitler eventually authorised Model to evacuate the Orel salient, which was the start of yet another German withdrawal.

By 18 August the Soviet offensive in the area held by Model's 9th Army came to a halt, the focus having shifted to the south against von Manstein's Army Group South. The Soviet advance had completely eliminated the Orel salient, and had approached Model's defence line east of Bryansk, called the Hagen Position. The situation was not as severe as it appeared, as Model had been able to recover almost all of his troops from the salient, and he had avoided an encirclement and inflicted heavy losses on the Red Army forces fighting against him. This was sufficient for the German high command to strip his command of the forces needed to help von Manstein to face the Soviet onslaught in the southern portion of the front. As the Red Army attacked towards Bryansk on 7 September, Model, on seeing the neighbouring forces on his flanks withdraw under pressure, had no choice but to do the same, and on 17 September the 9th Army pulled back to the Dnjepr line. On 24 September the Soviets reconquered Smolensk. To make the situation at the front clear, von Kluge added in his report to Hitler a memorandum written by Model, in which he described the appalling situation of the replacements, and his call for fresh units to be sent to restore the situation. Nothing happened, and fate took its toll. On 28 October von Kluge was injured in an auto accident and a week later, on 5 November, Model was recalled from his command and put in the commander's reserve. This tended to indicate permanent retirement, usually because one had fallen out of grace with Hitler, or simply prolonged leave and a period of rest at home. In Model's case it turned out to be the latter, and he was able to spend some time with the family at the White Stag house in Dresden. It was on 28 January 1944 Model was again summoned to Hitler's headquarters, to be informed he would take over command of the Army Group North.[4]

Chapter Four

Top Rank

The New Field Marshal

As a matter of curiosity, Model was expecting to be recalled but not to take over the Army Group North, but anticipated he would be taking over von Manstein's command at the Army Group South. Unknown to Model, the day before he was summoned to Hitler's headquarters, the Army Group North commander had met Hitler on the occasion of a National Socialist Leadership conference at Königsberg, where the dramatic situation at the front had been clearly reported. This had implied he was unable to conduct an effective defence in the area, a supposition confirmed three days later when he reported to Hitler in another meeting, that a withdrawal to the Luga River was necessary, and a continuous front could not be established. This was more than enough for Hitler who decided to give the command of the Army Group North to Model, who had established a solid reputation as the man who could face and resolve any crisis. As soon as he reached the Army Group headquarters, Model sent a telegram to Hitler reassuring that not a step back would be taken without his permission. Once again, the battle situation Model was sent to face was disastrous. Since mid-January the German front had been pushed back from Leningrad, the entire Army Group retreating. The most critical position was Narva, in the north, the key to the crossing of the river Luga, which linked the German defence positions with the Ilmen Lake. This time Model only had a few troops to hold a long stretch of the front, with no armoured reserves at his disposal. A defence line, known as *Panther*, had been prepared along the Narva and the Peipus Lake, but no withdrawal in that area was to be permitted because this would mean admitting defeat. Model understood that these defence lines mainly existed on paper, and that troops relied on them at a psychological rather than at a practical level. His first action was therefore psychological, as he prohibited any reference to the *Panther* line and even abolished the name. Furthermore, despite what he said in the grandiose message to Hitler, Model decided not to adopt a rigid defence but rather to rely on the 'shield and sword' tactic. This was based on a simple principle, namely, withdrawals could only be tolerated whenever the possibility to strike back occurred at the same place or at some other place, which was also Hitler's theory. Model applied the theory with a pinch of salt, being fully aware that the opportunity to strike back would seldom arise under such circumstances. The truth was that staged counterattacks were used to show that local retreats were nothing more than the first stage of a counteroffensive. Model wanted to apply his own version of the 'shield and sword' tactics with the 18th Army, which was withdrawing from Leningrad to a position along the Luga River while holding a bridgehead at Narva, but this proved impossible to achieve. The army was so weak it could barely face the Soviet advance, and all the commanders had noted the poor state of the troops who were totally exhausted. Model instructed them that they had to resist despite the pressures, while he started reorganising the front.

As the Soviets approached the Luga line, they found the 18th Army holding a consistent line of defence, and it soon became clear they aimed at encircling Narva which Model wanted to deal with by launching a counteroffensive. Hitler, usually delighted at such news, showed little enthusiasm, which is probably what Model wanted, as he was eventually authorised to pull back to the *Panther* position as soon as the situation became necessary. It is not clear whether Model was suffering from too much optimism or, rather unusually, Hitler had become excessively pessimistic, as the latter insisted that Narva should not be defended, and that the 18th Army was to pull back to the *Panther* position. The Soviet attacks, including a seaborne landing and the use of ski troops at the Lake Peipus, eventually put an end to the discussion. On 17 February Model started withdrawing to the *Panther* position, a movement which would be concluded by 1 March as he had promised. Model's period of command at the Army Group North ended at this point, with a stabilised front having been created after a staged withdrawal, which had seen none of the customary pockets being created by the advancing Red Army on the other fronts.

Model's achievement earned him the promotion to field marshal, which at 53 years of age made him the youngest field marshal in the German army, and with a new appointment approaching. On 28 March he was informed by Hitler's army aide that he would be soon given command of the Army Group South, to replace von Manstein. At this time the latter's command was facing a deadly situation with some twenty divisions trapped in the so-called 'Hube's Pocket' (after the German commander), and the threat of a Soviet breakthrough. Manstein was no longer appreciated as a field commander, and Model had permanently acquired the stature of Hitler's 'fireman' at the front. Meeting Hitler at his headquarters on 29 March, Model took an unbelievable move as he attempted to deprive the Army Group North of troops in favour of his new command, the Army Group South. It was the personal intervention of the Army Chief of Staff General Zeitzler, who eventually reduced Model's proposal to sending only one division from the north to the south. Model's first action as commander of the Army Group South was to enforce von Manstein's plan to relieve the 'Hube's Pocket', due to fresh troops made available by Hitler and transferred from the West.

The German front was now split, with Model's troops along the Polish border facing the advancing Red Army, and the rest of the Army Group South deployed along the Romanian and Soviet border down to the Black Sea. A reorganisation had to take place. While Model deployed his 1st and 4th Panzer Army around Lvov, on 5 April the former Army Group South was split, and two commands were formed from the Army Group A. In the north there would be the Army Group North Ukraine, which was Model's command, and in the Army Group South Ukraine which was formed from the remnants of Army Group A. As these changes were taking place Model was to face yet another crisis, as some 5,000 troops were encircled at Tarnopol, which Hitler insisted had to be a fortress town. Model attempted a rescue mission, which failed. This did not tarnish Model's reputation, quite the opposite. As the Army Group Centre was facing a difficult situation itself, and the commander Field Marshal Busch was no longer trusted by Hitler, who came up with a rather extraordinary solution: on 28 June Busch was relieved from his command, and Hitler announced that he would be replaced by Model who was, at the same time, to retain command of the Army Group South Ukraine.

On 22 June 1944, the anniversary of the German attack on the Soviet Union, the Red Army started a major offensive in the central sector of the Eastern Front, codenamed *Bagration*, which resulted in the most serious defeat for the German Army since Stalingrad. Model's appointment was welcomed by his subordinate commanders, who were unaware that he was partly to blame for the disaster along with the Army Staff, which had underestimated the Soviet capabilities and plans regarding this sector. Despite this issue, Model was regarded as the right man for the job, which did not prevent the German forces from facing catastrophe. It was not easy for Model, because Hitler rejected his requests to remove troops from the Army Group North and extended its southern flank to link up with the Army Group Centre. At the same time his former command, the XXXXI Corps, had been trapped by the Soviet advance and was facing annihilation. Without losing heart or his nerve, Model faced the situation as best he could. Despite Hitler's orders, the Soviets seized Minsk before a defence could be organised, but Model managed to create a line of defence around the city centred around Baranovichi, but it was soon lost. It was with dismay that the German commanders, including Model, realised that the Soviet offensive was much more ambitious as they fought, because it showed no signs of stopping even after the seizure of Minsk, which was some 200 kilometres to the west of its starting line. The only positive note came from the Army Group North, which managed to stretch its portion of the front and link up with the Army Group North Ukraine. On 8 July Model had to report to Hitler that the line stretching to the west of Minsk could not be held, and the Soviets were continuing with their offensive, which at that time was expanding to the other sectors of the Eastern Front, with their advance continuing towards Poland. Any effort made by Model to try and re-establish a continuous frontline was rendered useless by several Red Army attacks, which punched at the German defences wherever possible.

On 23 July the Soviet advance pushed as far as the Vistula River, just as news came of the failed attempt to assassinate Hitler. Model sent a message reaffirming his loyalty to the Führer, which undoubtedly secured his position at a time when the entire Reich was crumbling. Early in August the situation of the Army Group North Ukraine started to improve, mainly because reinforcements had started to arrive, and the withdrawals had improved the German situation by shortening the supply lines to Germany. General Guderian, who had been appointed the new Chief of Army Staff, insisted on resuming the offensive, but it was clearly nothing more than a pipe dream. A combination of factors came to Model's rescue and somehow enabled the front to be stabilised. After a failed counterattack against the advancing Soviet forces on the Vistula, the Warsaw insurrection saw Stalin pause the Red Army's offensive, enabling the Germans to crush the insurrection first, and start building a defence line along a more stabilised front. A more successful counterattack was launched to the north of Warsaw, and in mid-August Model was able to reassure Hitler that the Army Group could establish a continuous frontline. This was managed by early September, as the Germans were able to establish a defence line running in the south, all along the Carpathian Mountains to the Vistula River in the centre, and around Warsaw. Model was not to see the front on the East being stabilised.[1]

From East to Western Front

On 15 August 1944, Model was summoned again to Hitler's headquarters, where he was given the Knight's Cross with Oak Leaves, Swords and Diamonds, Germany's highest military award, and was told that he would be given a command in the West. Matching what he had done on the Eastern Front, Hitler appointed him at the same time Commander in Chief West and Commander of the Army Group B. This requires some explanation. Until the autumn of 1942 there had only been a single army group command in German occupied France, which was joined in November by a second army group following the occupation of the Vichy France area. At the end of 1943 a third army group was also formed, following Hitler's decision to appoint Field Marshal Rommel inspector of the Atlantic Wall fortifications, while putting him in command of the German forces in North-West France. In the summer of 1944, as the battle for Normandy was raging following the Allied invasion of 6 June, the German command structure in the West was based on three different commands. At the top there was the Commander in Chief West (*Oberbefehlshaber* West), which was Field Marshal von Rundstedt, who had under his command in the north Rommel's Army Group B, and in the south, the Army Group G. Developments at the front and elsewhere had turned the entire German command structure in the West into complete chaos. On 4 July von Rundstedt was relieved of command following the Allied success in establishing the Normandy front, and he was replaced by Field Marshal von Kluge as Commander in Chief West. Shortly after von Kluge's appointment, on 17 July, Field Marshal Rommel was wounded when a British fighter strafed his car, obliging von Kluge to take over at the same time command of the Army Group B. However, von Kluge was suspected of having taken part to the 20 July plot to assassinate Hitler, and he lost contact with the Wehrmacht High Command, and on 15 August, Hitler suspected he was trying to negotiate with the Allies and decided to remove him. Kluge, Model's former commander, committed suicide on 19 August. The chaos in the German command structure was only one of many problems Model had to face on his arrival at the Commander in Chief West headquarters. At the end of July, the Allies had managed to break through from the Normandy battlefield, and the advance had started into the Brittany peninsula towards the Seine. The German attempt to counterattack and close the gap had been repulsed, and the German forces found themselves trapped in the Falaise pocket. However, some managed to escape the trap, but with the Allied landing in southern France, the entire Western Front was withdrawing, and the German forces were retreating towards the German border. Paris was liberated on 25 August, just as Model was transferring his headquarters to the north. There was little, if anything that Model could do to restore the situation given the almost complete lack of reinforcements, the collapse of the units at the front, and the Allied air superiority which endangered the German supply system and overall communications.

Model dealt with the situation in his habitual way. He tried to recover as much as he could of the remnants of the Army Group B withdrawing it to the Seine, which was the first step of a major withdrawal, while he had the Army Group G withdrawing north to Dijon. To gain a first-hand impression of the situation he drove to the eastern margin of the Falaise pocket, and there are no doubts that the circumstances there told him everything. Eventually, fortune came to his aid, and the Allies failed to close the Falaise pocket, which enabled some remnants of the German armies to escape to the Seine and start a more organised withdrawal. This was something only those in the Normandy area could manage. Pockets of German resistance were left in Brittany and on the Atlantic coast of France, once bases for German submarines, and an entire army failed to escape to the east and had to surrender to the Allied forces. More importantly, Model's forces on the Seine were unable to be fully reorganised before the Allied drive started pushing them back towards the German border and into Belgium. By 3 September the Allied advance had reached Brussels, the Ardennes, and was approaching the Franco-German border along a line stretching from Verdun to Nancy. Fuel shortage (the Allied forces still relied on the supplies being brought ashore on the provisional ports built on the Normandy beaches) compelled General Eisenhower, the Allied supreme commander, to impose a temporary halt to the advance. The moment of respite was brief, and on 3–4 September the British 2nd Army not only reached Brussels but also advanced towards Antwerp, which had consequences of the greatest magnitude for Model. German forces had been trapped in the Channel harbours, such as Boulogne, Calais, and Dunkirk, some were to resist until the end of the war. The chaotic withdrawal had pushed the 15th Army to the north with the result, following the British seizure of Antwerp, that it had been trapped in north-west Belgium just as its forces were most needed. Model could not rely on any kind of help or reinforcements, as he probably hoped. The defeats suffered by the German army in the summer of 1944 were such that Germany came close to defeat, only saved by the over-extended supply lines of both the Allied and Soviet armies, which were obliged to halt to stock up on resources. By mid-

September the Allied advance had reached the southern border of the Netherlands, and was pushing to the German border, east of Belgium and Luxembourg. South of there, advance of the Allied forces had started to slow down along a line running from Metz to Nancy, and to the south, the Belfort area where the Army Group G had successfully managed to withdraw. Conscious of the situation and aware of his own capabilities, Model did what few other generals would do: he asked for a particular kind of help. He started advocating for von Rundstedt's re-instatement as Commander in Chief West, the only solution which could help him focus on the delicate situation of the Army Group B and restore the front. He eventually succeeded and, on 9 September, Hitler brought von Rundstedt back as the Commander in Chief West headquarters.

The Allied advance slowed, and Model was able to start reorganizing his forces to create a more stable and secure frontline. By 5 September he had the bulk of the 15th Army cross the Scheldt estuary while keeping control of the area, to deny the Allies the use of the port of Antwerp. The 15th Army managed to resist the attack of the 1st Canadian Army, started on 13 September, thus fulfilling its task, and denying the use of Antwerp until the end of 1944. This enabled Model to create a more reliable frontline along the Albert Canal, a move which would prove to be decisive in just two weeks. The Dutch frontline could be secured due to the new creation of the 1st Airborne Army headquarters (which owed its name to its commander General Student, the creator of the German airborne force) which took over the area and was able to slow down the advance of the British 2nd Army. This enabled Model to send troops to the areas of Aachen and Trier, where the American 1st Army was penetrating German soil with an offensive which started on 15 September. There the most important battle was fought since 19 September, with the 1st American Army advancing into the Hürtgen forest only to be forestalled by German resistance. On 17 September the Allies started Operation *Market Garden*, the airborne assault against the Dutch bridges which, in Montgomery's plan, was intended to pave the way to the crossing of the Rhine and to the subsequent advance into the Ruhr.[2]

The battle for Arnhem, a name which summarises the entire Operation *Market Garden*, deserves a special mention in Model's history as this was, along with the battle of the Ardennes, the only moments which gained him some post-war popularity. However, there was a completely false image of the field marshal. This was created by the American journalist Cornelius Ryan who, in his acclaimed book *A Bridge Too Far*, depicted Model as snobbish, and a not very competent type of Prussian commander who made a fool of himself. Ryan had based his book on a multitude of interviews with veterans, and he could not (for obvious reasons) interview Model, and he hardly studied the available records in order to gain a more appropriate picture of the situation. It suited his style and the ethos of the day as a collection of reminiscences like his previous effort *The Longest Day* more than an actual book of factual history. Model's portrait was greatly exaggerated in the movie subsequently made, based on Ryan's book. Model's portrait borders on stupidity, and the incident of him abandoning his headquarters near Arnhem is used to make him look foolish. On the other hand, the image portrayed in other commanders, such as von Rundstedt (who appears amiable and inclined to make jokes with his staff), and even the Waffen-SS generals such as Bittrich and Heinz Harmel, commander of the 10th SS Panzer Division are much better. The story is simple, as narrated in Ryan's book and portrayed in the movie: immediately after he was informed of the landing of Allied paratroopers near his headquarters, and in the Arnhem area, Model reacted by thinking they had been sent to capture him and his headquarters. It implied Model hastily fled, not before (as somebody recollected) that he had taken care that his cigars were rescued and taken along. The image one receives from the incident, especially as portrayed in the movie, is of a commander who is not just snobbish but borders on stupidity. Model is shown rejecting the captured plans of Operation *Market Garden* on the basis that had the Allies wanted to seize the Arnhem bridge, they would have landed in its proximity, and he was portrayed as arrogant. The truth is far from this portrayal. Model simply reacted to a rumour that was spreading widely amongst German commanders, even influencing Hitler. The ever-growing Allied airborne capabilities, along with the demonstrated skills of the British created a serious concern that airborne attacks could be utilised to capture the German commanders, as the Germans had rescued Mussolini. Hitler once said that he would happily sacrifice an entire paratrooper division if this enabled the capture of enemy headquarters. Putting together the fact that the 1st British Airborne Division had landed far away from the Arnhem bridge and that the only suitable objective in the proximity seemed to be his own headquarters, Model's reaction (enhanced in order to create the image of the 'Prussian style' commander) was certainly appropriate at that time.

Once Model realised the threat that Operation *Market Garden* posed, he rushed to find troops which could be used to attack the paratroopers, and if not to hold, at least ensure that the frontline slowed down the pace of advance of the British XXX Corps. What followed has been narrated over and over, but Model's contribution to the battle of Arnhem must be recalled. First, he decided to concentrate against two key positions upon which the entire enemy plan depended, which was Arnhem and the road leading to the seized bridges along the Eindhoven to Njimegen to Arnhem Road. The German counterattacks focused against the 1st British Division, in particular against the single battalion holding the northern end of the bridge, and on the flanks of the 'hell road' which had become the only suitable road the British XXX Corps could use to advance. Model's greatest mistake, the failed destruction of the Njimegen bridge, can be attributed to his enthusiasm and the hope of being able to launch a counterattack. Despite this issue, luck, and a series of catastrophic mistakes on the Allied side helped him to win the battle. By 26 September the 1st British Airborne Division had been practically destroyed, and the XXX Corps had been halted to the north of Nijmegen, well short of Arnhem. No other attempt was made in that area to seize the bridge or to cross the Rhine, and it took months of slow-moving advances to create a frontline which extended along the Meuse, with its bridgehead near Arnhem, and followed the river all along the Dutch border to the Roermond triangle, the only area where a major operation was to take place in the future.

The Arnhem crisis having been solved, Model could focus on the other areas, in particular on Aachen and the Hürtgen forest. The West

Wall defences, built by 1940, were not much of an obstacle and the weak German forces could only rely on a single advantage over the American 1st Army, namely their proximity to their supply sources. The main problem for the Allied advance was the temporary supply problem, which compelled Eisenhower to choose how to allocate the supplies that could be brought forward, mainly due to the non-stop running columns of trucks bringing what was needed, all the way from the Normandy beaches. Having first allocated supplies to the 2nd British Army for Operation *Market Garden*, both the 1st and the 3rd American Army suffered as a consequence. Model took advantage of the situation to slow the enemy advance, also bringing to the threatened areas all the armoured reinforcements he could find. This was a part of Model's command which is all too often overlooked, as he managed to put together the available reinforcements and replacements made available (Germany was literally scraping the bottom of the barrel) and turn them into some kind of effective fighting force, relying on the veterans who had survived the battle in Normandy. He also made intelligent use of the scarce armoured units available, focusing them where they could be most useful rather than scattering them all around the front. This did not prevent Aachen from being encircled at first, and eventually seized by the American 1st Army on 21 October. This transpired to be more of a propaganda success because the 1st Army was not able to exploit the victory and focused instead on the battle for the Hürtgen forest, where Model's skilful use of the few combat-worthy units enabled him to halt the American advance well short of their objective, the Roer River dams. By early December 1944, the 21st and 12th Army Group Allied advance had come to a stop, with the American armies being halted on the Meuse-Roer River line and Patton's 3rd Army (which was fighting against von Blaskowitz's Army Group G) having halted all along the German border. The Allied attention focused on the Roer River and the advance towards Saarbrücken. The Ardennes area was neglected and used as some form of rest area for exhausted troops or for the fresh new ones who had just reached the European front.[3]

Chapter Five

End Days

End of the Road

Most revealing in the way Model's image developed both during and after the war, was his association with the German Ardennes counter-offensive in December 1944. The *Time* magazine at that time placed von Rundstedt on the cover, associating him with the sudden German move. Model is usually associated with the counteroffensive itself, even though his direct impact seems hard to assess. Hitler started thinking of the counter-offensive already in September, the plans had been drafted since October when the situation had been critical. Model was informed at once as was von Rundstedt, both also being informed that new reinforcements would not become available, because they were needed to rebuild the units to take part in Operation *Watch on the Rhine*. This time the popular image was closer to the truth, even though it is not too often remembered that Model, as with von Rundstedt, showed little enthusiasm for Hitler's plans. On the basis of the lack of fuel, most of which had been consumed during the battles fought on the German frontier, Model had serious doubts that Operation *Watch on the Rhine* could actually be successful and enable the German army to reach the Meuse, thereby disrupting the Allied armies in the area. In order to try and bring Hitler's perspective closer to reality, Model developed his own plan, aimed at bringing local disruption to the Allied armies, with the aim of keeping them off balance, and prevent their further offensives. His *Autumn Mist* plan aimed at attacking in the Ardennes with the aim of disrupting the American 1st Army lines of communication, and once this aim had been achieved, attempt an encirclement against the enemy forces in the Aachen area. This 'small solution', preferred by both Model and von Rundstedt, aimed at keeping the offensives local, within reach of their supplies, well to the east of the Meuse and simply aimed at inflicting as many losses as possible on the enemy forces. This plan was not enough for Hitler, who realised that a large-scale success was the only way to change the fortunes of war, any local success being bound merely to delay the unavoidable fate of the entire war. Model, who was not involved in the planning for *Watch on the Rhine*, was the commander in charge of the entire operation, and he was to exercise his command in the style he most favoured. He immediately brought himself to the frontline as the offensive started on 16 December, and once there he helped to solve a traffic congestion which was slowing down the movement of the German forces. Model was the first who realised that reaching the Meuse was impossible, and he decided to focus on the battle of Bastogne in order to inflict a serious defeat on the American forces. Relying on the new forces brought into the area, the Allies might have attempted to cut off the 'Bulge', thus encircling all the German forces employed in the Ardennes offensive. Instead, following what Model had initiated, the battle focused on Bastogne where the initial relief of the trapped American 101st Airborne Division soon turned into a major battle which saw Patton's personal involvement.

Already, by 22 December, the German offensive had come to a stalemate, while from the north Montgomery's 2nd Army was approaching its northern flank and, from the south, Patton's 3rd Army had come to the relief of Bastogne. Had the German forces attempted to continue their advance, they might have been squeezed by a pincer movement from the north and from the south. Model realised this was a risk that could not be taken, and he gave a new direction to the entire battle. The advance was halted, and the German forces started focusing against Patton's 3rd Army at Bastogne, with the aim of achieving at least a local encirclement of the enemy forces. The new Battle of Bastogne failed to achieve its aim, but it distracted both Patton and Montgomery and prevented the German 'bulge' in the Ardennes being cut off. Slowly, the German forces started their withdrawal putting an end to the Ardennes offensive. By 17 January 1945, Model's Army Group B had been pushed to the east of Bastogne, the Allied counter-offensive reaching the German starting point by the end of January, and eventually the Our River line by early February. The offensive cost the Germans the loss of some 80,000 casualties and large amounts of irreplaceable tanks, weapons, vehicles, and equipment.[1]

All that followed disclosed the situation at the moment of the Third Reich's collapse in 1945. With a weak front running along the Meuse and the Roer River, held by the remnants of troops which had fought in the Ardennes, Model's solution of choice was a major withdrawal behind the only real line of defence: the Rhine. Hitler forbade such a withdrawal, took one Panzer Army from Model's Army Group to defend Hungary, and on 1 March, announced there would be no more reinforcements for him. With supplies reduced to a minimum, his troops having no fuel nor ammunition for the artillery, Model had no other option than defend the line and hope for a miracle, which did not come. On 8 February, the British 2nd Army started its offensive along the northern shoulder of the Rhine, which was reaching the area between Emmerich and Wesel. On the 23rd the American 9th Army started its own operation, named *Grenade*, crossing the Roer River, and advancing towards the Rhine which was reached between Oberkassel and Rheinberg. More than 50,000 German troops were caught in the pocket, which was closed on 3 March, with the American advance coming close to seizing an intact bridge on the Rhine at Oberkassel. On 2 March it was the turn of the American 1st and 3rd Army to begin their advance towards the Rhine, Operation *Lumberjack* concluding on 10 March with the complete elimination of all the German forces west of the Rhine (the last pocket, the Xanten triangle being cleared by the British 2nd Army), and with an unexpected surprise: the seizure of an intact bridge on the Rhine at Remagen. There was little, if anything at all, Model could do to deal with the Allied advance, and his attention as the Third Reich was crumbling focused on other matters. First, his family was at Dresden when the city was bombed on 13–14 February with catastrophic effects. Unable to search for his wife and children himself, he sent his aide who found them alive and helped bring them out of the city to safety, to Model's brother's house in Mühlshausen. Model's second concern was to put a brake on Hitler's repeated requests for special tribunals, to be used against any officer who was accused of having given up in front of the enemy. These Kangaroo Courts spread widely in the last months of war and were usually used to find somebody to take the blame for the loss of this or that position. They inevitably resulted in the execution of the alleged and often innocent culprit. Model, who recognised them for what they were, used his authority to block these summary executions which had no meaning, especially at that stage of the war. After the famous seizure of the Remagen Bridge, Model tried to halt the 1st American Army advance into Germany by throwing into the battle all that he could, but without success. The fate of his Army Group B was sealed, the bridgehead expanding by 21 March into a large bulge that could not be rescinded. On 23 March the last act came in the form of the British 2nd Army assault crossing of the Rhine at Wesel, which was followed by Patton's crossing to the south. The British 2nd Army advanced north of the Ruhr forming the northern pincer of the pocket which had as its southern pincer the American 1st Army, moving from Remagen, the trap to be closed around the Ruhr as the two advanced deeply into Germany by the end of March. At this point the British 2nd Army started its own race into Germany, leaving the American 9th Army the task of closing the trap around Model's Army Group B into the Ruhr. This occurred at Lippstadt on 1 April, the trap leaving some 370,000 German soldiers, of which no more than 75,000 were armed, surrounded. Model did not surrender and rather tried to resist, but the task was well beyond the capabilities of the shadow forces he had been left. Eventually, on 15 April Model took the step he would have never thought of once. He disbanded the Army Group B, left to his subordinates the choice of what to do, and, after ordering the civilian militia (the *Volkssturm*) to lay down their arms and to return home, he refused a proposal of surrender coming from General Ridgway. For the next four days Model and a small force with three vehicles, one of which was armoured, attempted to escape the trap, and reach the German lines, but to no avail. Bound by his sense of duty, he knew he had no other choice. On the morning of 21 April 1945, near Wedau, he walked into the wood and shot himself. A German field marshal cannot be taken prisoner. Germany surrendered just about a week later.[2]

Model as seen by Others

Several factors must be considered when examining how Model was seen by his colleagues and contemporaries. His rise as a field commander came late in the war, which meant he was hardly a noticeable figure until 1943–44 apart from his direct superiors. Furthermore, his death at the end of the war prevented him from leaving any account which could carve a role in the post-war narrative, or within the large pool of German generals who supplied memoirs and other narratives. Last but not least, Model's character does not appear to have made him a suitable figure for propaganda purposes. This vacuum means there is not much left because he never rose to the same level of other German generals whose image was widely exploited by propaganda, such as Rommel, Guderian or even Manstein.

The general impression is that he was appreciated as a field commander and acknowledged as being the kind of man who would stand under pressure and resolve situations apparently impossible to solve, but at the same time was seen as distant, excessively rigid, and not especially loved by his troops, who at least respected him. Noting down in his diary on 31 March 1944, in a meeting between Hitler's chief military aide General Schmundt and Model, Goebbels noted how the latter was completely taken by surprise by the announcement he might get a command in the southern part of the Eastern Front, which meant replacing von Manstein. Model's surprise was followed by an immediate reaction, which was a complete plan laid down in a matter of a few hours by him and his staff. Goebbels noted that 'Model is a very energetic troops commander, one who can put an end to all the existing nuisances in the shortest possible time. Besides he is rigorous indeed and he doesn't pull back from offending other generals in charge; but we can use now such a man.' At that moment, as Goebbels noted, Model and General Schörner (himself to become a last-minute field marshal) were the only ones who could stabilise the situation on the Eastern Front.[3]

This brief entry seems to summarise in a nutshell Model's character and his figure. He was efficient, he was admired for his skills, his efficiency, but he was also a character hard to deal with and one who could be hardly considered for public admiration. Even though Model had been fighting almost shoulder to shoulder with von Manstein, the latter only reserved minimal mention of his successor, and that was just regarding the meeting with Hitler when it was announced that Model would take over command. As von Manstein wrote in his memoirs, as Hitler mentioned that Model could become the new commander von Manstein replied 'I did not think any great harm would be done by my handing over to Model now...it's [Hitler's decision] only remaining commitment was to assist the fighting troops and give them moral support.'[4] Manstein's cold attitude towards Model is understandable, however, what one understands from these few words is the impression of professionalism united with remoteness and a cold attitude. In his book *The German Generals Talk*, Liddell Hart noted how Model had a career path similar to that of Erwin Rommel, even though with a much better professional background. While acknowledging his achievements, Liddell Hart also reports the comments made by other officers who considered Model a good commander, but 'difficult both as a superior and subordinate.' General von Manteuffel is reported to have said:

> Model was a good tactician, and better in defence than in attack. He had a knack of gauging what troops could do, and what they could not do. His manner was rough, and his methods were not always acceptable in the higher quarters of the German Army, but they were both to Hitler's liking. Model stood up to Hitler in a way that hardly anyone else dared, and even refused to carry out orders with which he did not agree.[5]

This account made him more than suitable to deal with the difficult situations at the front, but not the kind of example Hitler would want to give to his other generals or even to his soldiers. In one of the last diary entries before the end of the war, Goebbels noted once again that the only field commanders who suited the modern 'people's war' were Model and Schörner, the former being an 'intellectual type', which meant led by the mind and by rationale, as opposed to the latter who was led by his heart and feelings. They were, along with generals like Hans-Valentin Hube and Dietl, the only commanders who could be relied upon and proved capable to master the battlefield, compared to many others including the Waffen SS commanders, who had proved unable to create a single commander of this kind. Model was certainly not the most popular German general, but his capabilities were acknowledged in a unique way both by his superiors and by his adversaries.

Final Comments

It is a quandary to find a final comment on the man Model. It is necessary to recall that he was mainly a technician, the type of commander who dealt with the battlefield in such a way to bring troops to fight, supporting and equipping them, but without being the kind of typical field commander illustrated by some other German generals. First, Model was very gifted, a natural talent in the field of military tactics who further developed his skills as he rose in ranks and commands. In a way, Liddell Hart's remark above was accurate and it perfectly summarised Model's character. He had the chance to be promoted and he was given superior commands after he had learnt the trade in the field, and he was therefore able to understand how the higher commands worked down to their minutiae. Somehow, Model can be considered as a commander with a style between those of Rommel and of von Manstein. He was a career staff officer, like many others, but he also commanded a field unit (the 3rd Panzer Division) long enough to understand the difficult job of leading such a formation on the battlefield, which was more than both von Manstein (who never had such a command) or even Rommel did, the latter having commanded a Panzer Division on the battlefield for less than two months. Model's rise was slow, and the commands which he took over, from an army corps to an army and then to an army group, enabled him to understand in detail how each single level of command worked. All this, along with his skills and a rather unique capability to reorganise units, making them combat efficient despite the lack of weapons, ammunition, equipment, and supplies, enabled Model to fight defensive battles in a way hardly matched by any other German general. Also, one must not forget his capability of keeping his nerve, even when facing the most difficult situation, which was not that common amongst the German generals who, whenever facing a serious crisis, started crying for reinforcements and were too ready to blame others, Hitler in particular, for their defeats.

Model's skills and capabilities as a commander, at every level, were not matched by the sort of personality which may have given him a similar status as Rommel. His lack of popularity, amongst the troops as well as amongst his colleagues, was quite exceptional, and it should be recalled that even Hitler had made it clear he would not have wanted to serve under him. Model even refused Göring's meal while on leave because he kept within the wartime rations. Without doubt, Model's strong personality and brusque character hardly contributed to make him popular, but at the same time granted him a level of independence which hardly any other general seems to have been able to achieve. Model emerges as one of the very few who openly challenged Hitler and ignored orders, whenever it suited him or the needs at the battlefront, without ever being considered as a candidate for dismissal. As such, Model seems to be one of the very few who earned this distinction, which makes him probably one of the few German generals who could claim to be successful in all possible aspects.

However, these traits make it difficult to gain a full grasp of Model's personality, and to comment on his achievements. The first point to emerge is that he is constantly seen as a commander who showed his best while defending the front, both in the East and West, but he is not associated with attack or with any offensive of whatever scale. Despite being in charge during the 1944 Ardennes offensive, Model is best remembered for his opposition to the entire plan and for his own, small-scale proposal for a counterattack. On the Eastern Front Model managed to hold the front by launching small scale counterattacks which, albeit successful, never reached the magnitude of von Manstein's winter 1943 counteroffensive. The real problem with Model seems to be the fact that he is mainly associated with successful defences, albeit defences which were bound to end with a final defeat, and as such, were not the kind of battles that would ever enhance his reputation or popularity. Almost every field marshal has his name associated to a famous battle, but Model seems to have been more a secondary character in all of them rather than a first-class star. This vacuum of inside knowledge appears to be the only reason which makes it difficult to criticise his methods of command or his achievements, as they never granted him the fame others acquired and that Model seemingly never sought. To quote a classical thought, there is no such thing as great victories or small victories, only great generals, and small generals. Model, without doubt, belongs to the restricted circle of the great ones.

Final Observations

The Germans since the Wilhelmine era always felt a degree of pride in the professional strength of their army. Officers carried a high social status and were often from the Junkers class carrying *von* before their surname. Even Hitler assumed this at first referring to Kesselring as von Kesselring. The exigencies of time and necessity changed this attitude as aptitude and ability were soon recognised as being more important than social classification.

These three selected field marshals all came from middle-class backgrounds with their fathers as schoolmasters. They were intelligent, career-minded, and ambitious men, who all proved quick to learn and adapt. As such they realised the old Prussian tradition of obedience had to be taken seriously if they were to be successful, at least on the surface. It is known that Kesselring managed to avoid some of Hitler's demands, that Rommel was critical, and only Model challenged the dictator. They were generally successful on the battlefields and because of this feature probably avoided some of Hitler's unpleasant reactions which saw so many of their colleagues dismissed or retired.

They all had different personalities with Kesselring being charming and pleasant, Rommel somewhat thrusting and demanding, and Model with a reputation of being so tough even Hitler claimed he would not want to serve under him. Kesselring was liked by his subordinates and soldiers, Rommel was admired as his successes grew, whereas Model was known as *Frontschwein* (front-line pig). Although a convicted war criminal Kesselring had the support of his one-time Western enemies, and Rommel over the years has been built up on a pedestal as the epitome of a first-class and brilliant commander, whereas Model, of which little is known, has been denigrated by film producers.

However, they were all in their different ways sound commanders on the battlefield, Kesselring in defence, Rommel in attack, and Model as the last-minute firefighter holding the enemy back. Their main failure had been, like so many, accepting Hitler as their leader, who led them into a catastrophic world war, and established massacring innocent people as the norm. It led to a war which they could not win despite their professional talents.

To continue the same chess analogy as in the introduction, Kesselring played an excellent defence system, Rommel was an attacker but overused his gambits, and Model avoided his opponent's first attack moves. It was a game they could never win, because as soon as they took the opponent's piece it was swiftly replaced, whereas their pieces were lost forever. All three were outstanding fighting commanders, however, given the world's resources compared to Germany it was a lost game, but a game which cost millions of lives; their mistake was accepting Hitler as a military commander and as their nation's political leader.

Notes

Field Marshal Albert Kesselring

Chapter 1
1. Kesselring Albert, *The Memoirs of Field-Marshal Kesselring* (London: William Kimber, 1953) p.15.
2. Lingen Kerstin von, *Kesselring's Last Battle Crimes Trials and Cold War Politics* (Kansas: Kansas Press, 2009) p.17.
3. Berghahn V.R., *Modern Germany* (Cambridge: Cambridge UP, 1987) p.13.
4. Wette Wolfram, *The Wehrmacht: History, Myth, Reality* (London: Harvard UP, 2007) p.25.
5. Kershaw Ian, *Fateful Choices* (London: Penguin, 2007) p.438.
6. BHKM-(Kesselring personnel file) 61536: and quoted in Lingen, p.18.
7. Lingen, *Kesselring,* p.19.
8. Mitcham Samuel, *Eagles of The Third Reich* (Mechanicsburg: Stackpole Books, 2007) p.16.
9. Wette, *Wehrmacht,* p.140.
10. Ibid., p.143.
11. Thompson Alastair, *Left Liberals, The State, & Popular Politics in Wilhelmine Germany* (Oxford: OUP, 2000) p.8.
12. Hastings Max, *Catastrophe* (London: William Collins, 2013) p.118.
13. Tipton Frank B., *A History of Modern Germany since 1815* (London: Continuum, 2003) p.295.
14. Kesselring, *Memoirs,* p.17.
15. Macksey Kenneth, *Kesselring German Master Strategist of the Second World War* (London: Greenhill, 1978) p.24.
16. BHKM-(Kesselring personnel/file)-61536: 24th May17.
17. Ibid., 61536: 1-Jan1914 & Herde Peter, *Albert Kesselring (1885–1960)* (Fränkische Lebensbilder, Vol 18, series vii, Neustadt an der Aische, 2000) p.299.
18. Macksey *Kesselring,* p.24.
19. Lingen, *Kesselring,* p.19.
20. Wette, *Wehrmacht,* p.40.
21. Tipton, *History,* p.329.
22. Howard Michael, *The Invention of Peace & the Reinvention of War* (London: Profile Books, 2001) p.62.
23. Veale F.J.P., *Advance to Barbarism* (Torrance: Inst for Historical Review, 1979) pp.151–152.
24. Colville, *The Fringes of Power* (London: Hodder and Stoughton, 1985) p.26.
25. Bracher, Karl Dietrich, *Turning Points in Modern Times: essays on German and European History* (London: Harvard UP, 1995) pp.79–80.
26. Weitz, *Weimar,* p.31.

27. Kesselring, *Memoirs*, p.18.
28. Lingen, *Kesselring*, p.20.
29. BMKM-61536-Seyler-10.8.19H

Chapter 2
1. Goldensohn L. & Gellately R., (Ed) *The Nuremberg Interviews. Conversations with the Defendants & Witnesses* (London: Pimlico, 2007) p.320.
2. Herde, *Kesselring*, pp.299–300.
3. Overy Richard, *The Bombing War, Europe 1939–45* (London: Allen Lane, 2013) p.74.
4. Churchill Winston, *The Second World War Volume 1* (London: Cassell, 1948) p.34.
5. Bryant Mark, *World War II in Cartoons* (London: Grub Street, 2009) p.11
6. Mitcham, *Eagles*, p.17.
7. Haigh R., Morris D., Peters A., *German-Soviet Relations in the Weimar Era* (Aldershot, Gower, 1985) p.63.
8. Citino Robert, *The Path to Blitzkrieg* (Mechanicsburg, Stackpole, 2008) p.7.
9. *The German Generals Talk* (London: Harper, 2002) p.10.
10. Haigh, *German-Soviet*, p.169.
11. Haigh, *German-Soviet*, p.177.
12. D'Este Carlo, *Fatal Decision* (London: Fontana, 1991) p.86.
13. Haigh, *German-Soviet*, p.160.
14. Maycock Ian, Military History, *Poland 1939* (Issue 36, Sept 2013) p.37.
15. Senger von und Etterlin, *Neither Fear nor Hope* (London: Macdonald, 1963) p.27.
16. Kearley S., Military History, *The Secrets of Hughenden Manor* (issue 23, August, 2012) p.11.
17. Senger, *Neither*, p.43.
18. Boyne Walter, *The Influence of Air Power Upon History* (New York: Pelican, 2003) p.175.
19. Kesselring, *Memoirs*, pp.27–28.
20. Kesselring, *Memoirs*, p.27.
21. Burleigh Michael, *Moral Combat A History of World War II* (London: Harper, 2010) p.26.
22. Corum James, *The Luftwaffe Creating the Operational Air War 1918–1940* (Kansas: UP Kansas, 1997) p.161.
23. Killen John, *The Luftwaffe, A History* (Yorkshire: Pen and Sword, 2009) p.53.
24. Douhet Giulio, *The Command of the Air* (New York: Arno Press, 1972).
25. Overy, *Bombing*, p.13.
26. Mitcham, *Eagles*, p.18.
27. Overy, *Bombing*, p.227.
28. Corum, *Luftwaffe*, p.235.
29. *Times*, 26 April 1941.
30. Mitcham, *Eagles*, p.17.
31. Corum, *Luftwaffe*, p.224.
32. Corum, *Luftwaffe*, p.234.
33. Corum, *Luftwaffe*, p.235.
34. Macksey, *Kesselring*, p.53.
35. Murray Williamson, *The Luftwaffe 1933–45 Strategy for Defeat* (Washington: Congress Library, 1996) p.11.
36. NA-AMP, p.34.

Chapter 3
1. Zaloga Steven, *Poland 1939: The Birth of Blitzkrieg* (Oxford: Osprey, 2002) p.6.
2. HC-Debate, 2 July 1942, Vol 381/cc527-611.
3. NA-AMP, p.53.
4. Ibid., p.57.
5. Kesselring, *Memoirs*, p.41.
6. Corum, *Luftwaffe*, p.7.
7. Ibid., p.7.
8. Overy, *Bombing*, p.60.
9. Ibid., p.512: Burleigh, *Moral*, p.135
10. Hastings Max, *All Hell Let Loose* (London: Harper, 2011) p.18.
11. Kesselring, *Memoirs*, p.48.
12. Ibid., p.58: and Manvell & Fraenkel, *Herman Göring* (London: Heinemann, 1962) p.226.
13. Mitcham, *Eagles*, p.90.
14. Overy, *Bombing*, p.61.
15. Macksey, *Kesselring*, p.73.
16. Kesselring, *Memoirs*, p.61.
17. Boyne, *Influence*, p.210
18. Steinhilper U. & Osborne P., *Spitfire on my Tail* (Worcs: Self-Publishing Co, 1989).
19. Mitcham, *Eagles*, p.106.
20. Ibid., p.105.
21. Edgerton David, *Britain's War Machine* (London: Penguin Books, 2012) p.75.
22. Davies Norman, *No Simple Victory* (London: Penguin, 2007) p.297.
23. Lewin Ronald, *Ultra Goes to War* (London: Penguin, 1978), p.100.
24. Carell Paul, *Hitler's War on Russia* (London: Harrup, 1964) p.60.
25. Ibid., p.61.
26. Boyne, *Influence*, p.220.
27. Ibid., p.221.
28. Bartov Omer, *Hitler's Army* (Oxford: OUP, 1992) p.15.

Chapter 4
1. Trevor-Roper Hugh (Ed), *Hitler's War Directives* (London: Pan Books, 2004) pp.297–8.
2. KNA, *Top-Secret-Cypher-Telegram/19th-March-45*, Ref/FO-954/17A-File, Re-296.
3. Kesselring, *Memoirs*, p.104.
4. Macksey, *Kesselring*, p.107.
5. Westphal Siegfried, *The German Army in the West* (London: Cassell, 1951) p.122.
6. Vassiltchikov Maries, *The Berlin Diaries 1939–45* (London: Pimlico, 1999) p.95.
7. KNA, HW1/1844.
8. Capa Robert, *Slightly out of Focus* (New York: Modern Library, 1999) p.70.
9. Senger, *Neither*, p.152.
10. KNA, HW1/1029.
11. Jeffery Keith, *MI6: The History of the Intelligence Service 1909–49* (London: Bloomsbury, 2010) p.500.
12. Kesselring, *Memoirs*, p.116/ Lewin, *Ultra*, p.272.
13. Kesselring, *Memoirs*, p.141.
14. Beevor Anthony, *The Second World War* (London: Weidenfeld & Nicolson, 2012) p.378.
15. Young Desmond, *Rommel* (London: Book Club Associates, 1973) p.240.

16. Ibid., p.99.
17. Schraepler Hans-Joachim, *At Rommel's Side, The Lost letters of Hans-Joachim Schaepler* (London: Frontline Books, 2009) p.93.
18. USAH Division, 007718.
19. Liddell Hart B.H. (Ed), *The Rommel Papers* (New York: De Capo Press, 1953) p.120.
20. Ibid., p.203.
21. KNA, WO208/4348.
22. KNA, HW1/614.
23. Lucas Laddie, *Malta The Thorn in Rommel's Side* (London: Penguin, 1992) p.4.
24. KNA, HW1/449.
25. Evans Richard, *The Third Reich at War* (London: Allen Lane, 2008) p.150.
26. KNA, HW1/1029.
27. KNA, HW1/1331.
28. Brown Cave Anthony, *Bodyguard of Lies* (London: WH Allen, 1977) pp.127/8.
29. Ibid., pp.127–8
30. NA-AMP, p.143.
31. Westphal, *German*, p.122.
32. *Observer*, 18 May 1947, p.5.
33. Beevor, *Second*, p.404.
34. Kesselring, *Memoirs*, p.151.
35. *Times*, 1 October 1942.
36. KNA, HW1/1331.
37. D'Este, *Fatal*, p.87.
38. Beevor, *Second*, p.415.
39. Westphal, *German*, p.132.
40. Luck Col Hans von, *Panzer Commander, Memoirs of Colonel Hans von Luck* (London: Cassell, 1989) p.126.
41. Gregg V. & Stroud R., *Rifleman* (London: Bloomsbury, 2011) p.61/p.41.
42. KNA, HW1/614.
43. Luck, *Panzer*, p.149.
44. Makos Adam, *A Higher Call* (London: Atlantic Books, 2013) p.94.
45. Macksey, *Kesselring*, p.146.
46. Neitzel Sönke (Ed), *Tapping Hitler's Generals* (Yorkshire: Frontline Books, 2007) p.35.
47. Militärgeschichtliches Forschungsamt Potsdam (Eds), *Germany & The Second World War Volume VI* (Oxford: Clarendon, 2001) p.755.
48. Liddell-Hart, *Rommel*, p.417.
49. Evans, *Third*, p.150.
50. Katz Robert, *Fatal Silence* (London: Weidenfeld & Nicolson, 2003) p.70.

Chapter 5

1. Senger, *Neither*, p.128.
2. Klibansky R. (Ed), *Mussolini Memoirs* (London: Weidenfeld & Nicolson, 1949) p.55 and Whicker Alan, *Whicker's War* (London: Harpers, 2005) p.49.
3. Macintyre Ben, *Operation Mincemeat* (London: Bloomsbury, 2010).
4. Lucas James, *Hitler's Enforcers* (London: Arms and Armour Pub, 1996) p.50.
5. Klibansky, *Mussolini*, p.41.
6. Hansen Eric G., *The Italian Military Enigma* (Seminar Paper, Command & Staff College, Quantico, Virginia 22134, 1988) p.37.

7. Messenger Charles, *Rommel* (London: Palgrave, 2009) p.153.
8. Caddick-Adams Peter, *Monty and Rommel, Parallel Lives* (London: Arrow, 2012) pp.305–6.
9. Heiber, *Hitler*, p.231.
10. Ibid., p.465.
11. Ibid., p.xii.
12. Muggeridge Malcolm (Ed), *Ciano's Diary* (London: Heinemann, 1947) p.393.
13. Scotland Lt Col A.P., *The London Cage* (London: Landsborough, 1957) p.173.
14. Ibid., p.175.
15. Kesselring, *Memoirs*, p.158.
16. Senger, *Neither*, p.129.
17. Kesselring, *Memoirs*, p.164.
18. Hansen, *Italian*, p.38.
19. Fuehrer Conferences, 12 May, p.324.
20. (USAHD) -*Special*-007718, p.16.
21. Klibansky, *Mussolini*, p.107.
22. Lochner Louis (Ed), *The Goebbels Diaries* (London: Hamish Hamilton, 1948) p.325.
23. Parker Matthew, *Monte Cassino* (London: Headline Press, 2003) p.12.
24. USAH, 007718, p.7.
25. Dollmann Eugen, *The Interpreter, Memoirs of Doktor Eugen Dollman* (London: Hutchinson, 1967) p.255.
26. Ibid., p.257.
27. Westphal, *German*, p.148.
28. Salter Michael, *Nazi War Crimes, US Intelligence & Selective Prosecution at Nuremberg* (Oxford: Routledge-Cavendish, 2007) p.80.
29. Kurzman D., *A Special Mission* (New York: Da Capo Press, 2007) pp.48–9.
30. Macksey, *Kesselring*, p.178.
31. Battistelli Pier, *Albert Kesselring* (Oxford: Osprey Publishing, 2012) p.57.
32. Westphal, *German*, p.152.
33. Alexander Earl of Tunis, *The Alexander Memoirs 1940–1945* (London: Frontline Books, 2010) p.125.
34. Bradley N. Omar, *A General's Life* (London: Sidgwick & Jackson, 1983) p.161.
35. *Times*, 24 May 1944.
36. Lamb Richard, *War in Italy 1943–45* (London: Murray, 1993) p.6.
37. Hoyt Edwin, *Back Water War, The Allied Campaign in Italy* (Mechanicsburg: Stackpole, 2007) p.122, D'Este, *Fatal*, p.86, Atkinson R., *The Day of the Battle, The War in Sicily and Italy 1943–44* (London: Abacus, 2013) p.93, Hickey D. & Smith G., *Operation Avalanche, The Salerno Landings 1943* (London: Heinemann, 1983) p.293.
38. Graham D. & Bidwell S., *Tug of War The Battle for Italy 1943–45* (Yorkshire: Pen and Sword, 2004) p.38.
39. Roberts, *Storm*, p.378, Macintyre, *Operation*, p.282, Hastings, *Hell*, p.668, Harper G. & Tonkin-Covell J., *The Battles of Monte Cassino* (Auckland: Allen & Unwin, 2013) p.125, Beevor, *Second*, p.568.
40. Porch Douglas, *Hitler's Mediterranean Gamble* (London: Weidenfeld & Nicolson, 2004) pp.422–3.
41. Bradley, *A General's Life*, p.161, p.186.
42. Ibid, p.161.
43. Harper, *Battles*, p.xix.

44. Senger, *Neither*, p.196.
45. *Times*, 31 December 1943.
46. Lewis J (Ed), *World War II The Autobiography* (London: Robinson, 2009) p.448.
47. Kurzman, *A Special Mission*, p.165.
48. Bosworth R, *Mussolini* (London: Hodder Arnold, 2002) p.393.
49. Trevelyan Raleigh, *Rome '44 The Battle for the Eternal City* (London: Pimlico, 2004) p.107.
50. Atkinson, *Day*, p.476.
51. Ibid., p.367.
52. Knappe Siegfried & Brusaw, *Soldat* (London: BCA, 1993) p.249 and pp.246–7.
53. Atkinson, *Day*, p.477.
54. Katz, *Fatal*, p.165.
55. Militärgesschichtliches, *Volume-IX/X*, p.907.
56. Dollmann, *Interpreter*, p.310.
57. Morgan Philip, History Today, *Italy's Fascist War* (Volume 57, Issue 3, 2007) p.145.
58. Trevelyan, *Rome*, p.240.
59. Hastings, *Hell*, p.454.

Chapter 6

1. Infield Glen, *Disaster at Bari* (New York: Bantam, 1988) pp.29–30.
2. D'Este, *Fatal*, p.144.
3. Harper, *Battles*, p.174.
4. Detweiler, Burdick, Rohwer (Eds), *German Military Studies WWII, Kesselring's remarks on Med Campaign 4th July 1948* Vol 14 (London: Garland, 1979) pp.3–4.
5. Porch, *Hitler's*, p.522.
6. Westphal, *German*, p.155.
7. Hodges Richard, History Today, *Tempting providence: The Bombing of Monte Cassino* (Volume 44, Issue 2, 1994) p.246.
8. Senger, *Neither*, p.187.
9. Ibid., p.266, Westphal, *German*, p.158.
10. *Fuehrer Conferences on Naval Affairs 1939–45*, (London: Chatham Publishing, 1990) p.377.
11. Macksey, *Kesselring*, p.199.
12. Trevelyan, *Rome*, p.192 and *Kesselring*, p.196.
13. Trevelyan, *Rome*, p.381.
14. D'Este, *Fatal*, p.365.
15. Graham, *Tug*, p.315.
16. Alexander, *Memoirs*, p.125

Chapter 7

1. Nichlolas Lynn, *The Rape of Europa* (London: Papermac, 1995) p.258.
2. Kesselring, *Memoirs*, p.207.
3. Below Nicolas von, *At Hitler's Side, Hitler's Luftwaffe Adjutant 1937–45* (London: Greenhill, 2004) p.182.
4. Eberle & Uhl (Eds), *The Hitler Book* (London: John Murray, 2005) p.207.
5. Kesselring, *Memoirs*, p.209.
6. Dollmann, *Interpreter*, p.330.
7. Macksey, *Kesselring*, p.217.
8. Ibid., p.217

9. Senger, *Neither*, p.200.
10. Dollmann, *Interpreter*, p.330.
11. Hassell von Ulrich, *The Von Hassell Diaries* (London: Hamish Hamilton, 1948) p.297.
12. *Guardian*, 26 July 1944, p.8.
13. Ibid., 28 Nov 1944, p.4.
14. Murray Williamson & Millet, *A War to be Won: Fighting the Second World War* (Harvard University Press, 2001) p.374.
15. Alexander, *Memoirs*, p.159.
16. *Guardian*, 12 June 1950, p.6.
17. Battini M., *The Missing Italian Nuremberg* (New York: Palgrave Macmillan, 2007) p.31.
18. KNA, WO204/11496.
19. Neitzel S. & Welzer H., *Soldaten* (London: Simon & Schuster, 2012) p.77.
20. Morgan, *Italy's*, p.178.
21. Raiber, *Anatomy*, p.181.
22. Mazower Mark, *Hitler's Empire, Nazi Rule in Occupied Europe* (London: Allen Lane, 2008) p.499.
23. Trevelyan, *Rome*, p.19.
24. KNA, command CX/MSS/2960/T10-HW1/1884.
25. Davies, *Simple*, p.318.
26. KNA, HW1/2982.
27. KNA, WO204/11496.
28. KNA, HW5/474.
29. *Guardian*, 23 May 1946, p.6.
30. Lingen, *Kesselring*, p.44.
31. KNA, HW1/3007.
32. Kesselring, *Memoirs*, p.228.
33. KNA, WO204/11005.
34. Vassiltchikov, *Berlin*, p.214, Macksey, *Kesselring*, p.225.
35. KNA, Ref-FO954/17AFile, Ref 296.
36. Toland John, *The Last Hundred Days* (New York: Modern Library, 2003) p.221.
37. Heiber/Glantz, *Hitler*, p.585.
38. Kershaw, Ian, *The End: Hitler's Germany* (London: Allen Lane, 2011) p.303.
39. KNA-HW5/686.
40. KNA-HW1/3749.
41. Mazower, *Hitler's*, p.525.
42. Müller-Hill Werner Otto, *The True German, The Diary of a WWII Military Judge* (New York: Palgrave Macmillan, 2013) p.130.
43. Battistelli Pier, *Albert Kesselring* (Oxford: Osprey Publishing, 2012) p.5.
44. Müller-Hill, *True*, p.xxiv.
45. Rees Laurence, *The Dark Charisma of Adolf Hitler* (London: Ebury Press, 2012) p.375.
46. Macksey, *Kesselring*, p.225: Westphal was Chief-of-Staff again.
47. Kesselring, *Memoirs*, p.282.
48. KNA-CAB-66/53/8, pp.37–8.
49. KNA-HW1/3665.
50. KNA-HW5/706.
51. Toland John, *The Last Hundred Days* (Now York: Modern Library, 2003) p.329.
52. Kershaw, *The End*, p.303.

53. Speer Albert, *Inside the Third Reich* (London: Weidenfeld & Nicolson, 1970) p.438.
54. Sereny Gitter, *Albert Speer; His Battle with Truth* (London: Macmillan,1995) p.485 and p.487.
55. Kesselring, *Memoirs*, p.259.
56. BA-MA-N574-19-pp.53–54; and Kershaw, *The End*, p.364.
57. Kershaw, *The End*, p.396.
58. Hassell, *Diaries*, p.272.
59. Toland, *Last*, p.222.
60. Fest Joachim, *Not Me* (London: Atlantic Books, 2012) p.335.
61. Militärgeschichtliches-*Vol–IX/X*, p.55.
62. Macmillan Harold, *War Diaries* (London: Macmillan, 1984) p.750.
63. BA-MA-N750/2-LondDiary, p.3.
64. Macksey, *Kesselring*, p.230.

Chapter 8

1. Lucas James, *Last Days of the Reich (London: Arms and Armour Pub, 1986)* p.217.
2. Westphal, *German*, p.11.
3. Neitzel, *Tapping*, p.53.
4. Priemel, *Reassessing*, p.152.
5. Katz, *Fatal*, p.70.
6. Müller-Hill, *True*, p.104, 150, see also pp.142, 151, 155.
7. Hérbet V.G., *Hitler's Generals on Trial* (Kansas: Kansas Press, 2010) p.135.
8. Jackson Sophie, *Churchill's Unexpected Guests* (Gloucestershire: The History Press, 2010) p.100.
9. Scotland, *London*, p.173
10. Raiber, *Anatomy*, p.96.
11. *Guardian*, 20 May 1949, p.6.
12. Salter, *Nazi*, p.123.
13. KNA, FO 1060/493, petition to Foreign Office, May 1950.
14. Hébert, *Hitler's*, p102.
15. LRWC, Trial transcript for 17 March.
16. LRWC, Vol-VIII pp.13.
17. LRWC-Vol-VIII pp.10.
18. KNA-HW1/2982 and LRWC-Document-UK-66, pp.572–582.
19. LRWC-Vol-VIII, pp.12.
20. Hébert, *Hitler's*, p.71.
21. Veale, *Advance*, p.292.
22. Nicholas, *Rape*, p.239.
23. Ibid., p.241.
24. Kesselring, *Memoirs*, p.310.
25. Lingen, *Kesselring*, p.37.
26. Raiber, *Anatomy*.
27. Atkinson, *Day*, p.499.
28. *Guardian*, 7 May 1947, p.5.
29. KNA-HW1/3007.
30. KNA, WO216/214.
31. Roskill Stephen, *Hankey, Man of Secrets, Vol III* (London: Collins, 1974) p.651.

32. KNA, Prem 8/707 13 May 47.
33. KNA, WO 32/15490 13 May 47.
34. Lingen, *Kesselring*, p.131.
35. *Daily Mail*, 30 May 1947.
36. *Guardian*, 17 May 1947, p.4.
37. HC-Debate, 21 September 1943,Vol392/cc69-170/69.
38. KNA-FO1060/499-Legal Adviser's Zonal-Office.
39. *Guardian*, 23 April 1951, p.5.
40. Lingen, *Kesselring*, p.148.
41. USAHD *The War Behind the Front: Guerrilla Warfare*, MS C-032, Generalfeldmarschall Albert Kesselring, 007720.
42. Lingen, *Kesselring*, p.273.
43. Ibid., p.174.
44. Hébert, *Hitler's*, p.119.
45. JCS Directive No 1067.
46. *Manchester Guardian*, 23 April 1951.
47. Scotland, *London*, p.180.
48. HL Debate 5th Series vol.134 c.341.
49. KNA, FO 1060/501-29 Aug 1952.
50. HC Debate 12 Nov 1952, vol 507/cc926-7926.
51. Hébert, *Hitler's*, p.185.
52. Adenauer Konrad, *Memoirs 1945–53* (London: Weidenfeld, 1966) p.445.
53. KNA, FO1060/501, 29 Aug 1952.

Chapter 9
1. Macksey, *Kesselring*, p.243
2. Fulbrook Mary (Ed), *Twentieth Century Germany* (London: Hodder Headline Group, 2001) p.184.
3. Tipton, *History*, p.513.
4. Ibid., p.540.
5. *Guardian*, 30 December 1952, article by T. Prittie, Journalist/author on German/Israeli Histories.
6. *Frankfurter Allgemeine* Zeitung, 15 December 1952.
7. Lingen, *Kesselring*, p.189.
8. *Guardian*, 25 March 1954.
9. Lingen, *Kesselring*, p.278
10. *Guardian*, 30 August 1955.
11. *Guardian*, 18 June 1950.
12. *Guardian*, 18 July 1960, obits.

Chapter 10
1. Bartov, Grossmann, Nolan (Eds), *Crimes of War Guilt denied in the 20th Century* (New York: The New Press, 2002) p.xvi.
2. Roberts Stephen, *The House that Hitler Built* (London: Methuen, 1937) p.363.
3. KNA, HW5/474.

Field Marshal Erwin Rommel

Chapter 1
1. Fraser, *Knight's Cross*, pp. 3–13. Butler, *Field Marshal*, Chapter 1 (electronic edition).
2. Rommel, *Infantry Attacks*, (London: Greenhill, 2006) p.51.
3. Butler, *Field Marshal*, Chapter 2 (electronic edition).
4. Fraser, *Knight's Cross*, pp. 19–60.

Chapter 2
1. Fraser, *Knight's Cross*, pp. 81–156. Butler, *Field Marshal*, Chapters 3–4 (electronic edition). Alaric Searle, *Rommel and the Rise of the Nazis*, in: Ian F.W. Beckett, editor, *Rommel* (electronic edition).

Chapter 3
1. Russell H.S. Stolfi, *A Bias for Action. The German 7th Panzer Division in France and Russia 1940–1941* (Quantico: Command and Staff College Foundation, 1991).
2. Fraser, *Knight's Cross*, pp. 156–209. Butler, *Field Marshal*, Chapter 5 (electronic edition).
3. Claus Telp, *Rommel and 1940*, in: Ian F.W. Beckett, editor, *Rommel* (electronic edition).
4. Fraser, *Knight's Cross*, pp. 213–277. Butler, *Field Marshal*, Chapters 6–7 (electronic edition).
5. Militärgeschichtliches Forschungsamt, editor, *Germany and the Second World War. Volume III: The Mediterranean, South-East Europe, and North Africa 1939–1941* (Oxford: Clarendon Press, 1995), pp. 673–707.
6. Barr, Niall, *Rommel in the Desert, 1941*, in: Ian F.W. Beckett, editor, *Rommel* (electronic edition) p.742
7. Forczyk, Robert, *Desert Armour. Tank Warfare in North Africa* (Oxford: Osprey, 2023) p. 281
8. Fraser, *Knight's Cross*, pp. 277–297. Butler, *Field Marshal*, Chapter 8 (electronic edition). Militärgeschichtliches Forschungsamt, editor, *Germany and the Second World War. Volume III: The Mediterranean, South-East Europe, and North Africa 1939–1941* (Oxford: Clarendon Press, 1995), pp. 725–752.
9. Fraser, *Knight's Cross*, pp. 298–339. Butler, *Field Marshal*, Chapter 9 (electronic edition). Militärgeschichtliches Forschungsamt, editor, *Germany and the Second World War. Volume VI: The Global War* (Oxford: Clarendon Press, 2001), pp. 631–654, 661–692.
10. Fraser, *Knight's Cross*, pp. 340–413. Niall Barr, *Rommel in the Desert, 1942*, in: Ian F.W. Beckett, editor, *Rommel* (Electronic edition). Militärgeschichtliches Forschungsamt, editor, *Germany and the Second World War. Volume VI: The Global War* (Oxford: Clarendon Press, 2001), pp. 692–821.
11. Fraser, *Knight's Cross*, pp. 436–451. Butler, *Field Marshal*, Chapter 9 (electronic edition).

Chapter 4
1. Notes on the Rommel – von Schweppenburg 1 July meeting, annex to Army Group B war diary. NARA T313/Roll 420, frame 8713789. Liddell Hart, ed., *The Rommel Papers*, pp. 486–7.
2. Fraser, *Knight's Cross*, pp. 452–513. Butler, *Field Marshal*, Chapter 13 (electronic edition). Peter Lieb, *Rommel in Normandy*, in: Ian F.W. Beckett, editor, *Rommel* (electronic edition).

3. Fraser, *Knight's Cross*, pp. 514–552. Butler, *Field Marshal*, Chapter 14 (electronic edition). Russell A. Hart, *Rommel and the 20 July Bomb Plot*, in: Ian F.W. Beckett, editor, *Rommel* (electronic edition). Peter Lieb, 'Erwin Rommel. Widerstandkämpfer oder Nationalsozialist?', *Vierteljahrshefte für Zeitgeschichte* 3 (2013) 303:343.
4. Goebbels, Joseph, *Tagebücher*, Vols. 4 and 5 (Munich and Zurich: Piper, 1999), relevant entries per date.
5. See: Mark Connelly, *Rommel as Icon*, in: Ian F.W. Beckett, editor, *Rommel* (electronic edition).

Field Marshal Walter Model

Chapter 1
1. Görlitz, Walter, *Model. Der Feldmarschall und sein Endkampf an der Ruhr* (Munich: Universitas, 1989) pp. 10–21. & Forczyk, Robert, *Walter Model* (Oxford: Osprey, 2011) pp. 6–7.)

Chapter 2
1. Görlitz, *Model*, pp. 21–48. Forczyk, *Model*, pp. 7–10.
2. Görlitz, *Model*, pp. 49–68.

Chapter 3
1. Görlitz, *Model*, pp. 69–83. Forczyk, *Model*, pp. 10–11.
2. Görlitz, *Model*, pp. 84–97. Forczyk, *Model*, pp. 12–17.
3. Görlitz, *Model*, pp. 98–109. Forczyk, *Model*, pp. 18–30.
4. Görlitz, *Model*, pp. 110–160. Forczyk, *Model*, pp. 30–38.

Chapter 4
1. Görlitz, *Model*, pp. 161–193. Forczyk, *Model*, pp. 38–44.
2. Görlitz, *Model*, pp. 194–210. Forczyk, *Model*, pp. 45–50.
3. Görlitz, *Model*, pp. 210–222. Forczyk, *Model*, pp. 50–53.

Chapter 5
1. Görlitz, *Model*, pp.222–229.
2. Görlitz, *Model*, pp. 230–268. Forczyk, *Model*, pp. 54–56.
3. Goebbels, *Tagebücher* Vol. 5, 31 March 1944, p. 2030.
4. Erich von Manstein, *Lost Victories* (Novato: Presidio Press, 1982), p. 545.
5. Liddell Hart B.H., *The German Generals Talk* (London: Harper, 2002) p. 70.

Bibliography of Cited Works

Primary Sources
BA-MA: Bundesarchiv-Militärarchiv,
BHKM: Bayerisches Hauptstaatsarchiv, Kriegsarchiv, München (Kesselring personnel file) 61536
Newspaper Archives: *The Times, Observer, Guardian, Daily Mail, Frankfurter Allgemeine* Zeitung.
HC-Debate: House of Commons Debates
JCS: Joint Chiefs of Staff Directives
KNA: Kew National Archives,
LRWC: The UN War Crimes Commission, (1949) *Law-Reports of Trials of War Criminals, Volume VIII* London; Volume VIII Case No 47, London: *Law Reports of Trials of War Criminals*.
USAHD: US Army Historical Division, *The War Behind the Front: Guerrilla Warfare*, MS C-032 – Generalfeldmarschall Albert Kesselring. – 007720.
USAH: US Army Historical Division, *Special Report on the Events in Italy 25 July–8 September 1943*, MS C-013, Generalfeldmarschall Albert Kesselring, 1948. – 007718
US Army Historical Division: *Mediterranean War Part V, campaign in Italy Part II*, MS C-064, Generalfeldmarschall Albert Kesselring 1 May 1949 -007732
USDS: US Department of State.

Biographies, Memoirs, Conferences, Diaries
Adenauer Konrad, *Memoirs 1945–53* (London: Weidenfeld, 1966)
Alexander Earl of Tunis, *The Alexander Memoirs 1940–1945* (London: Frontline Books, 2010)
Battistelli Pier, *Albert Kesselring* (Oxford: Osprey Publishing, 2012)
Below Nicolas von, *At Hitler's Side, Hitler's Luftwaffe Adjutant 1937–45* (London: Greenhill, 2004)
Bosworth R., *Mussolini* (London: Hodder Arnold, 2002)
Bradley N. Omar, *A General's Life* (London: Sidgwick & Jackson, 1983)
Caddick-Adams Peter, *Monty and Rommel, Parallel Lives* (London: Arrow, 2012)
Capa Robert, *Slightly out of Focus* (New York: Modern Library, 1999)
Churchill Winston, *Onwards to Victory* (London: Cassell, 1944)
Dollmann Eugen, *The Interpreter, Memoirs of Doctor Eugen Dollmann* (London: Hutchinson, 1967)
Eisenhower Dwight, *Crusade in Europe* (London: Heinemann, 1948)
Farrell Nicholas, *Mussolini, A New Life* (London: Weidenfeld & Nicolson, 2003)
Fest Joachim, *Not Me* (London: Atlantic Books, 2012)
Fuehrer Conferences on Naval Affairs 1939–45 (London: Chatham Publishing, 1990)
Galland Adolf, *The First and the Last* (London: Methuen, 1995)

Goebbels Joseph, *Tagebücher*, Vol. 5 (Munich and Zurich: Piper, 1999)
Gregg V. & Stroud R., *Rifleman* (London: Bloomsbury, 2011)
Hassell von Ulrich, *The Von Hassell Diaries* (London: Hamish Hamilton, 1948)
Kesselring Albert, *The Memoirs of Field-Marshal Kesselring* (London: William Kimber, 1953)
Klibansky R. (ed), *Mussolini Memoirs* (London: Weidenfeld & Nicolson, 1949)
Knappe Siegfried & Brusaw, *Soldat* (London: BCA, 1993)
Liddell Hart B.H. (Ed), *The Rommel Papers* (New York: De Capo Press, 1953) or
Liddell Hart, Basil, editor. *The Rommel Papers* (London: Hamlyn, 1984)
Lochner Louis (Ed), *The Goebbels Diaries* (London: Hamish Hamilton, 1948)
Luck Col Hans von, *Panzer Commander, Memoirs of Colonel Hans von Luck* (London: Cassell, 1989)
Macmillan Harold, *War Diaries* (London: Macmillan, 1984)
Macksey Kenneth, *Kesselring German Master Strategist of the Second World War* (London: Greenhill, 1978)
Makos Adam, *A Higher Call* (London: Atlantic Books, 2013)
Manvell & Fraenkel, *Herman Göring* (London: Heinemann, 1962)
Messenger Charles, *Rommel* (London: Palgrave, 2009)
Muggeridge Malcolm (Ed), *Ciano's Diary* (London: Heinemann, 1947)
Müller-Hill Werner Otto, *The True German, The Diary of a WWII Military Judge* (New York: Palgrave Macmillan, 2013)
Neitzel Sönke (Ed), *Tapping Hitler's Generals* (Yorkshire: Frontline Books, 2007)
Neitzel S. & Welzer H., *Soldaten* (London: Simon & Schuster, 2012)
Rees Laurence, *The Dark Charisma of Adolf Hitler* (London: Ebury Press, 2012)
Roskill Stephen, *Hankey, Man of Secrets, Vol III* (London: Collins, 1974)
Senger von und Etterlin, *Neither Fear nor Hope* (London: Macdonald, 1963)
Sereny Gitter, *Albert Speer: His Battle with Truth* (London: Macmillan, 1995)
Schraepler Hans-Joachim, *At Rommel's Side, The Lost letters of Hans-Joachim Schraepler* (London: Frontline Books, 2009)
Scotland Lt Col A.P., *The London Cage* (London: Landsborough, 1957)
Speer Albert, *Inside the Third Reich* (London: Weidenfeld & Nicolson, 1970)
Steinhilper U. & Osborne P., *Spitfire on my Tail* (Worcs: Self-Publishing Co, 1989)
Vassiltchikov Marie, *The Berlin Diaries 1939–45* (London: Pimlico, 1999)
Westphal Siegfried, *The German Army in the West* (London: Cassell, 1951)
Whicker Alan, *Whicker's War* (London: Harpers, 2005)
Young Desmond, *Rommel* (London: Book Club Associates, 1973)

Other Published Works
Allen Butler, Daniel, *Field Marshal. The Life and Death of Erwin Rommel* (Oxford: Casemate, 2015)
Atkinson R., *The Day of the Battle, The War in Sicily and Italy 1943–44* (London: Abacus, 2013)
Bartov Omer, *Hitler's Army* (Oxford: OUP, 1992)
Bartov, Grossmann, Nolan (Eds), *Crimes of War "Guilt denied in the 20th Century"* (New York: The New Press, 2002)
Battini M., *The Missing Italian Nuremberg* (New York: Palgrave Macmillan, 2007)
Beckett, Ian F.W., editor, *Rommel. A Reappraisal* (Barnsley: Pen & Sword, 2013)
Beckett, Ian F.W., editor, *Rommel* (electronic edition) Niall Barr, *Rommel in the Desert, 1941.*
Beevor Anthony, *The Second World War* (London: Weidenfeld & Nicolson, 2012)

Bibliography of Cited Works

Berghahn V.R., *Modern Germany* (Cambridge: Cambridge UP, 1987)
Boyne Walter, *The Influence of Air Power Upon History* (New York: Pelican, 2003)
Brighton, Terry, *Masters of Battle. Monty, Patton and Rommel at War* (London: Viking, 2008)
Brown Cave Anthony, *Bodyguard of Lies* (London: W H Allen, 1977)
Bryant Mark, *World War II in Cartoons*, (London: Grub Street, 2009)
Burleigh Michael, *Moral Combat A History of World War II* (London: Harper, 2010)
Butler, *Field Marshal*, (electronic edition).
Carell Paul, *Hitler's War on Russia* (London: Harrup, 1964)
Churchill Winston, *The Second World War Volume 1* (London: Cassell, 1948)
Citino Robert, *The Path to Blitzkrieg* (Mechanicsburg, Stackpole, 2008)
Clark Alan, *Barbarossa* (London: Phoenix Press, 1965)
Corum James, *The Luftwaffe Creating the Operational Air War 1918–1940* (Kansas: UP Kansas, 1997)
Davies Norman, *No Simple Victory* (London: Penguin, 2007)
Dear (ed) *The Oxford Companion to WWII* (Oxford: OUP, 1995)
D'Este Carlo, *Fatal Decision* (London: Fontana, 1991)
Detweiler, Burdick, Rohwer (Eds), *German Military Studies WW II, Kesselring's remarks on Med Campaign 4th July 1948* Vol 14-(London: Garland, 1979)
Douhet Giulio, *The Command of the Air* (New York: Arno Press, 1972)
Edgerton David, *Britain's War Machine* (London: Penguin Books, 2012)
Evans Richard, *The Third Reich at War* (London: Allen Lane, 2008)
Forczyk, Robert, *Walter Model* (Oxford: Osprey, 2011)
Forczyk, Robert, *Desert Armour. Tank Warfare in North Africa*, (Oxford : Osprey, 2023)
Fraser, David, *Knight's Cross. A Life of Field Marshal Erwin Rommel* (London: HarperCollins, 1993)
Fulbrook Mary (Ed), *Twentieth Century Germany* (London: Hodder Headline Group, 2001)
Goldensohn L. & Gellately R. (Ed) *The Nuremberg Interviews. Conversations with the Defendants & Witnesses* (London: Pimlico, 2007)
Görlitz, Walter, *Model. Der Feldmarschall und sein Endkampf an der Ruhr* (Munich: Universitas, 1989)
Graham D. & Bidwell S., *Tug Of War The Battle for Italy 1943–45* (Yorkshire: Pen and Sword, 2004)
Haigh R., Morris D., Peters A., *German-Soviet Relations in the Weimar Era* (Aldershot, Gower, 1985)
Hankey Rt Hon Lord, *Politics, Trials and Errors* (Oxford: Pen in Hand, 1950)
Harper G. & Tonkin-Covell J., *The Battles of Monte Cassino* (Auckland: Allen & Unwin, 2013)
Hastings Max, *All Hell Let Loose* (London: Harper, 2011)
—. *Catastrophe* (London: William Collins, 2013)
Heiber Helmut & Glantz David (Eds), *Hitler and his Generals* (London: Greenhill Books, 2002)
Hérbet V.G., *Hitler's Generals on Trial* (Kansas: Kansas Press, 2010)
Hickey D. & Smith G., *Operation Avalanche, The Salerno landings 1943* (London: Heinemann, 1983)
Hoyt Edwin, *Back Water War, The Allied Campaign in Italy* (Mechanicsburg: Stackpole, 2007)
Howard Michael, *The Invention of Peace & the Reinvention of War* (London: Profile Books, 2001)
Infield Glen, *Disaster at Bari* (New York: Bantam, 1988)

Irving, David, *Rommel. The Trail of the Fox* (London: Weidenfeld & Nicholson, 1977)
Jackson Sophie, *Churchill's Unexpected Guests* (Gloucestershire: The History Press, 2010)
Jeffery Keith, *MI6 The History of the Intelligence Service 1909–49* (London: Bloomsbury, 2010)
Katz Robert, *Fatal Silence* (London: Weidenfeld & Nicolson, 2003)
Kershaw, Robert J., *It Never Snows in September. The German View of Market Garden and the Battle of Arnhem, September 1944* (Marlbourough: Crowood, 1990)
Kershaw Ian, *Fateful Choices* (London: Penguin, 2007)
—. *The End: Hitler's Germany* (London: Allen Lane, 2011)
Killen John, *The Luftwaffe, A History* (Yorkshire: Pen and Sword, 2009)
Kurzman D., *A Special Mission* (New York: Da Capo Press, 2007)
Lamb Richard, *War in Italy 1943–45* (London: Murray, 1993)
Lewin Ronald, *Ultra Goes to War* (London: Penguin, 1978)
Lewin, Ronald, *Rommel as Military Commander* (Barnsley: Pen & Sword, 2004)
Lewis J. (Ed), *World War II The Autobiography* (London: Robinson, 2009)
Liddell Hart B.H., *The German Generals Talk* (London: Harper, 2002)
Lingen Kerstin von, *Kesselring's Last Battle Crimes Trials and Cold War Politics* (Kansas: Kansas Press, 2009)
Lucas James, *Hitler's Enforcers* (London: Arms and Armour Pub, 1996)
——, *Last Days of the Reich* (London: Arms and Armour Pub, 1986)
Lucas Laddie, *Malta The Thorn in Rommel's Side* (London: Penguin, 1992)
Macintyre Ben, *Operation Mincemeat* (London: Bloomsbury, 2010)
Mazower Mark, *Hitler's Empire, Nazi Rule in Occupied Europe* (London: Allen Lane, 2008)
Messenger, Charles, *Rommel. Leadership Lessons from the Desert Fox* (Basingstoke: Palgrave Macmillan, 2009)
Militärgeschichtliches Forschungsamt Potsdam (Eds), *Germany & The Second World War Volume VI* (Oxford: Clarendon, 2001)
Militärgeschichtliches Forschungsamt, (Ed), *Germany and the Second World War. Volume III: The Mediterranean, South-East Europe, and North Africa 1939–1941* (Oxford: Clarendon Press, 1995)
Mitcham Samuel, *Eagles of The Third Reich* (Mechanicsburg: Stackpole Books, 2007)
Murray Williamson, *The Luftwaffe 1933–45 Strategy for Defeat* (Washington: Congress Library, 1996)
Murray Williamson & Millet, *A War to be Won: Fighting the Second World War* (Harvard: University Press, 2001)
Newton, Steven H., *Hitler's Commander. Field Marshal Walter Model – Hitler's Favourite General* (Cambridge, MA: Da Capo Press, 2005)
Nicholas Lynn, *The Rape of Europa* (London: Papermac, 1995)
Overy Richard, *The Bombing War, Europe1939–45* (London: Allen Lane, 2013)
Parker Matthew, *Monte Cassino* (London: Headline Press, 2003)
Porch Douglas, *Hitler's Mediterranean Gamble* (London: Weidenfeld & Nicolson, 2004)
Priemel C. & Stiller A., Eds, *Reassessing the Military Tribunals* (Oxford: Berghahn Books, 2012)
Raiber Richard, *Anatomy of Perjury* (Delaware: Delaware Press, 2008)
Remy, Maurice Philip, *Mythos Rommel* (Berlin: List, 2004)
Reuth, Ralf Georg, *Rommel. Das Ende einer Legende* (Munich and Zurich: Piper, 2004)
Roberts Andrew, *The Storm of War* (London: Allen Lane, 2009)
Roberts Stephen, *The House that Hitler Built* (London: Methuen, 1937)
Rommel, *Infantry Attacks* (London: Greenhill, 2006)

Bibliography of Cited Works   251

Salter Michael, *Nazi War Crimes, US Intelligence & Selective Prosecution at Nuremberg* (Oxford: Routledge-Cavendish, 2007)
Shirer L. William, *The Rise and Fall of the Third Reich* (London: Book Club Associates, 1973)
Showalter, Dennis, *Patton and Rommel* (New York: Berkley, 2005)
Schreiner A., *Hitler Rearms* (London: John Lane – Bodley Head, 1934)
Stein, Marcel, *A Flawed Genius. Field Marshal Walter Model: a Critical Biography* (Warwick: Helion, 2010)
Taylor Telford, *The Anatomy of the Nuremberg Trials* (New York: Knope, 1992)
Thompson Alastair, *Left Liberals, The State, & Popular Politics in Wilhelmine Germany* (Oxford: OUP, 2000)
Tipton Frank B., *A History of Modern Germany since 1815* (London: Continuum, 2003)
Toland John, *The Last Hundred Days* (Now York: Modern Library, 2003)
Trevelyan Raleigh, *Rome '44 The Battle for the Eternal City* (London: Pimlico, 2004)
Trevor-Roper Hugh (Ed), *Hitler's War Directives* (London: Pan Books, 2004)
Veale F.J.P., *Advance to Barbarism* (Torrance: Inst for Historical Review, 1979)
Wette Wolfram, *The Wehrmacht: History, Myth, Reality* (London: Harvard UP, 2007)
Wilks, John, Eileen Wilks, *Rommel and Caporetto* (Barnsley: Leo Cooper, 2001)
Zaloga Steven, *Poland 1939 The Birth of Blitzkrieg* (Oxford: Osprey, 2002)
Ziemke, Earl F. and Magna E. Bauer, *Moscow to Stalingrad. Decision in the East* (Washington: Center of Military History U.S. Army, 1987)
Ziemke, Earl F., *Stalingrad to Berlin: The German Defeat in the East* (Washington: Center of Military History U.S. Army, 2002)

Pamphlets/Magazine Articles/Study Papers
Blumenson, Martin, *Breakout and Pursuit* (Washington, DC: Center of Military History U.S. Army, 1993)
Cole, Hugh M., *The Ardennes: Battle of the Bulge* (Washington, DC: Center of Military History U.S. Army, 1993)
Hansen Eric G., *The Italian Military Enigma* (Seminar Paper, Command & Staff College, Quantico, Virginia 22134, 1988)
Herde Peter, *Albert Kesselring (1885–1960)* (Fränkische Lebensbilder, Vol 18, series vii, Neustadt an der Aische, 2000)
Hodges Richard, History Today, *Tempting providence: The Bombing of Monte Cassino* (Volume 44, Issue 2, 1994)
Kearley S., Military History, *The Secrets of Hughenden Manor* (issue 23, August, p.11, 2012)
MacDonald, Charles B., *The Last Offensive* (Washington, DC: Center of Military History U.S. Army, 1993)
MacDonald, Charles B., *The Siegfried Line Campaign* (Washington, DC: Center of Military History U.S. Army, 1993)
Maycock Ian, Military History, *Poland 1939* (Issue 36, Sept 2013)
Morgan Philip, History Today, *Italy's Fascist War* (Volume 57, Issue 3, 2007)
Russell H.S. Stolfi, *A Bias for Action. The German 7th Panzer Division in France and Russia 1940–1941* (Quantico: Command and Staff College Foundation, 1991).

Index

Adenauer, Chancellor 78, 80, 244, 247
Alarich Plan 40
Alexander, Field Marshal 45, 53, 56, 58, 59, 62, 74, 84, 85, 86, 240, 241, 242, 247
Ambrosio, General Vittorio 39, 42, 164
Andrus, Colonel 68
Anzio landing, Operation Shingle 54
Ardeatine Massacre 70, 71, 74
Arnim, General von 34, 35, 36, 163, 175
Attlee, Clement 74
Auftragstaktik 94, 95, 97

Bari air raid 52
Bastico, General 32, 34, 144, 146, 157, 161, 172, 174
Beck, General Ludwig 192, 193, 194
Beelitz, Kesselring's Staff Officer 70
Bell, Bishop George 75, 77
Below, General Otto von 31, 96, 188, 241, 247
Berndt, Lieutenant Alfred 172
Blomberg, General von 194
Bock, Field Marshal von 203
Bormann, Martin 64, 169
Bothmer, Major Count von 98, 99, 107
Brauchitsch, General von Walther 15, 23, 191, 204
Buffalo, Operation 56, 209
Busch, General Ernst 196, 217

Cavallero, Ugo 27, 31, 32, 39, 145, 147, 148, 149, 157
Churchill, Winston 11, 12, 17, 29, 38, 53, 54, 59, 74, 75, 78, 86, 172, 237, 243, 247, 249, 250
Ciano, Galeazzo 39, 41, 43, 240, 248
Clark, General Mark 26, 46, 53, 56, 85, 249

Cochenhausen, General von 190
Coningham, Air Marshal 52
Courten, Count de 43
Cramer, General von 188
Crusader offensive 139
Crüwell, General 31, 32, 140, 141, 142, 143, 150, 152, 173

Devers, General 66
Dietl, General Eduard 173, 231
Dietrich, SS General Josef 175, 236
Dollmann, General 43, 57, 61, 240, 241, 242, 247
Dönitz, Admiral 3, 33, 42, 65, 66
Dostler, General 74
Douhet, Giulio 13, 16, 17, 237, 249

Eisenhower, General Dwight 35, 65, 66, 77, 220, 224, 247
El Alamein 30, 31, 160, 161, 162, 178
Enigma 29, 32, 239, 251

Falkenstein, Major von 189
Felmy, General 22
Fritsch, General 194
Funck, General Hans von 127, 128

Galland, Adolf 23, 24, 247
Gambara, General Gastone 140, 142, 144, 145
Gambier-Parry, General 132, 133
Gariboldi, General Italo 129, 130, 131, 144, 172
Gaulle, General de 33, 121
German military rebuilt 12, 13
Germany post Great War 8, 9, 12, 108
Gillhausen, General von 188

Index

Goebbels, Joseph x, 29, 40, 42, 110, 139, 171, 172, 173, 174, 175, 176, 229, 230, 240, 246, 248
Goerdeler, Dr Karl 57
Göring, Hermann 13, 15, 16, 17, 18, 21, 22, 23, 24, 27, 31, 33, 34, 36, 50, 66, 68, 110, 163, 169, 175, 206, 232, 238, 248
Grandi, Dino 43
Graziani, Field Marshal Rodolfo 129
Guderian, General Heinz 26, 109, 114, 115, 116, 120, 121, 122, 123, 162, 167, 170, 192, 193, 194, 197, 199, 202, 209, 218, 229
Gustav Line battles 53

Halder, General 23, 32, 136, 138, 194
Hankey, Maurice 5, 75, 77, 80, 243, 248, 249
Hassell, Ulrich von 65, 242, 243, 248
Herr, General 61, 74
Himmler, Heinrich 48, 49, 65, 67, 169
Hitler in control 39, 55, 62, 121, 205, 216, 227
Hossbach, Colonel Friedrich 192
Hoth, Hermann 114, 115, 116, 117, 118, 119, 123, 124
Hube, General 46, 184, 216, 231

Jaschke, Colonel 193
Jodl, General Ferdinand 31, 39, 40, 173, 175, 190

Kaiser Wilhelm 5, 184
Kameradenschinder trials 82
Kappler, Head of Gestapo in Rome 48, 70
Keitel, Field Marshal ix, x, 3, 31, 40, 48, 62, 64, 71, 86, 173, 175
Kesselring, Albert 43, 69
  and 20 July Plot 57
  and Malta issue 30, 31, 36
  and Rommel 29, 30, 32, 39, 40, 44
  appointed Commander-in-Chief South 27
  as a young officer 4
  as seen by contemporaries 56, 57, 58, 61, 84
  as viewed by historians 45
  attends Nuremberg Trial 68
  at the Eastern Front 25
  character 4, 6, 11, 18, 27, 32, 33, 35, 39, 41, 48, 50, 51, 54, 63, 69
  communtation of death sentence 74
  early life 3
  family life 5, 79, 81
  his death 83
  his views on bombing 20, 21, 22, 24, 85
  in captivity 66, 67, 68, 69, 75
  in defence 34, 37, 41, 45, 46, 47, 53
  joins Luftwaffe as Commodore 14
  knowledge of atrocities 23, 37, 49, 61, 63, 65, 67, 70, 71, 74, 86
  later views on Hitler 85
  on trial 69, 70, 71, 72, 73, 74
  political stance 7, 8, 9, 10, 25, 48, 84
  politics of his release 76, 77, 78
  postwar freedom 79, 80, 81, 82, 83
  promotion 6, 7, 11, 13, 14, 16, 23
  reactions to Hitler 15, 25, 27, 30, 37, 38, 55, 57, 58, 62, 63, 79
  relationship with Italians 42, 43, 44, 50
  visits Russia 1923-24 12
Kippenberger, General Sir Howard 46
Kirchheim, General Heinrich 134, 137, 138
Klopper, General 156
Kluge, Field Marshal von 25, 169, 175, 199, 204, 209, 210, 213, 219

Laternser, Dr Hans, Lawyer 70, 72, 74, 76, 77
Leese, General 74
Lemelsen, General 74
List, Field Marshal 191
Lossberg, General Fritz von 189
Lucas, General 55, 239, 243, 250
Luck, Hans von 35

Mackensen, General von Friedrich 53, 55, 69
Malta Issue 147, 148, 149, 156, 162
Mälzer, General 56
Manstein, General von ix, x, 15, 76, 170, 192, 193, 194, 209, 210, 211, 213, 214, 216, 229, 230, 231, 232, 246
Manteuffel, General von 230
Maugeri, Admiral 39

Mincemeat, Operation 38, 239, 250
Model, Walter,
  and Sea Lion 197
  as a young officer 185
  as seen by contemporaries 229, 230
  as viewed by historians 230
  character 190, 193, 200, 201, 203, 205, 206, 228, 229, 232
  early life 183, 184
  family life 189, 190, 193, 213, 227
  his image 204, 207, 222, 225
  interbellum years 188, 189, 190, 191, 192, 193, 194, 195
  knowledge of atrocities 196
  leadership qualities 197, 199, 200, 201, 202, 204, 205, 206, 208, 209, 210, 211, 213, 214, 215, 218, 220, 221, 223, 224, 225, 226, 231
  leadership weaknesses 223
  panzer command 198
  promotion 185, 186, 188, 191, 194, 202, 205, 216
  reactions to Hitler 205, 214, 218, 225, 232
  Spanish Civil War 193
  start of WWII 196
  to Western Command 218
  WWI 186, 187
Montgomery, General 31, 46, 85, 129, 162, 174, 176, 221, 226
Mussolini x, 16, 27, 28, 31, 36, 38, 39, 41, 42, 43, 46, 49, 129, 130, 140, 144, 145, 147, 148, 149, 157, 162, 163, 171, 172, 175, 193, 239, 240, 241, 247, 248

Neame, General 132, 133
Nehring, General 153

O'Connor, General 129, 132, 133
Ohm, Colonel Berthold 82

Partisan Warfare 59, 60, 61
Patton, General George 85, 89, 224, 226, 228, 249, 251
Paulus, General ix, x, 3, 136, 137, 138
Pétain, Marshal Philippe 126
Petersdorff, General von 188
Preussen, Prince Oskar von 186, 187

Rantzaus, General von 187, 188
Rapido River battle 53
Rathgens, Colonel 169
Reinhardt, General 114, 116, 190, 202
Richthofen, Wolfram von 21, 52
Ridgway, General 228
Rome occupied by Allies 56
Rommel, Erwin
  and debate over 20 July Plot 169, 170, 178
  and July Plot 90
  and Kesselring 145, 147, 150, 152, 157
  as a young officer 91
  as seen by contemporaries 166, 171, 172, 173, 174, 175
  as viewed by historians 176, 177
  awarded for bravery 92
  character 91, 92, 103, 105, 106, 107, 112, 114, 131, 134, 135, 140, 160, 169
  early life 90
  family life 93, 97, 109
  his image 105, 107, 108, 123, 126, 128, 129, 139, 159, 161, 162, 164, 179
  in France 166
  in Italy with Kesselring 164
  knowledge of atrocities 125
  leadership qualities 92, 96, 97, 98, 99, 100, 101, 103, 104, 106, 115, 116, 118, 121, 124, 125, 132, 133, 155, 156, 166, 167, 177
  leadership weaknesses 136, 137, 138, 139, 140, 141, 142, 143, 145, 148, 150, 152, 160, 161, 167
  learns *Auftragstaktik* 95
  leaves Italy 165
  personal ambition 89, 91, 105, 110, 112, 113, 120, 122, 126, 146, 169, 170, 178
  political stance 110
  promotion 91, 93, 108, 109, 111, 128, 138, 145, 157
  reactions to Hitler 110, 111, 112
  The Great War starts 91
Rothenburg, Colonel 115, 116, 117
Röttiger, Hans 203
Röttinger, Captain Hans 193
Rundstedt, Field Marshal von 62, 166, 169, 196, 219, 221, 222, 225, 226

Index

Rupprecht, Crown Prince of Bavaria 5, 6, 7, 11

Schenckendorff, Colonel von 190
Schirach, Baldur von 110
Schmid, Colonel Joseph (Beppo) 24
Schmundt, General Rudolf 129, 172, 229
Schörner, Field Marshal 82, 83, 104, 229, 230
Schustern, Cardinal 60, 242, 248
Schwedler, General von 195
Schweppenburg, General von 168, 170, 199, 245
Scotland, Lieutenant Colonel 39, 69, 70, 76, 77, 240, 243, 244, 248
Seeckt, General von 11, 12, 13, 14, 19, 20, 62, 187
Senger und Etterlin, General von 14, 28, 46, 50, 53, 54, 57, 126, 237, 238, 239, 240, 241, 242, 248
Speer, Albert 63, 243, 248
Speidel, General 169, 190
Sprösser, Major Theodor 96, 97, 98, 99, 100, 101, 102, 103, 104, 105, 107
Stahlhelms 77, 81, 83, 86
Stalin, Joseph 26, 218
Stauffenberg, Claus von 57
Stigler, Franz 36
Streich, General 130, 131, 135, 136, 137, 145

Student, General 18, 22, 31, 149, 221
Stülpnagel, General 169, 188
Stumme, General 206
Stumpff, General 190, 198

Thoma, General Wilhelm von 127, 128
Tobruk, falls to Rommel 156
Tolsdorff, General 82
Tompkins, SOE Spy 50
Trettner, General Heinz 81

Udet, Ernst 16, 17
Ultra 29, 34, 40, 49, 60, 238, 250
  see also Enigma

Vietinghoff, General von 40, 46, 53, 58, 64, 206

Wavell, General 127, 131, 132
Westphal, General 28, 30, 33, 35, 36, 43, 44, 48, 50, 53, 54, 55, 57, 63, 64, 66, 70, 83, 142, 238, 239, 240, 241, 242, 243, 248
Wever, Walther 13, 16, 18
Wietersheim, General von 192
Winterbotham, Frederick 32
Wolff, SS General Karl 48, 61, 62, 64, 65, 70, 86

Zeitzler, General 209, 216

Dear Reader,

We hope you have enjoyed this book, but why not share your views on social media? You can also follow our pages to see more about our other products: facebook.com/penandswordbooks or follow us on Twitter @penswordbooks

You can also view our products at www.pen-and-sword.co.uk (UK and ROW) or www.penandswordbooks.com (North America).

To keep up to date with our latest releases and online catalogues, please sign up to our newsletter at: www.pen-and-sword.co.uk/newsletter

If you would like a printed catalogue with our latest books, then please email: enquiries@pen-and-sword.co.uk or telephone: 01226 734555 (UK and ROW) or email: uspen-and-sword@casematepublishers.com or telephone: (610) 853-9131 (North America).

We respect your privacy and we will only use personal information to send you information about our products.

Thank you!